S.E.N.D. IN THE CLOWNS

Suzy Rowland

Hashtag PRESS

Published in Great Britain by Hashtag Press 2020

A CIP catalogue for this book is available from the British Library.

ISBN 978-1-9162864-6-7

Typeset in Garamond Classic 11.25/14 by Blaze Typesetting

Printed and bound in Great Britain by Clays Ltd, Elcograf S.p.A.

Hashtag PRESS

HASHTAG PRESS BOOKS
Hashtag Press Ltd
Kent, England, United Kingdom
Email: info@hashtagpress.co.uk
Website: www.hashtagpress.co.uk
Twitter: @hashtag_press

My mother Dorcas (Cas) Walker was a much-loved teacher who taught in inner-city Birmingham and loved her job. As an educational campaigner and curriculum adviser she cared passionately about primary education. She was involved in supplementary schools in Birmingham and was a strong advocate for learning about culture and history as a way for children, particularly those from black or dual-heritage backgrounds, to build self-esteem and purpose.
This book is dedicated to my mother Cas;
an eternal student of life.

Acknowledgements

Ambitious About Autism, Clive Rowland, Education Policy Institute, Express CIC, Helen and Abiola, Imani, Jake, Khembe Clarke, Mencap, National Autistic Society, Phil Vickerman, Rabia Dignam, Rob Webster, Ruth Stone, Vikki Grimes, Venessa Bobb.

Foreword

Suzy Rowland, through S.E.N.D. in the Clowns, gives us a detailed, personal and profound insight into her journey supporting her son through his educational maelstrom of exclusions, assessments, Special Educational Needs and Individual Educational Plans.

For any parent going through the trials of planning education strategies for their child diagnosed with Special Educational Needs (SEN), this book explains the procedures, requirements and useful tips. The author shares her learned expertise on all matters concerning the educational blocks she faced at each stage and how to navigate around them.

Dispensing with 'labels,' and instead finding answers and solutions for her son, are Suzy's strengths, as we see her resilience and determination grow towards positive outcomes in the field of educational possibilities. Suzy has earned my admiration with her breath-taking tenacity, as she overcomes one hurdle after another along her path towards attaining a resolution for her son within the classroom setting.

Many teachers are not equipped to handle or recognise children with specific learning difficulties such as Dyspraxia, Dyslexia, Dyscalculia, ADD/ADHD or Asperger's. It is my experience that many children who exhibit these disruptive behaviours, or cannot keep focussed in the classroom, possess an undiagnosed learning difficulty that needs to be addressed.

This compelling book is a must read for any parent struggling to understand, decipher, explain or gain insights into their child's educational needs; I cannot recommend it highly enough.

Rabia Dignam
SENCO, SEN Teacher. Advanced Dip in Therapeutic Counselling, CPCAB. London, United Kingdom, 2020

As a highly developed species, human beings still have 'access denied' hovering over the entry point to the human brain - the thinking heart of our being. That which creates our world, our imagination, our feelings, thoughts and how we BE-have. Our brains are truly alive, constantly moving, responding to minute changes in our mood, reacting to chemicals we knowingly and unknowingly ingest, receiving signals from the rest of our body and external information from the world around us. An autism/ADHD diagnosis is an entry point to discovering the triggers and remedies for your child's behaviour. In addition to medication, there are literally hundreds of things you can try together to make life calmer, more organised, less stressful, more sociable and productive. I believe every child should be able to achieve their true potential. If you approach diagnosis as a stepping stone to a life of wonder and exploration, you may find the ride more comfortable, even life-affirming.

Suzy Rowland
Founder #happyinschool project, ADHD and Autism Specialist, BPS Approved Cognitive Behaviour Therapist, poet.

For J

Watching my children sleeping
barely daring to breathe myself,
all my energy focused on watching
the slow rise and fall of their chests
punctuated by snuffles, grunts
and the occasional start
as if they are falling through
stars from heaven.

-Suzy Rowland-

Table of Contents

Chapter 2: The Discovery Zone - What Is Autism, ASD, Asperger's Syndrome?

- The rise and rise of. . .
- Autism defined
- Stimming
- Pathological Demand Avoidance
- Alexithymia in autism
- Asperger's Syndrome
- Asperger's Syndrome - Moods and Mental Health
- The language barrier
- Catastrophic thinking
- Asperger's profile - a school eye view
- Let's talk about ADHD
- Three indicators of ADHD
- Beware of the label
- One, two, GO! Impulsivity
- Neurological factors and the part they play in outbursts
- Controversy
- Causes and commonalities
- Parent pupil profile
- Lessons learned

Chapter 3: The Big Questions Zone - Is My Child Autistic/ADHD?

- Bullying behaviour
- Misinterpreting bad behaviour - sensory factors
- A bony bump in the road
- Social isolation - difficulty making friends
- Why is my child a rule-breaker?
- Asperger's and Autism: easy to spot - not!

Chapter 8: The Post-Diagnosis Zone - Reflection And Learning

- Mantras
- Lessons learned

Chapter 9: The Medication Nation Zone - Knowing Your Options Before The Big Decisions

- Considering your options
- Talking to the professionals
- Medication nation
- Hyperactivity – best treatments and clinical evidence
- There is no cure for autism
- Lessons learned

Chapter 10: The Teacher Zone - Working With The School For Positive Outcomes

- Teacher training and SEN
- How you can support the teacher
- Working with the school
- Ideas on how you can help the school
- Ideas for teachers and how the school can help
- What you can do from home
- Trust makes it happen
- School and home communications tools
- Better than a poke in the eye
- Mental health
- Autism carries the secrets of power and potential
- Homework SOS
- Lessons learned

Chapter 11: The Therapies Zone - Working Through Myriad Therapies To Find What Fits

Chapter 13: The (Right) Secondary School Zone - Choices, Decisions And Motivations

- Time to move on
- Different types of school
- What type of school is 'best' for your SEN child?
- Alternative provision
- Our experience of the Secondary School process
- What if you don't get the school you want?
- A private assessment
- Managing the transition from Primary to Secondary
- Coping with a difficult transition
- Another move
- Exploring other options
- Living in the space between schools
- Mantras
- Lessons learned

Chapter 14: The New Beginnings Zone - A Fresh Start For Everyone

- Finding what feels right
- A new school and a new start
- Why the centre worked (where other schools failed)

Chapter 15: The Inclusion, Intersection And Conclusion Zone - You Deserve To Be Heard

- Inclusive education is not easy
- Beyond the now
- Intersectionality
- You deserve to be heard

References

Sources and Suggested Reading

Useful Contacts

Disclaimer

Using medication to manage ADHD is an accepted and effective practice. In Chapter 9: The Medication Nation Zone, I discuss the use of medicine and some of the things parents might need to consider. It is advisable to seek professional advice and information on this issue with your GP. I'm not a doctor but have done my best to explain the medical and biological parts of this text in plain English and as accurately as my perfectly flawed human brain allows.

Introduction

S.E.N.D. in the Clowns is for anyone with an interest in special children. This book is for you if:

- You barely have time to read a newspaper or drink a cup of tea without it getting cold.
- You've experienced a primary-aged child with disruptive behaviour in school.
- You're feeling stressed that your child doesn't seem to be learning anything, the teacher can't remember his or her name... and you need to read something that makes you feel calm.
- You need to tackle some of the crazy stuff that's been flying at you since your baby started school.
- Your child has recently had a diagnosis or you're in the process of getting one.

I'm here to provide you with practical and friendly suggestions from someone who's been through it all. I'll tell it like it happened; our stories may be different, but if mine helps you in any way, it's worth sharing. This is not a work of fiction: it's a work of fact.

Compiled through extensive research and conversations with parents who have attended my #happyinschool workshops, this book will help you navigate the world of special educational needs. You will gain enough knowledge to help you understand what's happening, to get access to the right support for your child and find your voice when you need it most. Reading this book will open your eyes to what might happen before, during and after a diagnosis, and provide practical suggestions to help you move forward.

Families with a 'special needs' child experience a specific angst when their child becomes school aged.

Since I started to write this book there have been many 'shock docs' on television about badly behaved children in schools, variously casting blame on parents, teachers, society at large, and sometimes the children.

I have lived the shame of parenting a child who has been excluded from school as punishment for behaviour he could neither understand nor control.

Neurological diversities provide distinct challenges to the education system, in sharp contrast to many physical disabilities. They present uniquely challenging situations that require innovative and skilled approaches, plus a level of understanding of neurological difference that is not sufficiently covered in most undergraduate or post-graduate teacher training courses.

Often the educator's response to the neurodiversity (the correct term to describe people who are 'wired differently') is fear, misunderstanding or another reductive approach.

These behaviours are often put down to a behavioural issue alone instead of a neurodiversity issue. It is my opinion that further mandatory training is needed for teachers to recognise and support such pupils effectively.

Like many parents and carers, I endured the misery of feeling that my son's 'difference' was my fault. You can't always confide in friends or family; they don't always realise it, but their help can come across as judgmental.

If you can't fully explain your feelings to close family or friends, I've written 'lessons learned' and soothing mantras at the end of each section especially for you.

Mantras (a word or sound repeated to aid concentration in meditation) can be used to train the brain to focus on positive thoughts, instead of those self-destructive ones that pop into your head. Used repeatedly, they can help you stay calm through what can be an emotionally draining time.

Sometimes it feels like you don't talk, think or worry about anything else but your child. There will be times when things go smoothly and your stress levels drops from crisis to calm.

Statistically, boys are more often identified as having disruptive behaviour in school than girls, with higher levels of autism and ADHD diagnoses. Current indications show girls are either being overlooked for a neurological diversity, diagnosed with another condition (depression/anxiety), or are diagnosed late or remain undiagnosed.

In this book, I have highlighted my experiences of being a single parent and young mum of Black Caribbean heritage. Statistics show that Black people have one of the highest rates of school exclusion from an average UK state school, particularly in major towns and cities.

Some of my experiences will ring true with you whatever your race or background. When your child is experiencing difficulties at school due to behaviour, arising from a diagnosed or undiagnosed special educational need, most schools initially focus the spotlight on you. And what happens when we feel attacked? We fight back! I know it's hard but try to reign yourself in. Stay calm. Talk to someone you can trust.

When you're in conflict with a school, local authority

or other institution, you must fight with words, evidence, logic, and in some cases, with the law. Get a trusted pair of eyes and ears to sit in meetings with you. If there's no-one to help, some charities and not-for-profit companies provide a service of attending school meetings, particularly if the meeting concerns a forthcoming disciplinary process or arranging special educational support.

The examples and stories in this book are true accounts. I have changed names, but the experiences are real. I have written from the perspective of a mother and a son, but the parent/child relationship can take many forms—everyone is welcome!

I hope reading this book will be therapeutic for you, and will create a safe place to think about your emotions and work out what to do.

Expert books on this subject delve into child psychology and development, behavioural milestones etc. The purpose of this book is simple—to help you slide through the maze of special educational needs from diagnosis and beyond, ensuring your child is safe, happy, and confident.

I've split the book into sections, so dive into whatever section you need to read. There are tips to help you intervene successfully at nursery, school, college or whatever setting your child is in. You will run into difficulties, even in the best school, often when there is a change such as a new pupil, teacher or routine.

There is no quick fix and it doesn't matter where your child is on the spectrum. If you're informed and feeling positive, there is a lot you can do to turn a situation around.

I've put a list of useful contacts at the end to help you on your way. Everyone's experience is unique but take what learnings from me that you can. In the harsh glare of a straining educational system, we all share the same boat.

My strongest wish is that you cease to compare your autism/ADHD child with any other child, either autistic or typical. With an informed parental steer and a supportive educational and social environment, your unique child will forge their own way to live, according to their own rules.

CHAPTER 1

The Bad Behaviour Zone
What Are The Primary Signs?

When I had my son Lucas, 11 years after my daughter, I was over the moon. He was a peaceful, smiley baby who melted everyone's hearts. I lived in a bubble of exhausted satisfaction for a couple of years, until the relationship with their father ended. Then, life as a single, working mother of 2 got tough.

There weren't many of the 'dressing-gown-cuddles-on-the-sofa-play-games-together-until-lunchtime' days but lots of, "I'm so tired and hungry," "I will have cereal for dinner," "I can't even be bothered to get changed for bed!"

Somehow, I got through work every day and was a zombie in the evenings. Things would improve when Lucas started nursery.

I was feeling good about getting my life back on track. Early on, his nursery key worker called me and said, "Lucas had a good day but likes to play on his own and he doesn't like sharing." I didn't think it was a big deal. During his regular health screening tests at the clinic, the health visitors hadn't flagged up or mentioned any developmental delay.

Lucas's behaviour started to change during Primary School.

Primary signs

Lucas started at the local Primary School aged 4 years and 2 months. In a mid-year report, in the section on social and emotional development, his teachers indicated that he was 'achieving at a level slightly below that which is expected for his age.'

I didn't dwell on it. His attitude to learning, language, literacy and creative development all scored highly, so I was happy. His reception teacher even described him as 'an endearing child with many special qualities.'

Reflecting on these opinions about Lucas's early years, I can see that a broader appraisal of his development may have indicated some early autism signs, especially as he was relentlessly bullied (1) and didn't seem to have many friends.

A study of how commonly autistic children aged between 4-17 years are bullied found the reported rate was at least 4 times higher than their peers. (Little, 2002.)

At the end of reception, I decided to move Lucas from the school, mainly due to the bumps on the head he kept coming home with, which I suspected were due to bullies, rather than regular Primary School accidents. The teachers mentioned he was hit by a child who later apologised AND at another time he'd 'fallen off' the pirate ship. Maybe another school would be the better suited for him?

Aged 5 years and 2 months, Lucas started his second Primary School, a strict Roman Catholic school. My mother was a practicing Roman Catholic, so it was not the religious or academic aspects of his new school that tripped him up, nor the routine and respect for the teachers. Lucas seemed to trip himself up.

He kept lashing out at the teachers and other kids. I was sure the disciplined environment would protect him from bullies, but according to reports from Primary School 2, Lucas had become the bully.

School quickly became one of the most hostile educational environments that we'd experienced. Within weeks, Lucas was repeatedly getting into trouble. Unsurprisingly, he wasn't making any friends.

I sank inwardly when the school's number came up on my phone one day while I was at work. I came off the phone shaky, insecure and sad, but walked back to my desk acting as though everything was fine. The school had told me they weren't happy with his behaviour. He'd only been there for four weeks.

Kicking off at school
This new school had a system of sending red cards home with the children, summarising in great detail the misdemeanours that had occurred during the day. These stern red pieces of cards, with black scrawls of Lucas's daily black deeds, used to terrify me. Every week, he got Santa-sized sacks full of, what I liked to call them, Red Cards of Doom, signed in angry spider writing by the headteacher.

I fantasised about the other angelic children who only took home shiny stars and certificates. I was sure one day I would crack under the weight of the shame.

Ungodly behaviour
Lucas was kicking off every day for reasons I couldn't understand.

I couldn't figure out what was causing his behaviour, but he lashed out at teachers, even once kicking the headteacher. His class teacher told me if she had been pregnant when he kicked, she would have lost a baby because he had kicked her in the stomach. I was confused and alarmed by what I was hearing. I didn't appreciate at the time something I now understand; their handling of him could have been part of the issue. If any child is held or restrained in a certain position, it's their instinct to kick and thrash.

As a faith school, I felt a strong sense of hostility from them towards Lucas and I, as if somehow his meltdowns were ungodly, sinful and damaging to the core beliefs of the school.

Something wasn't right at all; I didn't understand what. I just knew that he was behaving in a wild, unfamiliar way, which was causing lots of problems.

The Special Educational Needs Co-ordinator (SENCO) asked me all the right questions—was he hypersensitive to noise? Had he behaved like this in other situations? I said no. He behaved like a normal little boy in other settings. But reports of him crawling under tables and throwing things around made me feel unhinged. He didn't sound like the child I knew and loved.

A peek inside the classroom

I arranged with Lucas's newly qualified teacher to go into school to observe his Year 1 class. Some of the children had clear and specific educational needs. One of them, a little girl, would periodically kick off, screaming and crying so sorrowfully it set my nerves on edge.

I watched this class of 5-year olds react to this girl's extreme behaviour and witnessed something fascinating. They sensed her anxiety and remained calm until her storm had passed. When the class was quiet again, some of the children, although shaken, picked up flying pencils, spilled water and scribbled work, and calmly told the teacher that she needed time out. They knew instinctively she was emotionally stressed.

Children might be young, but they are their own people. They won't all be influenced by a child kicking off, just as not all adults become verbally or physically aggressive after too much beer or wine. We all have different tolerances and personalities.

The kids in this class had adapted their behaviour to this little girl and worked together to restore peace to their classroom.

Lucas was aware of her too, but his reaction was to bounce off her energetically. It was not a good environment for him; he was not one to walk away. He reacted emotionally, rather than rationally, to her.

It was strange to see him rise to her energy levels, getting more agitated and vocal. My presence in the classroom did make a difference; I gently reminded him to listen to the teacher, to pay attention and try to stay calm. It appeared that he couldn't focus for long periods of time and needed to let off steam every 20 minutes or so.

I was grateful to the teacher for inviting me into her classroom as I learnt a lot. Her objective was for me to see first-hand the difficulties she was having with Lucas in her class.

What I actually saw was a group of young children feeding off each other emotionally with a newly qualified teacher who was struggling to control the dynamics of her classroom.

I was exhausted when I left. The undercurrent of tension between the teacher and her class felt like a battleground for control.

Class size is a hugely political issue, but this class of thirty-one children seemed too difficult for a single teacher to effectively manage, nurture and educate.

Another teacher whispered to me in the playground one morning, in a 'helpful' way, "I wish I'd been firmer with my girls when they were growing up!"

Another said, "It's a shame. If he doesn't settle down, he'll be failing by the time he's 11."

Lucas was 6 at the time.

My mum, who was living with us, said one evening, "Why don't you ask the school for an assessment?"

I wasn't sure what it entailed, but I asked for one anyway. The school said Lucas would not be offered an assessment with the borough educational psychologist, but they urged me to take Lucas to the doctor to find out what was 'wrong' with him.

I was thinking of moving him to another school at this stage but it would still be useful to get a doctor's opinion. The doctor referred us for an appointment at the Child Adolescent Mental Health Service (CAMHS) to be assessed for ADHD. And just like that BAM! Someone had named the cause of the behaviours. We got an appointment in a few weeks—the demand for assessments was lower then.

Back at school, I asked the newly qualified class teacher to explain why the school denied us an assessment. She explained that they already had 3 other children with special needs in his class and couldn't afford another. They continued to restrain him, increasing the volatility of his behaviour.

Lucas and the staff were trapped in a downward spiral of meltdowns, punishment, more meltdowns and so on.

Excluded from Primary School

The situation was escalating and became highly distressing. One afternoon, I got a call from school telling me Lucas was being excluded with immediate effect.

I was clueless then about due process and went along with it in a daze.

Looking back, I'm sure Lucas was excluded illegally many times, but I wasn't aware of our legal position. It may have been difficult to prove that the exclusions were illegal as he wasn't diagnosed at that point.

As I was working on the other side of London, I couldn't get to his school in time. My teenage daughter was at a Secondary School nearby but she couldn't collect him until after her school day had ended.

I called Lucas's childminder in a panic to see if she could collect him. When I arrived at her house, frazzled and on edge, she told me that when she went to pick him up, the staff were asking her questions about him, trying to see if he was as difficult with her as he was at school! She told them the truth. "He's no problem at all, just like the other kids I look after. Actually, he's quite caring with the younger ones."

I couldn't believe the school had gone behind my back to try to catch me out! They'd refused him an assessment but were sneakily trying to find social proof for his behaviour.

They clearly thought he was an unruly kid or was being brought up by a useless parent, or both.

ADHD and autism: wearing many masks

"My child has a lack of interest (focus) in school."

What does this look like in class?
- Not listening to the teacher.
- Unable to follow instructions or stay on task.
- Disrupting other children.
- 'Clowning around.'
- Staring out of the window.
- Throwing books, pens or pencils in the air, flipping rulers.
- Making silly noises and calling out.

Possible causes?
- Lack of concentration.
- Hearing problems.
- Eyesight issues.
- Tiredness.
- Distractibility.
- Hyperactivity.

"My child struggles to stick to school rules."

What does this look like in class?
- Not sitting still.
- Hair-pulling.
- Talking during assembly.
- Making noises.
- Calling out.

- Complaining that uniform is uncomfortable.
- Unkempt appearance such as laces undone, tie skewed, shirt untucked.
- Running/walking on the wrong side of the corridor.

Possible causes?
- Unclear about rules.
- Forgets rules easily.
- Rules not enforced at home.
- Oppositional defiance.
- PDA (Pathological Demand Avoidance).

"My child has mood swings."

What does this look like in class?
- Obvious sadness or anger making it impossible for the child to relax or complete a task.

Possible causes?
- Social communication.
- Poor speech.
- Language difficulties.
- Unable to make and keep friends.
- Worry about school life.
- Phobias around food.
- Sensory overload.
- Noisy classroom.
- Body issues.
- Home or family issues.
- Trauma or abuse.

"My child seems emotionally unstable."

What does this look like in class?
- Temper tantrums.
- Short fuse.
- Angers easily.
- Shouting.
- Swearing.
- Gives up easily.

Possible causes?
- Likes to challenge for shock value.
- Attention-seeking behaviour.
- May feel insecure or vulnerable about any new situations or changes.
- Changes at home.
- Used to hearing/using profanity at home and/or in other environments.
- Domestic violence or other abuse.
- Experience of trauma.

Children's and young people's behaviours are affected by:
- Dyslexia, dyspraxia, dyscalculia.
- Physical disability.
- Mobility issues.
- Childhood depression.
- Generalised anxiety.
- Social anxiety.
- Eyesight or hearing problems.
- Autism (Autism Spectrum Condition).

- Attention Deficit Hyperactivity Disorder (ADHD).
- Inadequate diet, malnutrition.
- Poverty and social deprivation.
- Insufficient or poor-quality sleep.
- A genetic condition.
- Learning disability.

Children's behaviour can look like clowning around:
- Attention issues such as ADHD and Attention Deficit Disorder (ADD).
- Medication wearing off.
- Lack of sleep.
- Attention-seeking behaviour (what's the primary cause?).

Causes of anxiety in children with neurodevelopmental differences:
- Sensory issues.
- Communication difficulties.
- Rigid routines.
- Resistance to change.
- Processing speed (how quickly they learn things).
- Transitions.
- Theory of Mind (ability to think beyond themselves).
- Inflexible thinking.
- Masking.
- Autism/Autistic Spectrum Condition (ASC).

Identifying the underlying reasons for children's behaviour at school is complex and time-consuming, however it is becoming more readily recognised that in many young people, bad behaviour is used as a distress beacon and isn't always a sign of plain naughtiness.

ADHD - helpful diagnosis or harmful label?

I was naïve about the complexities of the system and the conditions, but after going to my GP and with ADHD being mentioned, I went to the CAHMS appointment. I was hoping we would come away with an ADHD diagnosis.

I filled in the parent section of the Conner's questionnaire (a multiple-choice diagnostic questionnaire) knowing Lucas's teachers had filled it in too.

A couple of weeks after the exclusion, they told me the form had been sent off. I hadn't seen their scorings and wasn't expecting to. Usually people who know a child well (such as teachers, early years childcare providers, nurseries, playgroups, childminders and parents) are invited to complete this form.

I did see their comments many years later whilst going through mountains of old paperwork for this book. I was shocked at how the responses about all of his behaviours had clearly been exaggerated to force a diagnosis.

Comments on his Conner's 'Teacher Rating Scale' (a diagnosis tool where '3' is 'very much true'):

- Inattentive, easily distracted: 3
- An emotional child: 3
- Feelings easily hurt: 3
- Excitable and impulsive: 3
- Does not know how to make friends: 3
- Seems over-focused on details: 3

At the first CAMHS appointment I saw the psychiatrist at the borough's specialist mental health hospital. She looked at the Conner's questionnaire and asked how things were for him at school and Lucas's behaviour in other environments.

I truthfully told her he was generally well-behaved in other settings including at his childminder's and at Cubs. School was the main problem.

Her view was that Lucas's behaviour was a reaction to being bullied at his first Primary School. She believed—because of his relative immaturity—that he was unable to communicate how he was feeling and her opinion was that he didn't have ADHD.

She wrote a follow-up letter to the SENCO at Primary School 2 explaining that Lucas would be discharged from the CAMHS service and didn't have ADHD. I don't know what the teachers felt when they read this, but at that point in time it felt like a relief.

Having reviewed the paperwork for this book, the teachers were keen to stress that Lucas was on the extreme edge in their Conner's responses. Nevertheless, our first CAMHS report was a no to ADHD.

Things at school bumped along after that. No-one seemed to know what to do next. Maybe you have been in the same situation?

Everyone had a different opinion on what was causing Lucas's upsetting behaviour. I started doing my own research, and remained open to the suggestions of the teachers, health professionals and friends.

I was willing to share details of my relationship history and was honest to teachers and professionals about how difficult it was being a single parent, working full-time. Naturally, teachers and health professionals were very interested in my personal life. Before I saw it coming, there were judgemental comments about my choice to work, my marital status and my ability to parent, which I found deeply hurtful. I'd have a smart answer for some of that nonsense now. But back then I didn't use my voice in those discussions.

Stress at home
The stresses of the school day were beginning to make the atmosphere at home tense. My mother was ill and living with us at the time. I was constantly shouting at Lucas and telling him off for being naughty at school.

Something just didn't sit right with me about the school so I decided to move Lucas. I thought a change of environment away from negative teachers would help, but instead it was a further period of spiralling behaviour problems and exclusions.

The local authority contacted me to say there was a Year 2 place available at another local Primary School. It was actually the school that my daughter had attended almost 10 years earlier; and she had been happy there. This had to be the one!

I called to arrange a visit and the receptionist was warm and helpful. I immediately felt moving him again was the right decision.

The bad behaviour merry-go-round
In the prism of a busy, noisy classroom, I understood it was easier to tell Lucas off and remove him from class than have a behaviour management strategy for the entire classroom. But picking on one child repeatedly is often the only method used.

Teachers might identify 1 or 2 'trouble-makers' in the average class without whom it would be much easier to teach. Although there are mountains of management techniques at the disposal of teachers, which doesn't isolate one child, the pressure on teacher's time is immense. It's a challenge for them to avoid a repeated negative focus on one child. Under pressure, most of us revert to the path of least resistance, so why should teachers be any different?

The socially isolated child learns that repeated bad behaviour will at least get the teacher's attention for a few minutes. It is widely understood amongst child psychologists that any attention is better than none.

There are many behaviours that look to be naughty, which are caused by a neurodiversity including autism and ADHD, or a combination of the 2.

Investigating the cause of the behaviour, instead of focusing on the effect of it and punishing the child, is a logical way to approach a problem rife in many schools. In these situations, staff who are unfamiliar with how neurodiversity presents itself in the classroom can rush to the conclusion that the child has been poorly raised or is just naughty. Swift removal of the child or full class evacuation might seem like the best course of action for everybody at the time—especially if the child is acting dangerously—but unless an impartial investigation follows swiftly a repeat performance is a certainty.

In that moment the teacher is standing against bigotry, prejudice and ignorance. Speaking on behalf of the child who may have social communication difficulties is challenging. Parents and teachers may blame each other rather than work together.

Being an autism/ADHD parent is like being part of a

unique club; one of the joining requirements is that your child is unlikely to have many, if any, friends. Your child's idiosyncrasies can intimidate or confuse other children or even frighten them. It's difficult for children and adults to break out of a negative perception cycle:

Bad behaviour > teasing > temper tantrums > bad behaviour > no friends > low expectations > harsh discipline > temper tantrum > bad reputation > and on it rolls...

I'm fascinated by the question that James MacAllister poses in his abstract *Why discipline needs to be reclaimed as an educational concept,* which basically means, learning about behaviour and specifically discipline, about social rules and what is expected of us as social beings, is a subject in its own right. This needs to be taught the same way as maths or sciences is taught.

Labels are losing their meaning
It's encouraging to see the autism community, autistic people and their families, owning autism, and applying a positive narrative that breaks down the stigma.

As new words are added to the Oxford English Dictionary every year such as gender-fluid, non-binary, gender-neutral etc more established words either re-assert their traditional meanings or simply fade into obscurity.

Autism isn't a new word, but it's becoming a word less often associated with vulnerability and disability. There are more positive words associated with it such as individuality.

It's thrilling to be part of an autism community that describes this neurological condition with dignity. The words neurotypical and neurodiverse are slipping into the everyday language.

Language holds the key to understanding and self-determination. New words that challenge stereotypes provide all of us with hope and direction. Healthy dialogue accelerates the pace of cultural change that needs to happen, so children who are different in any way, aren't continuously locked out of society.

The fact that autistic and ADHD children's behaviour is still misunderstood in many schools is the cause of distress to thousands of parents. It happens in all sorts of schools from specialist to state.

This is not a simple question of teacher or parent blame, or even scarce funding, it's an uncomfortable reflection of how we treat our most vulnerable people in society.

In the words of the late Nelson Mandela, "There can be no keener revelation of a society's soul than the way in which it treats its children."

Disability inequality persists for adults in the form of poor employment prospects, promotion opportunities and options for accessible workplaces. The Equality Act is clear about the requirement in law for fair treatment for disabled people, but in reality, culture change moves as quickly as a moon-walking sloth.

Is bad behaviour catching?
Imagine your child is neurotypical, and you're worried about your child's education being disrupted by those kids in the class with additional needs.

In my #happyinschool sessions, which provides autism and

ADHD education, training and empowerment for families, educators and organisations, we discuss the needs of the other children in the class and what is fair.

It's usually a lively session with a heavy dose of reality and covers points such as:

- Children have an in-built radar about their peers. They know who's weak, shy, confident, who to pick on, who will cry easily, who will kick off if teased (it's Darwinian).
- The influence kids exert on each other is powerful. If your child is the one who's 'different' this can make them the object of bullying behaviour.
- A child's natural instinct is to be one of the pack, with a strong desire to fit in. Even if they feel uncomfortable about bullying another child, they will join in (as in William Golding's book *Lord of the Flies*).
- A big part of going to school is learning the rules of social engagement. Play is a key socialisation tool and if a child doesn't get the rules of play (lots of autistic kids don't) this immediately singles them out, so they may struggle to be accepted.
- Interestingly, some autistic children are comfortable with their own company and don't wish to be part of the pack. In a classroom setting this self-imposed isolation can be unsettling for the majority of neurotypical children (4).
- Here's the clever thing: children can work out what is real and what is pretend.
- Most children will quickly stop messing about when

they are threatened with genuine punishment (i.e. followed through rather than an empty threat) by a teacher such as missing a special trip or not playing outside.

- The autistic child with sensory overload, or the child with ADHD whose brain has peaked at red for danger, won't always stop. It's like they have no off button.
- All of these signs mark them out as 'different,' which makes them potential targets for bullying behaviour.

Typical children won't be overly influenced by the impact of their autistic school chums. They will understand instinctively that they are different. They won't become autistic because they're not wired that way. What they may do is mock the autistic child's actions or wind them up.

The other 29

Headteachers with extraordinary leadership skills are good at balancing the competing needs of concerned parents, teachers and support staff. They know how to reassure the other 29 parents who are worried about the effect that your child's actions, will have on their child's education.

Most distressing is the pressure on your child who senses their difference and, depending on their age, isn't sure why it's a problem.

As a teacher, what do you say to the parents who think the challenging child should be educated somewhere else because they are stopping their child from learning?

The other 29 can reasonably access the curriculum without support. They don't want their learning to be disrupted. This is why some autistic children need one-to-one sessions. But the need for additional support in one child can create envy in parents of the other 29. Parents need to be kind to each other and try to understand we each have kids with different strengths and challenges.

The argument to remove a child from a classroom to protect the other 29 is a loaded one. There are many reasons for and against, and every case is different.

All teachers have different skills and will approach a class disruption using the skills they are most comfortable with. Whether to remove a disruptive child or not depends on the cause of behaviour, how quickly it's escalating, and what strategies are being used to deal with it.

Behaviour management is a complex subject dependent on many variables, including the dynamics of the class and the other personalities in it.

Classroom Behaviour by Bill Rogers is a great book which brings a range of classroom scenes to life and the various approaches used by teachers. A child who uses verbal bullying behaviour, spiteful words as missiles to trigger explosions in other children, can create as much disruption by their words as a child who kicks out.

Supply teachers or newly qualified teachers (NQTs) are especially vulnerable to rowdy classroom behaviour mainly due to their inexperience. What if a child's Learning Support Assistant (LSA) is off sick on the day of a classroom incident? Is the child with SEN always wholly responsible for their actions? What about the actions of others who may trigger them? Does the whole class have a moral responsibility to support the one with additional needs?

Sticks and stones may break bones, but words can harm the soul, long after they are spoken. The safety of the 30 is paramount, but the education of the 29 will continue to be disrupted if the underlying issues of the 'one' are not effectively managed. But what if the disruptive 'one' isn't always the same child? The other 29 are not always the same group of youngsters!

It's not a black and white issue, and my experience is to avoid getting into direct conflict with other parents or teachers on this one. Your perspective will be right depending on where you stand. But be open and compassionate to the views of others, as they can be right too!

Teachers are frequently faced with several seriously disruptive incidents with various perpetrators in any given week. Whether they are all dealt with evenly is another matter. Is a child excluded even if they haven't been disruptive before? Is a child less likely to be excluded if they are SEN? It's an emotive subject and best dealt with if the emotion and polarising opinions are reduced in favour of fair systems, proper training and full regard for the SEND code of practice.

Core values of respect, compassion, equality and anti-discrimination are usually the key pillars of every school community. We are all responsible for trying to uphold these principles wherever they fall on the parent, educator or SEN continuum. As members of an advanced society, we need to listen to voices that sound different to our own.

Managing behaviour is a key element of the teaching process but managing autism and ADHD behaviours requires training and guidance.

I notice a greater appetite for teachers (not just specialist or SENCOs) to do continued professional development (CPD) training on autism and ADHD. It makes sense, as school is often where a child with a disability will show up, especially if any issues haven't been picked up in early years settings.

School is great at spotting anomalies because they are highly conformist environments. If you notice any different behaviours in your Primary School aged child, make a note of it and take into account.

Not all autistic/ADHD children behave in the same way. Their individual temperament will be intricately woven into their autism or ADHD self to make a unique whole. We all need to understand the nature of difference and recognise the changes in behaviour or communication that difference may cause. Only then will school become a more comfortable place for all children.

Autism is sometimes difficult to spot in a busy classroom with up to 30 children clamouring for a teacher's attention. To complicate things further, girls with undiagnosed autism respond to classroom pressures differently to boys. They can at times appear to be cripplingly shy, uncommunicative, evasive, withdrawn, often with low mood or what looks like a disinterest in learning.

Autistic girls are also known to mask or camouflage their natural behaviour or habits that they feel are socially unacceptable. They do this in order to fit in with their peers and not draw attention to their difference.

Masking is extremely tiring for those who do it, and can disrupt their wellbeing and mental health, through the sheer sustained stress of not being true to themselves.

Girls who mask are more likely to internalise their struggles which leads to anxiety or depression. This can lead to misdiagnoses of anxiety and depression when in fact the primary cause of the depression is autistic spectrum condition.

If your child's behaviour is described as challenging, remember there is always a cause: every action has a reaction. You may not know what's triggering it, but if you position yourself together with the teacher, leaving blame on both sides firmly off the table, you have a fighting chance of settling on a cause(s) and then you can begin to craft a tailored plan for your child.

A pause in sanctions may seem like a soft touch, especially if your child's school practices negative discipline, but sometimes the teacher and the child need a break from the repetitive negative behaviour patterns they may have both fallen into.

Boys will be boys
Boys love larking about, playing the clown and getting laughs. Dealing with challenging children and pranksters is difficult for teachers who are under such pressure to deliver good league table results for their school.

Depending on the skill and experience of the class teacher, there are positive ways that boys' energy can be channelled so that the teacher retains control and the children doesn't feel publicly embarrassed. Not the easiest balance to strike but I believe that even the worst behaviour, can be worked out.

There is always a cause, but often there is not enough time or resources to figure it out. In some cases, boys bring high levels of aggression and complex behavioural problems into school that cannot be easily addressed. These can be indicators that the child has experienced some kind of trauma. But they are still someone's son, and require compassion and understanding, even if they are not able to remain in school.

Early childhood experiences can ruin potentially brilliant children. A lot of bright young stars fizzle out prematurely by turning their destructive forces on themselves or outward in a series of harmful behavioural patterns.

You've got to hand it to teachers, many carry out multiple roles of educator, mother, father, social worker, counsellor and friend and for that we salute you.

Teacher's responsibility

Based on what we've learned about neurodifferences so far, it's clear that the issue of teacher experience and confidence is game-changing. It's essential to know how to:

1. Identify a child in sensory or emotional distress
2. Apply de-escalation and calming skills
3. Bring the rest of the class off the boil (laughing, teasing, shouting)

It's also critical that the teacher knows when to make a judgement call about removing a child from the classroom or calling for assistance.

Shouting at a child who is outside of the norm, in distress or unable to respond, is clearly unacceptable. Everyone gets stressed and angry but in that instance, every other child is watching the teacher for their reaction and their body language. The teacher is setting a strong example to every child about how to respond to difference, how to behave fairly and compassionately.

I read examples every day of teachers who cast a bright

and positive light over their classrooms; instilling respect for every child. I also hear stories about cruelty from children and adults towards others in school that bring tears to my eyes. All children need to learn the core lessons of humanity, compassion, patience, individuality and forgiveness.

In addition to exuberance, autism and ADHD can look like wilful naughtiness. Calling out, banging desk lids, constant movement and irrepressible energy must make some teachers question why they entered the profession!

Sometimes the class is dysfunctional, rude, belligerent, unkind and the responsible adult needs to find a way to restore calm and hold a moral compass up high. Teaching is not for the fainthearted.

When your child starts to act up at school there are many possible causes. Some may overlap, which can make the cause more difficult to identify. If not autistic, your child may have another reason driving their behaviour such as Avoidant Personality Disorder (AvPD), Oppositional Defiant Disorder (ODD), Anti-Social Behaviour Disorder, Pathological Demand Avoidance (PDA) or ADHD.

There are many reasons for disruptive behaviour in the classroom, only a few of them are due to kids being naughty.

Breaking the negative cycle
Children with an undiagnosed hidden disability like autism, ADHD or social, emotional and mental health difficulties will find lots of things about school very challenging to manage.

They usually start school already stressed. Hungry, tired, worried about family problems or other social and emotional problems that they don't know how to articulate. School will simply add to their number of things to feel anxious about.

Many of us have an in-built sensitivity radar when it comes to children, but when we fall off the wagon or have a run-away mouth (ahem), we need to remember to react to children in a way that empowers them and makes them feel worthy.

In addition to autism or ADHD, your child may be hurting due to a number of reasons. The following exercise might help you to understand.

Try This. . .

Write down 5 things that may have caused your child to feel unsettled in the last 2 years

You might have a little cry when you're writing this, that's okay! But it's important for you to be honest. In the future, you may wish to share these thoughts with a trusted professional.

1.

2.

3.

4.

5.

Try This. . .

Now write down 5 things that have gone well for your child in the last couple of years

1.

2.

3.

4.

5.

Reflect on what you're written down and think how these events brought you to where you are today. Put these thoughts somewhere safe. Journaling is the first step of the journey you and your child will go on towards more confident and happy times at school.

Friendly Advice

- Consider creating a partnership with the school, shifting your relationship from adversarial to collaborative. Not easy but essential.

- Make it known to the teaching team that your expectation is to be regarded as an equal partner in how your child is supported in school.

- Schools can provide access to experts to help you and your child inch from hopeless to hopeful. Take your notebook into meetings and ask a few direct questions such as, how will Lego Therapy support my child's social communication/ADD/speech and language/autism/ Asperger's/socials skills?

- Think about what life looks like from your child's point of view.

- It's easy to get frustrated with the school but do you know enough about your child's behaviour, emotional and social issues at school? Do you have all the information? And if not schedule in a meeting with the school.

Questions to Ask Yourself

- Am I happy that the causes of my child's behaviour at school are being fully and swiftly investigated? Might there be a medical reason(s) for my child's behaviour?

- Does the teacher have evidence for issues that are being discussed?

- Am I putting things into my notebook?

- What can I do to look after myself and ensure I feel confident as a parent?

- Who is supporting me? Do I need to ask for help from friends, family and other sources?

Mantras

"My child is a unique part of me, but still a separate, unique being, with their own challenges and joys. I trust my child and I set them free."

"This is just a temporary phase, my child is spreading their wings and testing the boundaries. We will work together to make school a safe and happy place."

Positive Ways to Address a Child With Autism

- Avoid calling a child out publicly.

- Look for opportunities to showcase the good things they do/say/achieve.

- Investigate root causes of behaviour.

- Remember it takes time to get to the root cause of the behaviour. Be patient.

- Good quality of teaching is a vital requirement to help to diffuse difficult situations; your child is more likely to believe a good teacher can be a trusted adult if they see the teacher treat them fairly.

- Behaviour management strategies need to be tailored to the child. Reward-based systems only work if the child is motivated by rewards, otherwise the behaviour programme might feel like a punishment.

Parents, be aware that the cause for your child's behaviour may change as they get older, as they are more able to mask their patterns, keep secrets or tell lies.

Lessons Learned

- Behaviour is a form of communication where emotions become our voice. There is a reason for all behaviours.

- One of the most powerful motivations for behaviour is fear (the other is love). Sometimes even if we aren't aware of what is making us feel anxious our bodies will still react to what is making us stressed.

- Adverse behaviours of children and young people with autism and ADHD have many causes:
  - Processing difficulties (level of understanding about what is going on)
  - Social or general anxiety
  - Sensory overload
  - Low self-esteem
  - Communication difficulties
  - Hard to make friends
  - Challenges fitting in with peers

- When the build-up of emotions isn't fully addressed, the pressure cooker of pent-up emotion boils over into a meltdown.

- Instead of using words to communicate the emotion (I'm tired, confused, overloaded, irritable, unwell, angry) a physical emotional display will happen instead. Especially if a child thinks they cannot trust you (the designated adult) with their emotions. Eventually, it becomes too much and they lose control entirely.

- When a meltdown occurs, your child has lost the ability to regulate their emotions.

- In addition to poor emotional regulation, your child with autism/ADHD may also need support with speech, language and communication i.e. processing time to help them:
  - Recognise their feelings
  - Communicate their feelings in advance of them reaching the point of meltdown
  - Name their feelings

- As a parent or family member, you have the full picture and knowledge of your child's moods, triggers and history. Trust your instincts. Make sure your voice and opinions about your child are heard.

- Others will tell you things about your child that may be unsavoury or distressing, but it's important to listen to them.

- Your honesty will help everyone to reach the right diagnosis and help your child to access the right treatment plan.

- If your child displays challenging behaviour at school, there is always a cause.

CHAPTER 2

The Discovery Zone
What Is Autism, ADHD And Asperger's?

The rise and rise of. . .
When he was at school, entrepreneur Richard Branson's teachers considered him stupid and lazy. His mind was active, but he had difficulty focusing, which in retrospect he attributes to not having his dyslexia taken into account. As he grew older and built his empire of businesses, he learnt about the mechanics of his learning disability and adapted his management style. He believes this made him a better manager and he has gone on to claim his dyslexia is his 'greatest strength.'

SEN, autism and ADHD are hot topics. People ask me why autism and ADHD diagnoses are rising. Honestly, I don't know, but I do think the answers are many and varied.

Causes are both fascinating and controversial, but my interest is not in medicalising or marginalising what is, for many of us, another way of being [human].

I'm interested in improving equality and enjoyment of life for all. Undeniably autistic people experience the world differently, for me, as long as the experience of the world is as complex, pleasurable and painful as it is for everyone else, the cause of autism and ADHD is of less significance.

I see autism/ADHD not as an oddity, but as a new normalcy. Part of the evolution of our species, not just neurologically, but spiritually.

So why do you feel alone? I can relate to how you're feeling right now. You don't know how you got here. You feel like you're in a parallel universe. How can a neurodiversity cause so much sadness, frustration and confusion? I think we all need to change our perceptions.

ADHD and other neurological disorders are on the increase amongst boys and girls. American data points to boys being twice as likely to be diagnosed, with approximately 13% of boys and 5% of girls diagnosed.

World Health Organisation (WHO) states 1 in 160 children (2) is autistic (from a global study). Another study from the Centres for Disease Control and Prevention (3) estimates autism spectrum disorder (ASD) amongst children in the US at 1 in 54. These studies also show that autism in boys is '4 time more common' than girls.

There are no agreed universal criteria and the situation changes so quickly before analysts have a chance to debate and agree guidelines. One thing is certain: there is a growing need for people the length and breadth of the autism spectrum to be fully integrated into society, free of the education, employment and personal discrimination they currently face.

Neurodiverse girls present so differently to boys we are potentially misunderstanding and misdiagnosing large numbers of girls who are suffering unnecessarily.

Right now, you might be investigating other health issues

with your child. Autism exists with disabilities including Dyspraxia, Dyslexia, speech and language disorders, Sensory Processing Disorder, gastrointestinal problems, as well as ADHD and a host of other conditions. The list is not exhaustive and the presence of other conditions can make treatment and support tricky.

My son was tested for Sickle Cell Anaemia and other genetic conditions that affect Caribbean and Mediterranean descendants. Thankfully his genetic profile was clear.

Children with additional educational needs are becoming common in UK schools. There are approximately 1,318, 330 pupils with SEN: 14.9 %. Most of these children (1,047,165) don't have Education Health and Care plans (EHCPs). That's 670,110 pupils in state primaries and 413,790 pupils in state secondaries. There are 13,070 pupils in pupil referral units and 90,485 pupils with SEN in independent schools: approximately 15.6%. (All data gov.uk, Jan 2019)

Evidently, SEN are an issue schools face every day. Some do this well, in co-ordinated, compassionate ways, using a variety of interventions whilst accessing expert advice. Others approach teaching children with special educational needs as something they have to do legally, but ideally, they'd rather pass this responsibility on to a school with specialist expertise.

Significant numbers of children in our schools have social, emotional and mental health difficulties. Primary and Secondary SEN figures (Department for Education, 2019):

- 108, 979 pupils (16.3%) have social, emotional and mental health difficulties in Primary Schools.

- 81,223 pupils (19.6%) have social, emotional and mental health difficulties in Secondary Schools.
- 52,808 pupils (7.9%) have Autism Spectrum Disorder in state Primary Schools (includes those with SEN support and EHCPs).
- 42,555 pupils (10.3%) have Autism Spectrum Disorder in state Secondary Schools (includes those with SEN support and EHCPs).

Autism Defined

The UK's National Autistic Society (NAS) defines autism as:

"... a lifelong developmental disability that affects how people perceive the world and interact with others. Autistic people see, hear and feel the world differently to other people. If you are autistic, you are autistic for life; autism is not an illness or disease and cannot be *'cured'*. Often people feel being autistic is a fundamental aspect of their identity. Autism is a spectrum condition. All autistic people share certain difficulties but being autistic will affect them in different ways."

It's interesting that the NAS refers to autism as a developmental disability whereas some of the clinical papers refer to autism as a developmental disorder. Autistic children or adults do not necessarily have a learning (intellectual) disability. Learning may be more difficult for some due to a range of sensory, emotional or social interactional factors. It could also be another cognitive (learning) impairment.

An autism diagnosis does not automatically mean the child has intellectual impairment. Some young people, in particular those with ADHD or those with what used to be called Asperger's Syndrome, now known as high-functioning autism (HFA), have poor executive functioning skills. This will impact their forward planning and organisation skills. It can also affect their working memory, both of which can make learning in a school environment challenging. This is why the condition is referred to as a spectrum.

Other autistic children will experience sensory issues (sight, sound, touch, smell, motion etc) which makes the average classroom feel overwhelming and a difficult environment to learn in. This is not the same as having a learning disability.

I also see notable autism characteristics including:

- Social honesty and integrity.
- Strong sense of social justice and equality, non-judgmental, passionate about fairness.
- Rigid, methodical and systematic on subjects of great interest to the individual.

Under the banner of autism or Autism Spectrum Disorder (ASD) there are 3 sub-groups:

1. Asperger's Syndrome* (high-functioning autism).
2. Pathological Demand Avoidance (PDA).
3. Autistic Disorder (Classic Autism).

*Asperger's Syndrome is no longer an official diagnostic classification as it doesn't feature in the official diagnostic manual. High-functioning autism is the alternative term. But are we happy talking about high-functioning, which leads you to think others are therefore low-functioning? Language ties us in knots! Although many Asperger's kids I know are comfortable with the term, even referring to themselves as 'Aspies,' there is a historical and political sensitivity around the word Asperger's, as it comes from an Austrian paediatrician of that name, who conducted studies on mental disorders in children. One you may wish to research.

Autism is a spectrum condition, which means it presents with a different intensity from person to person. The range in the spectrum is so vast that some autistic people will have limited communication or rarely speak, while others will have highly developed language and cognitive skills.

Current autism academics are happily busting myths such as no empathy, being really good at drawing or maths, not making eye contact, flapping arms. When you meet an autistic person, you've met one autistic person. There are autism traits and there are autistic individuals.

Children on the spectrum behave in a noticeably different way to their peers and require support to make and sustain friendships. They will usually require some support to learn at school, which their neurotypical peers won't need. That is called SEN.

Autism is not a mental health disorder. It's a neurological condition. A development disorder (I prefer the word condition) that affects the brain, which is as complex as it is individualistic.

The current Mental Health Act defines autism as a mental disorder, which means that autistic people can be inappropriately detained in hospitals against their (and their family's) will.

The National Autistic Society is campaigning for this to be reviewed: 'We are clear about this: autism is not a mental health condition and it is inappropriate for autism to be included in the definition in this way.'

Autistic youngsters are often delayed in meeting developmental milestones because they are engaged in a neurotypical way. They are expected to make eye-contact and reciprocate in primary carer learning settings.

Many autistic youngsters do make good progress in primary years, even with a delayed start, some overtake their peers, while others always remain slightly behind. I remind parents to see their child as an individual and encourage their strengths (personal as well as academic) and not to compare them too much with other people's kids. Easy to hear, not so easy to do—I know!

Now is a good time to have a quick walk around other aspects of autism that you may come across on your travels. These descriptions don't apply to all autistic children and yours may exhibit some of these or none of these. All is possible in the bandwidth of the autism spectrum.

Stimming
A short-hand word for self-stimulating behaviour, such as:

- Walking on tiptoes.
- Blowing bubbles.
- Waving or flapping hands.
- Repetitive noises.
- Echoing or repeating words (echolalia).
- Head banging.

- Hair stroking.
- Repeated blinking.
- Rocking.
- Pencil-tapping.

All are normal in children and teens with autism and ADHD. I see stimming as a fascinating way that the body provides itself with what it needs, such as:

1. A release. If you're feeling a build-up of an emotion—negative or positive, which makes sense when you understand that we experience emotions in a sensory way in the body.
2. Stimming can block out extra sensory input if you're feeling overstimulated.
3. Pain reduction: stimming can assist in releasing endorphins (feel good chemicals) in the brain.
4. Self-regulation: self-soothing/calming if you feel anxious.

Stimming can lessen as you get older but in some cases it stays with you all of your life. It's a natural response in humans and isn't something that needs to be managed or cured unless the stimming is dangerous or harmful in some way.

Some clinicians suggest introducing an alluring alternative to stimming if you wish to reduce or stop one that is harmful, for example introducing a physical activity such trampolining, or playing with a specific toy or game.

Pathological Demand Avoidance (PDA)
In the 1980s, Professor Elizabeth Newson noticed that while

a group of children didn't meet the usual clinical profile of autism or Asperger's, they all had something in common. The central characteristic in all the children was 'an obsessional avoidance of the ordinary demands of everyday life.' (Autism Education Trust, E Newson, 2003.)

Read more about PDA on the National Autistic Society website (5).

Alexithymia in autism

I agree, this word is a bit of a mouthful but it's interesting to be aware of and will help you to understand how to communicate with your autistic child.

This is a personality trait that can make it difficult to identify or describe your—or other people's—emotions. It can look like emotional detachment about their own feelings and shows up as an inability to describe how they are feeling, apart from in a few limited adjectives.

It's a complicated area of psychiatry and doesn't affect everyone with a diagnosis of autism. It's a newly classified disorder but one worth mentioning as it does seem to affect a proportion of autistic people in adulthood.

Asperger's Syndrome

Asperger's Syndrome used to be listed in the Diagnostic Statistical Manual of Mental Disorders (DSM) in 1994, but in 2003, Asperger's Syndrome was folded into the overall diagnosis of Autistic Spectrum Condition.

The Asperger's part of my son's diagnosis helped to explain why his characteristics didn't look like 'classic' autism.

Children with autism will behave differently in the same

situation, react differently to sensory overload and communicate in a variety of ways.

Asperger's Syndrome is characterised by difficulties in social interaction and non-verbal communication along with restricted and repetitive patterns of behaviour and interests.

Since 2013, Asperger's Syndrome was removed as a separate diagnosis in the Diagnostic and Statistical Manual of Mental Disorders (DSM-5), which means anyone presenting with these symptoms since that date is diagnosed with High-Functioning Autism (HFA).

Although it's considered a milder form of autism, differing from other ASDs by 'normal' use of language and in many cases higher than average intelligence levels, the condition still requires specific skills of management, particularly if it co-exists with ADHD.

Even to the trained eye, symptoms of ADHD are present in Asperger's Syndrome and vice versa. According to in-clinic investigations, American psychiatrist Daniel Rosen found that, "60-70% of children with Asperger's have symptoms that are compatible with an ADHD diagnosis (6)" (NHS).

Learning approaches for ADHD and autistic children need to be consistent and adaptive to the needs of the individual child for them to be able to cope with mainstream teaching methods.

The use of the word 'mild' doesn't accurately credit how hard an individual with High Functioning Autism has to work to operate within a mainstream education system, or how many micro-adjustments they have to make for their autism to appear 'mild.'

Asperger's Syndrome traits can include:

- Remarkable (hyper) focus.
- Excellent attention to detail or excellent memory for facts and data.

In some these traits seem to conflict directly with the ADHD personality:

- Restlessness/inability to sit still.
- Impulsivity.
- Inability to concentrate on one task at a time.

Asperger's Syndrome - moods and mental health

Children (and adults) with Asperger's can experience problems with anger, which can be extreme. There are many causes, which include the temperament of the individual, genes, their level of social integration, whether they have friends, family and people to talk to and how well they are able to function in their environment.

If you live with a young person with Asperger's, who has low mood or angry outbursts, you will be keen to reduce the frequency, intensity and consequences of this anger. No children with autism are the same, but we do know when they vent their anger—whether publicly or in private—it can be highly disruptive and distressing for the individual and the people around them.

Asperger's Syndrome can be complex to manage for families as these children and young people can appear remote and reluctant to engage in everyday conversation.

Children with Asperger's Syndrome may be described as high-functioning but this doesn't mean they will listen attentively and calmly to every one of their school lessons. They won't. They will present as the model student in a lesson they're interested in. They can almost block out everything else around them and focus rigidly on the lesson if they find it interesting.

If on the other hand the lesson is of zero interest to them, their autism logic will focus their attention on something more interesting—to them.

Problem solving can be crippling.

- "I can't leave this until I've done it." (Hyper-focus)
- "I can't do this, so what's the point in trying?" (Fear of failure)

The tendency to be excellent in some subjects and completely disinterested in the rest of the curriculum can make educating Asperger's kids (especially those with an additional diagnosis of ADHD) a frustrating balancing act.

Young people with Asperger's Syndrome can be vulnerable to depression, with about 1 in 3 children and adults with Asperger's Syndrome experiencing clinical depression.

The 'red-card' technique or Zones of Regulation model, acts as a signifier of agitation and is a tried and tested method used to help children flag-up when they're about to kick off or need urgent assistance from a teacher (more of this in the Therapies Zone chapter). Some autistic kids can't find their 'red card' in time; they may need to leave the classroom or get adult help.

In Lucas's words: "I got annoyed because I worked for 5 days on my Tudor Project and didn't get a Headteacher Award. So I started throwing pencils everywhere. I should have told the teachers that I was getting upset, but I would still have been angry and want to say the 'F' word."

In summary, children with Asperger's display:

- Sensory integration difficulties.
- Social communication difficulties (not understanding the rules of play).
- Struggle with gross motor co-ordination—appear clumsy, bash into things, unsure of where they are in space.
- Impairment in executive function (the frontal lobe part of the brain that organises memory; the 'boss' part of the brain that tells you what to do and organises you). Executive function impairment can also show up as difficulty switching from one task to another, such as changing lessons or classrooms.
- Children with Asperger's can appear distracted, inattentive or slow to transition from one activity to another.

The most interesting area for me as a parent was understanding how difficult it can be to make precise diagnoses.

At the more severe edges of the ADHD spectrum and the less extreme edges of the Asperger's Syndrome, clinicians can argue for one diagnosis over another. It is common for a child with Asperger's syndrome to be first diagnosed with ADHD due to attention and behavioural issues. This was the case for us. As further tests are done and more specialists get involved, a more specific diagnosis of Asperger's is made.

With Asperger's, their behaviours can appear so unusual that children can be unkindly labelled as a 'nerd' or 'weirdo.'

Although the media sometimes glamorises autistic people as being prodigies or having super high intelligence, more than half of autistic people have an IQ of less than 70. And 30% of autistic children never speak more than a few words. Plus, they can suffer with bowel and digestive problems at a much higher rate than the average population.

Many autistic people also experience crippling levels of anxiety. (Robyn Charron, 2017, www.focusforhealth.org/autism-rates-across-the-developed-world/.)

Children and adults with Asperger's Syndrome are often average intelligence and sometimes above.

Asperger's Syndrome can also co-exist with a number of associated conditions including Oppositional Defiance Disorder (ODD), Depression, Bipolar Disorder, Borderline Personality Disorder (BPD) Anxiety and Obsessive Compulsive Disorder (OCD).

The language barrier
Language is a minefield for children with Asperger's; what you say should be what you mean. We don't actually mean there is a field full of mines or that cats and dogs will come falling from the sky when it rains.

I spoke to a child with Asperger's who said, "But we think what you say, and the way you say it, is important. That's why some of us are not great at the small talk side of social interaction. All of those conversations and words spoken that aren't really saying anything of substance, why would people waste time on that?"

Some autistic people are highly literal and expect you to say exactly what you mean, without sarcasm, word play or other confusing idioms, used so common in the English language. Avoiding expressions such as 'blow me down,' 'light as a feather' or 'cutting off your nose to spite your face' is advisable, as these expressions can sound alarming to the autistic ear! Just to be clear: these are specific aspects of the autistic profile and won't apply to every autistic child.

What words do you use to describe your child? Do you realise you are creating a story or narrative about them that will be repeated until those words become true?

"Disturbed, deranged, naughty, aggressive, angry, violent, disruptive, cocky, lippy, mouthy, nasty, rude, attitude, cheeky, troublemaker, challenging disruptive, a right handful."

You get the idea.

How do these words make you feel? You've done something wrong, you're sorry, but people keep reminding you of what you've done wrong. Eventually you own the bad behaviour. It's your label.

Words can and do hurt, especially when the label used to describe you isn't the real you, and the pain of being divorced from your true identity makes your heart and soul feel stretched until you don't know where the label ends and you begin.

Somewhere between the gappy 2-year-old through to aged 6 or 7, Lucas was morphing from cutie to monster. I saw the issues of self-identity and awareness as both empowering and limiting him.

Catastrophic thinking
Autistic children can project extremely negative outcomes on things they are trying to do. You might hear them say, "I'm

rubbish at drawing" or "If I try to play football, I will probably trip and break my neck!"

They are grappling with severe lack of confidence and anxiety, which can make just thinking about something throw them into a whirlwind of failure and disappointment. If your child does this, don't laugh it off, it can be distressing for them to feel such a lack of confidence in their own ability.

Extreme emotions

Some children and young people are extreme in their catastrophic thinking. "I would rather leave home in a body bag than set foot in that school again." This is an actual quote from a 15-year-old girl with autism and severe anxiety. She was unhappy at school and showed her level of anxiety to me in a very clear way. If you hear this kind of talk, take notice.

Some adults find it disturbing or disrespectful if a young person talks about life and death in a way which seems designed to shock you. Try to listen without interrupting and if you feel yourself saying, "Don't be silly" try to hold it in—there may be a serious cry for help behind those dramatic words.

There are many therapies that can help, ranging from Psychotherapy, Cognitive Behaviour Therapy (autism/ADHD specific is better), Acceptance and Commitment Therapy (ACT), Art, drama and play therapy are all excellent at helping to express feelings and build confidence, imagination and resilience.

Trained therapists can be found through British Association of Behavioural and Cognitive Psychotherapies (BABCP). You can also get a referral for your child through CAHMS but waiting lists can be long.

It's also worth speaking to your local authorities Children's Services Team (look on your local council website) as some boroughs are working on Improving Access to Psychological Therapy (IAPT). They may have a pathway for your child with or without an autism or ADHD diagnosis.

The causes of catastrophic thinking are unclear but may be linked to past experiences that create a genuine fear in the child, a fear of failure, fear of getting it wrong, or being laughed at. There is a genuine fear of standing out or feeling foolish, which is a concern for children and young people who struggle to make and keep friendships.

The anxiety and dramatic thoughts and emotions can be an autism type characteristic; it's common in people with Asperger's.

A worrier-type mindset also known as Generalised Anxiety Disorder (GAD) can get worse over time and start to define the thought process, which creates more automatic negative thoughts. This level of anxiety can be debilitating and draining.

Cognitive Behavioural Therapy (CBT) and medication combined are highly effective at moving people on from being stuck in a negative thinking cycle. Sometimes the talk therapy can be so effective that medication isn't required. Direct all medication questions to a qualified psychiatrist or GP.

Asperger's profile from a school eye view
Please note that some children will have elements of Asperger's and ADHD.

- The Asperger's child will focus on one activity with a

level of intensity that can exclude everything else in his environment.

- Will get angry if their routine or favourite activity is interrupted.
- Will usually want to have friends (despite having poor 'social entry' skills, knowing how to start and carry on conversations).
- Will break rules because they don't understand them, or think they are illogical.
- Might display oppositional behaviour such as Oppositional Defiance Disorder (ODD) which is hostile, defiant and disobedient behaviour directed to an adult. It's also characterised by irritable and moody behaviour.
- Children with Asperger's crave order, routine and reliability. Too much change or unexpected change can make them brittle and unsettled.
- They can be tyrannical about details.
- It is common for a child with Asperger's to be initially diagnosed with ADHD due to impulsivity and behavioural issues.

Before you get too down hearted, we need to remind ourselves that some of the brightest and most progressive minds in history may have had an autism diagnosis:

- **Thomas Edison**, one of the world's most prolific inventors, was kicked out of school at an early age, as his teacher lost patience with his persistent questions and wandering mind. Where would we be if prescription drugs had numbed his creative spirit? (Probably in the dark!)

- **Frederick Douglass**, one of the foremost leaders of slavery's abolitionist movement began defying the rules for Black people when he was a child.
- **Albert Einstein**, father of modern physics, was a quiet child who kept his distance from his peers. He resented the rote learning methods enforced in school and was labelled a foolish daydreamer. Imagine if he had been forced into conformity! For some children (and adults), discovering they think and act differently to their peers is a transformative step.
- **Dr Willard Wigan MBE** is a British sculptor who makes microscopic art. His sculptures are typically placed in the eye of a needle or on the head of a pin. A single sculpture can be as small as 0.005 mm. Autistic and dyslexic, Willard's sculptures are magical and entertaining. I dub him 'The King of Tiny Art.'
- **Billie Eilish**, American singer, is candid about her Tourette's Syndrome, which she hasn't allowed to hold her back on her rise to stardom. She manages her tics when she's being interviewed (by letting them out between questions). Her singer-song-writing ability is incredible.

Let's talk about ADHD

Autism Spectrum Disorder and ADHD are linked; both neurological in origin, therefore affecting behaviour. But ADHD is not on the autism spectrum, although some practitioners believe ADHD is a form of autism.

Clinicians are starting to realise the similarities in presentation and acknowledge that it is possible for a child to have both Asperger's and ADHD. So it is easy to see why ADHD is regarded as an Autism Spectrum Disorder.

Using 2 negative words—deficit and disorder—to describe another unique type of mind detracts from the passion and energy of people with this condition.

The global increase in autism cases around the world is impossible to ignore. Many suspect that published figures don't reflect the real extent of the issue due to adults and children who are undiagnosed, or diagnosed with other conditions.

Before Lucas was diagnosed I felt the contempt of teachers who seemed to hint that his behaviour was due to me being a single working mum. It's understandable that beleaguered teachers may try to offload the problem of disruptive children onto parents.

There may be other things going on with the family that impact the child's mental wellbeing which could amplify their autism/ADHD traits. Assessment and diagnostic pathways can be complicated so it's easy to see why the focus is often on defective parenting, rather than investigating the root cause of the behaviour.

Three indicators of ADHD
1. Hyperactivity: lots of movement all the time.
2. Inattention: unable to focus or concentrate.
3. Impulsivity: acting or speaking without thinking about the consequences.

People usually think of hyperactivity when they hear the word

ADHD but as with many neurological conditions, there are many variants. Here are 3 sub-types of ADHD:

1. Inattentive: silly mistakes, poor attention to detail, or organisation, losing things.
2. Hyperactive-impulsive: fidgety, restless, calling out, on the go, excessive talking, impatient.
3. Combined inattentive and hyperactive-impulsive: a combination of the 2 previous sub-types, difficulty concentrating with impulsive outbursts if they don't understand something, or feel frustrated with themselves.

TV programmes about children with ADHD sensationalise their condition, which makes great viewing, but ultimately they can demonise an entire generation our intelligent and loving children.

Beware of the Label
There are plenty of kids who fidget, have the attention span of a flea, get bored, talk too much, say nothing at all, defy the rules, are moody, disobedient and disaffected. Maybe they have an 'artistic temperament' or any number of issues.

Some children lack the emotional vocabulary to understand the changes around them or express their feelings of anxiety. They lock away or internalise these negative feelings in their body which is stored as trauma.

Some children will experience a response to major changes within their family such as moving house, a family member's illness, someone leaving home/moving out, divorce, abuse etc.

Life's colourful tapestry happens but can leave young

children feeling frightened as if the ground is shifting under their feet.

The effects of childhood trauma and attachment are still being explored, but we do know that certain types of stress—even if they happened a long time ago—can cause significant emotional damage to the child's early behaviour and their ability to communicate their feelings or cope with change.

Some teachers are natural healers and can help children to tackle the big fears eating away inside of them such as a new school, friends, parents arguing etc.

If children—particularly boys—act out their concerns in a predominantly physical way, they can become tagged with negative labels that hold them back for years, if not decades.

If you're feeling stressed out reading this, try not to worry. It can seem overwhelming and isolating. It's not fun to realise that 'wild child' in the year group, the one everyone talks about, belongs to you. Worse still, you suspect the teachers think it's your fault because you are a bad parent. But your stress can transfer onto your child. If they're not old enough or able to express their feelings to you in words, their negative emotions can get trapped.

Remember to take care of yourself. Whatever you need to do to de-stress, take at least half an hour out to unravel. Your child needs you less stressed and you need to take care of your own mental health and self-care.

Getting an ADHD diagnosis can be a relief to an adult but potentially a burden to your child. It's a diagnosis that is still heavy with stigma and negativity. Much of the stigma is due to ignorance and misinformation. It can be difficult to manage in children, but it is manageable with practice and consistency.

One, Two, GO! Impulsivity

Impulsivity is a symptom of ADHD, which can be minimised by using skilful and behavioural, cognitive techniques or a mix of the 2. The success of behaviour modifying therapies depends on a range of issues:

- Who's conducting the therapy.
- If the child or young person trusts/has a rapport with the therapist.
- How experienced the therapist is.
- What time of day the therapy happens and the location.
- The child's emotional state before they start the treatment.
- Whether the child has experienced significant trauma.
- Whether the child's family experience hardship.

If the child's impulsivity creates a potentially dangerous or difficult situation for the teachers and the other pupils, such as having such a strong feeling of anger that they throw a chair, or lash out at a teacher or another child, there are 2 ways that the class teacher can react:

1. Escalate the situation.
2. De-escalate the situation.

This is much easier to write than it is to do but the impact of learning the techniques of de-escalation are far-reaching for both parents and educators. An escalated situation can result in a more violent outburst, a highly emotionally distressed child and possibly an exclusion.

A diffused situation can enable the child to learn valuable lessons about how their body reacts to stress and how to calm themselves down.

This child may be moved from the classroom for a while, but a faster return to normal will discourage the body from remembering this extreme fight reaction, and their associated behaviour re-programming will be faster.

Finding out the cause or trigger of an outburst is the first priority. The second is to ensure that the child is taught to notice how they feel if that trigger happens again and eventually learn a new way of reacting.

All classrooms would benefit from lower stimulus levels at certain times of the day (after breaks, PE, assembly etc).

More schools are investigating the 'Whole School SEND' approach. Schools with such an approach—those with inclusion woven into their policies and training—understand the requirement to make adjustments and accommodations, so children with autism/ADHD and other disabilities can learn and progress within the parameters of their neurodiversity.

Accommodations include regular movement breaks, fiddle toys, cool down time, completing work in another setting, calm quiet spaces, use of visual timetables, social stories, behaviour regulating systems permitting extra transition time to get to and from lessons or into the canteen early.

These accommodations introduce an equity in the mainstream school system, which for a number of reasons is missing. Schools can help children by making specific accommodations for a child, sometimes at the request of parents or recommended by occupational therapists or other experts These are known as reasonable adjustments.

For me, having this approach isn't just about the accommodations, it's also about putting practical measures in place, to support pupils who are different. These adjustments benefit not only children with disabilities but can also be helpful to the whole school community. For example, some schools offer yoga and meditation sessions to all pupils to aid calmness.

The Mindfulness in Schools Programme (MISP) is gaining popularity and interestingly, medical science backs the theory that it is impossible for the human body to feel anxious and angry at the same time as feeling calm.

Neurological factors and the part they play in outbursts
As I got deeper into writing this book, I started to understand more about the neuroscience and why Lucas's emotions were so extreme. Don't panic brain surgeons; I'm not after your job! But what I'm learning is fascinating.

Understanding how the human brain functions is a critical part of learning how to properly support your autistic, ADHD child and learner.

Here are some of the things I've learned:

- When we are upset, anxious or fearful that something or someone is going to hurt us, the older (reptilian) part of our brain kicks into action to protect us.
- Our primal fear reaction triggers the emotional centre of the brain, which is why we scream, shout, or cry when we're frightened. Naturally we respond to any threat (anxiety can feel like a threat) in 3 ways: fight back, run away or freeze on the spot. When the brain is in

survival mode the body plays its part too, by flooding your system with blood, so you can run for your life if you need to.

- The logical part of the brain hits the pause button, which is why people can't always explain their actions in the heat of the moment. It's because they're not thinking, they are reacting. When a release of hormones mobilise the brain and body for action, cue chair/pencils/being hurled in the air in the heat of a meltdown. If you ask a child "Why did you do so and so?" after they've just flipped out, 9 times out of 10 they will tell you, "I don't know." And they really don't.

Some people refer to autism meltdowns as 'incidents.' This can make children, especially those who are undiagnosed, end up feeling shame and sadness by their apparent inability to control their negative behaviours.

Is it right to punish a child for their lack of control if that's part of a neurodevelopmental condition?

Having little or no time to react is described as poor impulse control and is related to brain function as I described earlier. Being unable to suppress the urge to lash out, scream, kick, can escalate into a full-blown meltdown with severe consequences for the child.

Children with Asperger's and High-Functioning Autism are prone to frustration, anger and sometimes violence. The rapidity and intensity of anger, often in response to a relatively trivial event, can be extreme. When they're angry, Asperger's children aren't able to stop and think of alternative strategies to resolve their situation.

This is why the 'traffic light' anger management systems can fail. Emotionally dysregulated, autistic/ADHD children can go from zero to 'red' in minutes or seconds. It looks like an instantaneous physical response without thought or consideration for others.

When the anger is intense, the youngster with Asperger's may be in a blind rage and unable to see the signal, indicating that it would be appropriate to stop *(Asperger Syndrome and Difficult Moments:* Brenda Smith Myles, Jack Southwick, published 2005).

Controversy

What does a diagnosis mean for you and your child? Controversial child psychiatrist, Dr Mike Shooter, expounds some interesting views about why autism diagnoses are rising, stating that some parents are actively seeking a diagnosis because some parents love a diagnosis and it lets them off the hook because it means their child's behaviour is not their problem or their fault.

He claimed in the Times Newspaper (February 10th 2018) that parents 'like a diagnosis of Asperger's Syndrome because it's something you can boast about.' He uses the example of a child who was badly behaved at school and perfectly behaved on holiday with his parents, to demonstrate his point.

In my opinion, such comments are unhelpful in the dialogue between parents, psychiatrists and behaviour professionals, as we seek to manage our children's behaviour and mental health. The reality is that a child can behave differently in different settings and it's critical to understand what is causing the behaviour at school, before jumping to the conclusion that the child hasn't been taught how to behave.

Causes and commonalities

Asperger's Syndrome is associated with the development of various secondary mood disorders including depression, Generalised Anxiety Disorder (GAD), as well as problems with anger management.

At the other end of the emotional scale, high-functioning autistic children sometimes find it difficult to return displays of love and affection. My son has been known to return a hug, but rarely spontaneously hugs. He sometimes stands stiffly, as if the touch is too far in his personal space (which it possibly is). I've heard other parents say the same about their kids. At the other end of the spectrum, some autistic kids are hugely cuddly and have problems with personal space at school.

Lucas's behaviour plan highlighted a lack of understanding in brain functions in stressful situations (for these kids it's the classroom).

One of my son's school reports said, 'Lucas can arrive in a very angry mood, which he has great difficulty controlling. Confrontation can cause his anger to escalate. He needs to be reminded of expectations and needs to be told clearly what he should be doing to behave appropriately (if he chooses to ignore this, consequences are put in place as outlined). He has his own anger card which he can show to an adult if he is becoming cross or needs to explain the problem.'

Emotional management for autistic or ADHD children can be a build-up of negative emotion, which can be difficult for them to express constructively.

Activities that involve problem solving can become a source of frustration if they fixate on one idea paired with an intense fear of failure. Instead, regular physical activity, active meditation as well as mindful meditation can help all spectrum children to tap into their bodies and emotions.

Parent pupil profile

Building a detailed profile of your child, which you can share with everyone who interacts with them, helps them to be protected and understood in a range of environments. This sort of document is a one-page of A4 and is usually known as a pupil profile. This needs to be updated at least annually. It should summarise your child's likes, dislikes, triggers, soothers, habits and hobbies.

It's a good idea to include a sentence from your child (with their permission) in their voice. A document such as this is sensitive and you will need to consider carefully who sees it apart from teaching staff. It just needs to be a few bullet points from the parent and a couple of visuals or sentences from the young person. This can be a helpful document for professionals who may encounter your child for the first time and be unaware of your child's specific needs.

Buy an elegant notebook to chart important events. Trust me it will stop you from feeling like you're going mad.

Document what happens at school with the date and time, who was involved, what your child tells you, what happened afterwards etc. After a while you may see triggers or patterns.

Keep the notes factual rather than emotional, otherwise it becomes a journal. Writing down thoughts and feelings is powerful and healing but if time is pressing, stick to the facts: what punishment, how many times a week, anything else happening, what did you child do/say, has their mood changed etc.

Lessons Learned

- Teachers who are trained in a school that applies a whole-school approach to SEND are more confident in their ability to recognise—from their behaviours—the signs of the hyperactive, oppositional, autistic, ADHD child.

- They will be aware of, and able to implement, suitable management tools.

- A regular review of your child's behaviour history, sensory profile and key considerations with the staff and key workers, will help them in school, even if their regular teacher isn't available. For example, avoid touching or hugging, as a child may kick or lash out.

- Discuss and agree your child's calm down techniques (drink of water, fresh air, toilet break, fiddle toy, etc). You will need several. Discuss them with the child in understandable terms, use visuals and prompts to remind. Everyone needs to know the drill.

- What does the child's body language say? A fixed angry face, clenched jaw or fists? Anger usually expresses itself in the body and if you know what you're looking for, you can spot it before it boils over.

- If the child needs to be removed from class to regain

calm, how is this done? It is vital that there is clarity, as it is at this point when de-escalation is most powerful. If not done carefully, further violent physicality can ensue.

- Decisions need to be taken quickly to maintain classroom control. It's not easy, but can be learned with training, compassion, insight, maturity and a calm approach.

- Consider a presentation about their life/ADHD/autism (depending on age, confidence etc). Children talking directly to other children is powerful and can break down the stigma.

CHAPTER 3

The Big Questions Zone
Is My Child Autistic/ADHD?

Bullying behaviour
Until you have a diagnosis, you can only rely on your instincts. There are several clues that will help to guide you towards seeking an assessment and a diagnosis. Unfortunately, we know that bullying happens at every school. Children with autism/ADHD are more often victims of bullying than their neurotypical peers. Bullying directed at children with mental health difficulties, autism, or social communication difficulties can be less obvious.

Lucas was an easy target: kind, odd, moralistic, easy too upset or anger, with a strong sense of justice.

As the 'perpetrator,' he would be severely reprimanded, admitting to his wrongdoing but struggling to explain why he had done it, which is common with autistic children.

Being asked 'why?' over and over again didn't help Lucas, as he couldn't explain the intensity of his emotions that caused his extreme reactions. Saying 'yes' to everything was much easier.

The school environment is competitive, with many complex

social interactions. Kids want to fit in and look or behave in a certain way. Autistic and ADHD kids stand out plenty but often for the wrong reasons!

As Tony Attwood, a British psychologist notable for his work on Asperger syndrome, so eloquently states, 'The unusual profile, especially in the social domain, is very apparent to their peers. Some peers will respond as 'predators' with malicious intentions of teasing and bullying someone they regard as an obvious and easy target.'

Between the ages of 8 and 14, the frequency and intensity of bullying is most prominent. An autistic child is often being bullied even if they're the one throwing punches and lashing out.

There was only one teacher in Lucas's Primary School who had the right instinct about Lucas's behaviour. Most of the teachers didn't bother to disguise the irritation they felt towards him nor their contempt towards me. He was viewed through the prism of an ill-disciplined child with intellectual potential, but his extreme behaviours meant his academic successes were overlooked.

Parents I've spoken to have had similar concerns such as this Mum to an II year old autistic girl, "My daughter is of average intelligence but as long as she's quiet and not causing any trouble, there seems to be less interest in developing her academically. I know she could do more but she's highly anxious and doesn't put her hand up in class—ever. She's become invisible."

When Lucas started in Year 2, the teachers at his third Primary School were capable and enthusiastic. The headteacher loved her charges and her mantra was "Tomorrow is another day!" This was reassuring as Lucas's behaviour since leaving the Catholic school was highly problematic. It's unbelievable his autism wasn't picked up earlier, especially with letters like this landing in my hand at the end of the school day from his second Primary School. Here's an extract from the letter:

There was a serious incident this morning, which led to a member of staff being kicked by Lucas. He had taken a toy from another child and was refusing to give it back. He then climbed onto the table and refused to come down. Another teacher came into class and asked him to come down as he was endangering other children who were seated at the table. At first, he refused, so the teacher had to lift him down. This was when he kicked her. She then took him to the Rainbow Room to try to calm him, and he became extremely aggressive and used violent language and tipped chairs up. Eventually he calmed down and apologised to the teacher.

Another letter read:

An incident was witnessed today. Lucas was asked to come in from the playground as he was kicking another child. He was extremely angry at having to miss his play, due to this he hit out at a member of staff and repeatedly shouted out and kicked the door. It took him about an hour to calm down before he was able to resume art activities that afternoon.

When Lucas was at his third Primary School the class teacher would look around the room in despair saying he would just kick off for no reason. When I asked Lucas what was going on he would explain in his monotone voice how the children would mess up his neat lines of pencils on his desk or come too close to him.

These are 2 clues to his autism: the need to organise his environment and avoid unwanted sensory contact.

His third Primary School wasn't without incident and Lucas was still undiagnosed but he was doing art therapy, which he found enjoyable and calming. These art therapy sessions resulted in him painting a beautiful mural. It was mounted on an exterior school gate for several years, which made me smile every time we drove past.

Misinterpreting Bad Behaviour: Sensory Factors
Teachers would tell me Lucas was bright and ask why couldn't he stop calling out in class, banging his desk lid, and bouncing up and down on the chair?

They constantly asked him, "Why can't you sit still?" In these pre-diagnosis days, we didn't recognise the self-stimulating behaviour as that—a self-soothing activity to release anxiety or tension. We all do it to a degree, but for some autistic children it is persistent and can be intrusive.

Lucas would line up pencils and pens too. He wasn't doing it to deliberately distract his classmates. He used to crawl or hide under the table and these were unsuccessful attempts to get away from the sensory overload. He was told off for doing that, which sent him into a spiral of self-loathing.

Children with ASD and autism may display rage behaviour, which is when they blurt out inappropriate phrases when they are stressed or overloaded.

Schools are full of hundreds of children who shriek and

express themselves in complicated and mysterious ways. It's hardly surprising that your autistic, sensory-sensitive child gets anxious on Sunday nights before school on Monday. They know what's coming and the thought of that level of intense stimulation can make going to sleep on Sunday nights very difficult.

Lucas's third Primary School appointed a behaviour specialist to support Lucas and I. Lots of professionals popped in and out of our lives in those pre-diagnosis years.

The behaviour specialist strongly advocated that Lucas had no obvious mental health issues. She said, "He's very bright, of above average intelligence for his age. He knows how to manipulate adults. He's just a naughty little boy and he needs boundaries." The behaviour specialist turned to the teachers, "You need to be firmer with him. He doesn't have ADHD."

His later diagnosis disproved everything she said, but what upset me more than that was discovering that she had recommended restraint training to help the teachers manage Lucas's meltdowns. She believed his emotional needs would benefit from counselling and anger management. She also encouraged the class teacher to devise behaviour targets to share with the staff.

Whilst his third Primary School was infinitely better than the other 2, I began to notice that the child I came home to after school was more withdrawn.

Knowing now how sensory autistic children are, especially to unwelcome or forced touch, it makes my blood run cold when I think about the discomfort of restraint endured by Lucas.

The restraint didn't work because he was being held against his will, which made him kick out and lash out more.

Restraining a 6-year old sounds extreme but it happens in mainstream schools and more widely in assessment and treatment units (ATUs). And no, I wasn't consulted about it.

I casually dropped the school happenings into a conversation with Lucas's Beaver Cub Group Leader and his response was, "He's no worse than any of the other boys here. He can get over-excited, but I'm shocked!"

To think I only found out that my son was being physically restrained at school by reading through his confidential files in research for this book is shocking. It's possible it was happening at the Catholic School too, which is how a member of staff got kicked in her stomach.

There is still a culture in some parts of the education and medical systems where non-consensual restraint happens without the agreement of parents or children. I understand that staff can be hurt in the midst of a meltdown, but my personal view is that hands-on physical restraint should be a last resort. Especially if there is any suspicion of autism. Lucas never mentioned it to me, but the distress was showing on his little face.

A bony bump in the road

There didn't seem to be as much bullying at his third Primary School, so when Lucas fell off a large climbing frame, I put it down to a silly accident. But his arm took ages to mend and one weekend he was crying and in immense pain. His arm hurt but so did his knees and his back, and during the course of the weekend, he was unable to stand upright or straighten his legs.

His older sister and I had to carry him to and from his

bedroom to the toilet. He had a blue, wooden chair, which we moved into my room and he slept upright in it. As the weekend rolled on and he didn't improve I decided to take him to the hospital that evening.

I drove slowly but every speed hump in the road caused him to moan in pain. After a very long night (I slept on the ward on the floor next to him) and an even longer day of tests, Lucas was diagnosed with juvenile arthritis. It was viral in origin and had attacked and inflamed all of his joints. After high doses of pain killers and anti-inflammatories he was in a wheelchair the day after admission.

The day after that he was hopping about in crutches up and down the ward. After a few more days he was discharged. Over the following months he had a few more joint flare-ups. He was pulled out of PE as we were careful about putting too much strain on his growing joints. We opted for lower impact sports (non-contact) where possible. The school's reaction to his obvious disability was hugely sympathetic. He was allowed to sit at the end of the line in assembly next to the teacher, to avoid getting his legs bashed when they all got up, and he could stay in every play time.

Strangely, I felt calmer too with this visible disability, it seemed to be much less of an issue in school than his as yet undiagnosed autism.

Social isolation: difficulty making friends

Lucas's time at his third Primary School was good overall, despite his intense outbursts. Outside play was problematic because he didn't like football. He either stayed inside during break times or played outside in a sheltered garden with the nursery and reception children. He seemed to really enjoy both of these options more than free play with the older children.

If your child in Primary School has difficulties making and keeping friends, this is another clear sign that they may need additional support. Play and friendships are the flipside of the bullying issue, as a socially isolated child who plays differently is unlikely to have as many friends. It is their self-imposed or group-imposed isolation—not belonging to a pack—that makes them vulnerable to bullying.

In his friendless state, Lucas invented solitary games that didn't involve sharing or interacting with other children. I wasn't too concerned about his solitary school play habits. At least he wouldn't get into trouble. He would engross himself in Lego, drawing, or having long, detailed discussions about Pokémon with his key worker.

He had tantrums about not wanting to do things or join in socially and I found excuses for everything. I was a single mother, a young mother, he was summer born, I worked full-time. But I couldn't hide from the truth. He wasn't managing well socially at school.

Issues with social communication were becoming more marked. He was unable to sustain friendships and was missed off party invitation lists. I can count the number of birthday parties he attended during his Primary School years on one hand (not including his own!). Swimming lessons, karate and Cubs were all fine. He got positive feedback from the leaders saying that he could follow instructions and deliver on the tasks.

Why is my child a rule-breaker?
Before a tornado strikes, the wind dies down and the air

becomes very still but when you know it's on its way, there's not much you can do about it.

Learning your child is having difficulties at school, with a cause that is unknown, stirs up big emotions. Teachers, Local Authority teams, early years professionals—it can be a big muddle of professionals buzzing around you. Then there's the delay, when things are getting much worse, but nothing seems to be happening.

Neurotypical kids usually love PE. It's an opportunity to run around after your friends, screaming at the top of your voice, picking teams, moving around and releasing lots of feel-good hormones. But what if changing your clothes is painful and complicated? Or swimming pool water burns your eyes? Or no-one picks you in games?

When the games start, the rules are difficult to follow. You can't explain why you don't understand, but you don't. You drop the ball as you can't quite judge the speed it's approaching at. Then everyone laughs. The frustration is difficult to cope with, and the teacher is asking you to try again, but you don't want to. You've had enough. You don't see the ball before it makes contract with your face, and now everyone is laughing at you again. There's too much noise, too many instructions, and hot tears prick behind your eyes.

The person who kicked the ball laughed so much that you kicked them. You weren't thinking. You just had an overwhelming need to make them stop laughing at you. In the headteacher's office you feel numb. You're in trouble again, and the headteacher is saying he will need to call your mum and ask her to pick you up.

You're sorry and you don't know why you did it. Well, you

do know why, but it's difficult to explain, and there's the bell again that feels like it's ringing inside your skull.

Many autistic children, particularly those who are considered high-functioning, like to control their environment as a way of managing it. A change of routine is destabilising. Having a rules-based personality is an instinctively clever way to manage the thing that stresses you out—change!

A rules-based child can find themselves in a conflict with authority figures in schools, such as teachers and headteachers, because children are not encouraged to challenge the rules. Here's the thing, they won't deliberately challenge unless the following applies:

- If they believe the rules clash with their own value system.
- If they think the rule is archaic, silly, and can argue the reasons why.
- If they believe the rule is unfair or unjust in some way.
- They have created their own rule(s), which others must follow.

I've seen this sort of conflict arise in high-functioning children; it can be a real flash point with a teacher. For example the students taking a day off to attend a climate change march. For them it's educational, it's their future, and they are passionate supporters of this cause. Besides they don't like Spanish and will be giving it up at the end of Year 10, so missing a class isn't a big deal.

These are all cogent and persuasive arguments to break the school rules. They are rule-breakers because in their mind the rule is not logical. What we're seeing is a reaction to a fundamental opinion, a neurotypical one and a neurodiverse one. The challenge intensifies when the rule is being enforced by someone in authority and the rule-breaker is perceived as a threat to the status-quo. This is a fundamental point.

Recognise if your child is heavily rules-based, discuss this with the teacher to see what compromises can be reached.

Asperger's and autism: easy to spot? Not!

Identifying undiagnosed autism or ADHD in the classroom is both easy and difficult. It's easy once it's been pointed out. But it's difficult if you think you're seeing something else or have misread the child's behaviour.

Neurological factors relating to autism highlight the importance of the amygdala; a pair of nerve structures that process information coming into the body through our senses and create appropriate reactions within the body by way of a response. The amygdala is part of the limbic (emotional regulatory) system, which is highly involved with emotions, feelings and memories.

It's useful to know this when we try to understand what meltdowns are and the triggering activity that comes before it. A basic understanding of brain function helps to explain why autistic children have extreme emotional reactions to seemingly insignificant events.

If a loud noise is painful to an autistic child, we start to understand why they may have a meltdown just before the lunch bell goes off. The anticipation of the noise can release stress hormones, making the child feel anxious about what is coming.

Early intervention

Early intervention is the key to preventing some of the unnecessary stress autistic children and their families face.

- Long wait times for appointments.
- Inappropriate support or needs not being met.
- Denial.
- Ignorance and discrimination.
- Administrative incompetence.
- Bullying.

A child is a sensitive vessel, and with loving guidance and instruction, can be helped to minimise or refocus the intensity of their negative and overblown reactions.

It's encouraging to see a range of therapies and interventions being developed and explored by autistic people and their families to support ADHD/autistic children. More of this needs to be enabled with public funding, as the existing mental health, medical and educational structures appear to be struggling to cope with the demand for their services.

Difficult morning routine and eating issues

Most parents dread the morning routine. I have seen parents taking their kids to school in pyjamas, totally frazzled. If you're a working parent, you're probably out of the house early, dropping your child at breakfast club, juggling a day's work, arriving home long after your child, or picking your child up from the childminder's or afterschool club.

This is equally as stressful as looking after your children all day. Looking back, the constant drop-offs and pick-ups each day, and high levels of social exchange, must have been stressful for Lucas.

For many autistic or ADHD children, especially pre diagnosis, the morning routine is an overloading nightmare. Their impaired executive functioning makes it difficult to remember things. Sensory difficulty will make dressing at speed difficult and if they have an obsessive tendency they might genuinely lose all track of time unless they are carefully time managed.

Then there might be issues around eating so early, wanting to eat the same breakfast every day or a meltdown if their chosen food runs out. Or they may refuse food entirely, which is a normal response to anxiety.

Additional needs children are time-consuming, and if you have other children to get ready, your morning will feel like being on a rollercoaster in the dark.

Transition to Junior School

The year had flown by. It was time for Lucas's Year 2 group to leave the Infant School and transfer to the Junior School. This would be Lucas's fourth school.

The whole school did a transition visit but the preparation for Lucas was minimal considering the big change ahead. However, he seemed to settle in quickly at the Junior School, at aged 7.

Within weeks, he snagged his first exclusion. He got into a squabble with another child and was dealt with swiftly and unequivocally.

The Year 3 teaching team didn't know much about his previous behaviour issues. In the middle of the first half-term, I got a letter from his Primary School asking for my permission to pass on his Common Assessment Framework (CAF) to the Junior School. A CAF is a document designed to provide a whole team with key information about a child.

I couldn't understand why they were contacting me now, weeks into his new school and after an exclusion, to seek permission to share important documents! Because basic information hadn't been shared, we had to suffer the ignominy of an exclusion in the first half term. Not a great start.

The headteacher believed all children should start with a clean slate. Many schools like to make their own assessments for new pupils, but as you can see, there is some risk in doing this. The headteacher was adamant that his teachers were highly experienced and didn't need notes from previous schools. His faith in his first-rate teachers was admirable, but as good as they were, they had never taught Lucas before!

Lessons Learned

- If your child is well-known to the teacher for bullying behaviour or constantly getting into trouble, make a note of how long this goes on for.

- Don't get stuck in a spiral of bad behaviour, punishment, apologies and blame. There is always a cause. You and the school owe it to your child to investigate root causes properly. It saves everyone time, money and heartache.

- If your child is constantly being told to come back in the room, or told off for gazing out of the window, and the teacher can barely remember her at parents evening—make a note of everything.

- Find out why your child is so withdrawn. Sometimes there is more than shyness going on.

- Write down your thoughts and concerns and discuss with the class teacher. If you are concerned, book an appointment with your GP as well.

- If the behaviours persist, don't hope they will grow out of it or go away. Persistent negative behaviour is your child's way of communicating with you over something they don't always have the words for. Listen to them.

- Build an accurate picture of their daily experiences.

- Identify specific situations that are difficult for them. Do they need more time to answer questions? Do they understand what they're meant to be doing?

- Is their social communication difficulty making friendships a big issue?

- How do they communicate when they feel stressed or angry?

CHAPTER 4

The Assessment To Diagnosis Zone
Going With The Flow (It Can Be A Long Path)

Wanting a diagnosis

Having a diagnosis was important for me as it would prove to the judgemental teachers that I wasn't a bad mother. Children with autism and ADHD are intellectually able, but due to their neurodiversity and/or emotional, social difficulties, they are unable to spend as much time in the classroom as their peers.

What if school isn't the best learning environment for a child with specific learning impairments?

The SENCO appeared to have no tools in the toolkit. He asked the headteacher to help with my son, then he wrote to the Local Authority Educational Psychologist, 'All we are doing is containing. We have already been to CAMHS—where to next? Where can we get support and guidance to help us get to the underlying issues?'

The pre-diagnosis phase was a nightmare. After lobbying hard, the school secured additional funding from the Local Authority. Reviewing the paperwork for this book, Lucas's original statement (before he was re-assessed) indicated that he needed a statement because of his behavioural, emotional and social difficulties. The term now used since the introduction of the code of practice is social, emotional and mental health (SEMH difficulties). It was another year before his autism spectrum disorder and ADHD was correctly identified.

Interventions can only go so far if you haven't worked out what the causes of the behaviours are. This is a stumbling block for schools, pouring water on the fire, instead of moving the logs underneath it. Lucas was struggling.

I was open to the idea of counselling but the waiting lists in the borough were long. Fortunately, the Junior School had their own counsellor.

After I split with Lucas's father, all 3 of us would have benefitted from some counselling, but it didn't happen. I had no time to fit in counselling. But I liked the idea of Lucas seeing someone, especially if I didn't have to pay for it.

In Year 3, he had no support in the classroom, after so much support in Year 2. The leap between Infant and Junior School is a big one, due to the scaling down of pastoral care and reassurance.

Year 4 arrived and Lucas was drowning. It was starting to feel urgent to get a diagnosis. I just wanted him to get an education, to have friends, go to school without getting into trouble. I wasn't asking for much.

Parents can apply individually or in partnership with the school to the Local Authority for an EHCP assessment, and this must be done in writing; a few charities have template letters you can download free online (7).

You may be required to provide documentary evidence with

the assessment request, which would include school reports, doctors or other medical reports and correspondence from the school.

You will need to provide details of what support your child is already receiving, such as Provision Maps (an outline of what support your child receives, who delivers and how often) or Individual Education Plans (IEPs). You may also wish to include social services reports. Keep copies of everything.

The EHCP is, in theory, a last resort, in addition to other interventions, which have proved insufficient in terms of enabling access and educational attainment.

In Year 4, my son's class teacher told me how lucky I was to have a one-to-one support for Lucas in English. Just a few months earlier she had told me how disruptive he was in her lessons. She couldn't see that his one-to-one benefitted not just him, but the whole class, freeing her up to educate the other 29.

The Educational Psychologist suggested that Lucas be referred to a Child and Family Consultation Centre. There was a weird sense of the school flailing around for help when the resources and expertise should have existed within their existing framework.

I've since reviewed highlights of the school's request for additional funding. One-to-one LSA support for the significant part of the day was reducing the risks of further exclusion but didn't address the issues of Lucas's emotional mental health needs.

The letter stated, 'Lucas hit 2 children this morning. On both occasions he reacted to the other child not wanting to play with him or be his friend. I am not sure how much longer the other children or parents will be as patient and understanding as they have been.'

I hope that if your child is going through such difficulties now, their school will be more knowledgeable on the range of social and behavioural tools now available to trained teachers and support staff.

The beginning of our assessment process

I finally got a letter from the Local Authority stating that the Junior School had requested a statutory assessment of Lucas's Special Educational Needs.

The letter was copied to the school headteacher, community paediatrician and the Single Point of Access team. We were finally making progress! It was another step forward on the l-o-n-g diagnosis road.

The doctor in the Community Paediatric team had reviewed Lucas's notes 2 years previously. I knew he wouldn't waste any time. He was an old-school gentleman, very softly spoken. He shook both our hands as we walked into his office to begin another interrogation.

"Step on the scales, young chap!" he said brightly.

After measuring Lucas's height, he asked Lucas a series of questions.

"Can you hop on your right leg? Good, now hop in a straight line. Did you wash behind your ears today?"

I held my breath as Lucas said confidently, "Erm, no!"

But instead of chastising him, the doctor said, "Top marks for honesty!" This guy was a class act.

At the end of the session, he suggested that as part of Lucas's diagnostic process that we (the doctor, the school and

I) should reward Lucas for periods of non-fighting activity. Every break and lunch time that passed peacefully should be acknowledged with positive praise.

If anything happened, Lucas had to tell me the truth in detail, and I would know what sanction to put in place at home. We were to continue this until the next review.

We should zone in on the positive aspects of Lucas's contribution to home and school life such as his kindness, empathy, creativity and imagination.

When asked in the meeting, Lucas said that he had lots of friends at school (or people he would like to be friends with). Poignantly, he said his class teacher was top of his friend list. Forever forgiving Lucas. His kind nature was music to my ears. I wished his teachers could hear the same notes as me.

It was a relief to get feedback on Lucas from somewhere other than school. Next in the assessment process was a one-on-one meeting with the Educational Psychologist (EP).

I was still annoyed that the Infant School hadn't passed on information to the Junior School, but I was determined that the dots would connect.

The EP outlined a range of available support to help Lucas manage daily life at school, including social skills workshops to build his confidence with friends and raise his self-esteem. The EP assured me there would be no stigma in Lucas being in these groups. He mentioned the school had a behaviour co-ordinator, that Lucas should have sessions with.

Lucas attended the school behaviour programme. I had no clue what they discussed or who else was in the sessions, or anything else of value.

If your child is involved in any sort of behaviour or

social skills support, try to find out what the content of the programme is and how the programme leader measures success.

If your school suggests that your child should have a needs assessment, there are 6 things to consider:

1. The diagnosis process begins with a needs assessment, which can be requested by the school (possibly the SENCO) or your GP can refer your child. Usually Special Educational Needs are just that; the child requires specific help to access their education. Not all children with special educational needs require an EHCP.

2. The assessment will establish whether your child has a specific medical, mental health, neurological or any other health issue, which may make learning at school more difficult. Schools and parents should provide any reports and information to help in the assessment process.

3. It's not your job, or the school's, to assess or diagnose a child, but if you do have an idea of your child's condition, you must get this confirmed to enable you to receive funding for the right support.

4. You and your child will be assessed by a number of medical and health professionals during the assessment process.

5. The Local Authority must respond to your request for a needs assessment within 6 weeks to advise you whether or not they will progress with an Education Health and Care needs assessment for your child.

6. It is common to be denied an assessment initially,

but get one later on. If, like me, you are denied an assessment, the legal criteria as to whether they carry one out is (Children and Families Act 2014, Section 36 (8)):

- The child or young person has or may have Special Educational Needs.*
- Special Educational provision may be necessary for the child or young person, in accordance with an EHCP.

*Defined legally as a child or young person with a significantly greater difficulty in learning than the majority of others of the same age. Or a learning difficulty, or a disability which hinders them from making use of facilities provided for others of the same age. Special Educational Provision is to be made for them.

Mental health conditions like Oppositional Defiant Disorder (ODD) or Pathological Demand Avoidance (PDA), which is currently recognised as part of the autistic spectrum, can be difficult to diagnose and complex to manage. Be prepared for a long ride.

Keep CAMHS and carry on

The diagnostic process for Lucas continued. I received a report from the Local Authority EP stating that Lucas had been known to the Educational Psychology Service since he attended the Infant School. Current involvement was focused on drafting a referral form to CAMHS to explore if features of Lucas's behaviours were related to an autistic spectrum condition.

A quick Google search for CAMHS pulled up lots of information about various mental health conditions and who the professionals were. There was also a page on dealing with a mental health emergency.

A snippet from the Local Authority Educational Psychologist report is below. It shows a useful snapshot of what was happening as well as management strategies:

'Since the beginning of term, Lucas has progressed to the stage where he can leave his Pokémon toys in a bag under the teacher's desk, without the need for them being on display in his immediate vicinity. I went into school to gain an update on the progress with Lucas's class teachers. There had also been increased examples of play with other children under the supervision of a teaching assistant. While he's made progress there are still incidents where he gets very frustrated.

We need to work on Lucas's increasing self-awareness and communication skills so that he could indicate to adults when he's angry or upset. The realities along with the inherent difficulties of this skill were discussed, i.e. it is very hard when one is frustrated to communicate effectively and preventatively.

Lucas is to be introduced to a visual cue system that he can use when times are becoming problematic for him. This system can have 2 elements: a cue, which Lucas can have himself (a keyring in his possession to indicate to staff that he may want to go to a calming place, with a box of his activities). Secondly, a visual cue for adults to support and remind him of specific behaviour required in different situations.'

The ideas in this report were excellent but in reality the effectiveness of any behaviour strategy is down to skilled delivery and consistency.

In the many years since his diagnosis, some excellent ideas had failed due to the inconsistency of teaching style and sometimes just a lack empathy.

The final piece in the diagnostic puzzle was an appointment with the consultant psychiatrist, who worked as part of CAMHS. We had a series of meetings with her. Some were one-on-one interviews with just me, me and Lucas, and a couple where she assessed Lucas as he carried out a series of tests.

Waiting list times for psychiatrist consultations can be weeks or even months long, so I recommend that you get the most value out of your session/appointment.

To prepare, find out as much about your family history as possible, including your grandparents' medical histories. Make sure you can remember key details about your pregnancy and your child's birth, what your child was like as a baby, and whether or not they reached key developmental milestones. I was asked all of these questions about Lucas, his father, my mother and their parents. It was like being under a microscope, but I surrendered to the experience reminding myself they were looking for clues, triggers, patterns.

Some scientists believe that there are DNA links to autism, and it may be hereditary in some families. Answering personal, detailed questions is important, as they can help to provide answers and ultimately a diagnosis.

Key professionals and organisations in the process
You will meet a number of different professionals and organisations during the diagnosis process. Here's a snapshot of their roles and how they can help.

Child and Adolescent Mental Health Services
Child and Adolescent Mental Health Services (CAMHS) is a cluster of a NHS service provision for children and young adults who are identified as having issues with their emotional, psychological or mental wellbeing. CAMHS is an umbrella term for all the professionals who help you to understand your child's behaviour and the emotional issues that are impacting their life. The team of psychiatrists and clinical psychologists we saw at CAMHS were professional, kind, calm and helpful. The 3 big issues parents commonly have with CAMHS:

1. The time it takes to get an appointment.
2. If your appointment leads to a diagnosis, what happens after that? Especially if your child is discharged from CAMHS.
3. What does the diagnosis mean for your child at school? Parents can find themselves facing more unknowns after a diagnosis.

Clinical Psychologist
The NHS definition of the clinical psychologist's role is that they work with people who might have mental or physical illnesses including:

- Addictive behaviours.
- Anxiety and depression.
- Difficulties with personal and family relationships.
- Childhood behaviour disorders.

Clinical Psychologists often work in the community, alongside social workers, in clinics, health centres, community health teams and in CAMHS.

Behaviour Therapist

Behavioural therapy is an umbrella term for the types of therapy that treat mental health disorders. This form of therapy identifies and changes potentially self-destructive or unhealthy behaviours. The basis of the approach is that all behaviours are learned and unhealthy behaviours can be altered. The focus is often on current problems and how to change them.

Educational Psychologist

Educational Psychology is concerned with the psychological and educational development of children and young people within the context of homes, schools and the community. In my experience, this professional was the link between the mystical, complicated work of psychology and the day-to-day practicalities of everyday life.

The 'Ed Psychs' or EPs are usually one of the first professionals assigned to your child before they are referred on to either the clinical psychologist or the psychiatrists. They commonly visit your child at school and in their classroom to make observations.

Sometimes your school will refer you to an EP as a stand-alone investigation, or you might see an EP as part of the 'needs assessment.'

EPs bring a specialised perspective to working with children. They are concerned with child's learning and development, and where there are difficulties, their goal is to bring about positive change.

EPs attempt to make the bridge between theory and practice by translating behavioural research into innovative and relevant practice in the classroom.

For us, the Ed Psych acted as the friendly broker between the white-coat professionals and the teachers. Be aware who the Educational Psychologist is employed by. If they're employed by the Local Authority, their interest in supporting your child may be tempered by the Local Authority's financial restraints and the need to stick within a budget.

If you're at the start of the assessment process, you are entitled to find out whether the EP is independent. Many families can't afford to hire a private or fully independent Educational Psychologist.

If your initial assessment is denied and you take the Local Authority to a Tribunal, the Independent Educational Psychologists are sometimes requested by a judge to verify that the advice about supporting your child is truly independent and not restrained by cost.

Parents can appeal to the SEND Tribunal.

You can check current legislation for Local Authority duties in *The Noddy Guide* by David Wolfe and Leon Glenister, which is a public resource free to download.

Where the assessment process goes wrong
According to a report from the Local Government and Social Care Ombudsman (www.lgo.org.uk) the guidelines around assessment decisions and timescales need to run as follows. The whole process from first request for an EHC assessment, to issuing a final plan, must take no longer than 20 weeks. Within that, councils must:

1. Decide whether to carry out an assessment within 6 weeks.
2. If assessing, collect evidence from educational, health and care professionals within a further 6 weeks.
3. Consider the evidence and decide whether it is necessary to issue a plan.
4. If so, share a draft plan, consider representations or school preference of the parent or young person, and consult with schools.

NOTE: This is a Covid-19 era book and some rules may have changed. Please check the current UK Gov web pages.

The expectation is that Local Authorities assume the role of the lead agency in the EHC process. They have the appropriate commissioning and partnership arrangements in place to allow SEND officers to obtain advice for EHCs in a timely way and to have mechanisms to address any problems that arise.

That's the expectation, but the reality is very different when Local Authorities across the country have different EHC forms, partnership arrangements, processes, job roles and so on as well as resource pressures.

There are guidelines and processes to follow if you hit a stumbling block at any point, including the IPSEA website or using your local council complaints process.

Tips on assessment and the diagnosis process
- Co-operate as fully as you can in your interview with the Educational Psychologist. I found the process positive, but a bit personal. As a new single mum, I was raw and

vulnerable, but I still had to divulge information about often he saw his father and did mental health issues run in his father's family? My personal life was being tipped out for everyone to peer at.

- We revisited elements of our family history that had been locked away for decades. I understood this was because emotional and family issues, buried deep, can contribute to your child's behaviour. Be as honest as you feel comfortable with, but take care, because the health and social care systems are pre-disposed to subconscious bias. There is oodles of data about this. Try to get someone to attend appointments with you or if you're in a relationship and one of you needs to work, take turns. This way you will be able to compare notes.
- Make the educators aware that classroom noise levels, even from a teacher who may have to shout to get kids attention, can trigger high levels of anxiety in an autistic child. This can slow down their cognitive function as they struggle to block out the distressing noise. Noises and other forms of emotional overload cause stimming, or other self-soothing behaviour or a meltdown.
- Autistic girls are known to internalise their anxiety, sometimes retreating into themselves to such a degree that they are unable to communicate at all or may resort to self-injurious behaviours.
- Keep notes of what is happening at school and how it was dealt with in your notebooks. Note down the dates. Hundreds of things can affect your child's behaviour such as teaching style, other children's illness, genetics, an undiagnosed or attributed mental health issue, stress,

anxiety, childhood depression. The teachers suggested it was Lucas's home environment that was causing his issues at school. They were partly right, and this might be the same for you—that does not mean that the school doesn't need to investigate what might be happening at school as well.

- Jot down any major events at home because they can tie in with particularly bad patches at school. Be careful about what is being attributed to the home environment or 'bad' parenting and what is happening at school. Having 2 very different environments can in itself create stress for your sensory, ADHD child as any transition can be destabilising for them.

- Acknowledge moving between school and home is a key transition for autistic children. They need time to adjust between settings. Try to apply similar rules in both places if possible, to help your child to feel settled.

Getting an assessment is difficult regardless of whether your child is a boy or girl, the youngest or oldest. It's challenging if you are a single parent or not, the parent of a child of Caribbean or mixed Caribbean-African heritage (a group that is statistically excluded from school more often). Whatever your background, what is happening hurts and it's easy to blame yourself.

I was a single, full-time working mum of Caribbean heritage—a danger category—according to the Department for Education statistics. I held down a good job, owned a flat and a car, provided for my family, and I still felt like a failure.

Social isolation

Thousands of children worldwide with learning difficulties, emotional trauma or a neurological difference, which makes their behaviour unpredictable (to neurotypicals), are diagnosed with mental health disorders. Then they are provided psychiatric drugs for months or even years at a time.

Human behaviour is our strongest weapon but also our greatest weakness. Children with extreme behaviours due to neurological differences and associated mental health issues, do not deserve a life sentence of seclusion, exclusion or social isolation.

There is a growing movement of groups and individuals fighting back against the injustice and social exclusion of thousands of children. It's an issue beyond the scope of this book, and like many discussions around disability and discrimination, requires careful handling and analysis. It's a discussion that's already taking place in many online forums.

I encourage you to tread carefully online, even when you feel at your lowest ebb or your most triumphant.

Parents are highly sensitive to criticism, especially if they concern our children. And believe it or not, other people aren't always happy in your success. You will read things that upset you and things that totally chime with your opinion. Sometimes it's better to save your venting for when you're with a group of trusted friends.

It's really easy to fall out with people over your opinions on big political and humanitarian issues. Before you find yourself on the opposite side ends of playground, remember we all have days when we feel particularly on edge or vulnerable. Comparing ourselves to other families and situations is unhelpful.

Try to focus on your and your child's unique and individual journey, celebrating your successes with your child's immediate supporters first—in real life, if you get my drift.

Behind closed doors the parents who seem on top of their game are usually fighting a battle every bit as difficult as yours. The grass is green right under your feet; just keep watering it.

Sensitive children
Dreamers, sensitives, highly-strung—you've met kids like this. Did you know many autistic children share these traits? People are usually amazed when they interact one-to-one with the child who previously appears to be angry or withdrawn.

- "He's a real sweetie."
- "Ah, she's such a thoughtful little girl!"

Autistic children are known to absorb stress, negative energy, moods, sounds and experiences that they don't know how to let go of.

They are okay in familiar settings like home, but in the stimulating, complicated environment of school, the energy of other children creates an uncomfortable sensory overload.

I went on a couple of school trips with Lucas (it was partly a condition of him going). We went to the science museum and the local park. I saw how the other kids viewed him. I had to bite my tongue so many times when they said things to trigger him or didn't include him.

Teachers will never care for your child as you do. They're not his parents and they may let hurtful words pass. They can't be everywhere and hear everything. Their concern is when there is physical contact between children, which there was a week later in PE. The teacher called me in to discuss an outburst during outdoor PE when Lucas threw a ball in another child's face. He told the teacher he'd done it deliberately. When I questioned him about this, he said he got confused when the teacher questioned him. He didn't deliberately mean to hurt the other child (it was a soft ball). So why did he admit to doing it? When he tried to explain to the teacher, he got angry and was sent to the staff room. When he went into the headteacher's office he burst into tears.

Lucas said it was easier to own up than try to explain that he didn't understand the rules of the game. It was one of those games where you catch, then throw, then pass through your legs, then turn around, and then it starts again.

I was shocked that my happy-go-friendly child was crying at school.

Assessment flowchart

Request an assessment to your Local Authority (LA) in
writing
⅂

Local authority acknowledge they've got the request (chase
them up if you don't get one)
⅂

The LA may request more evidence from you or school
⅂

The LA needs to reply to the assessment request within 6
weeks
⅂

If the LA says 'No' to an assessment you can appeal
⅂

If LA agrees, the needs identified in the assessment this may
form part of an ECHP
⅂

A number of parties will be asked about the child's needs
(including the child, if they are in Year 9 or above)
⅂

The LA will request information from a variety of sources
⅂

Educational Psychologist
⅂

SALT (Speech and Language Therapist), Occupational
therapist (OT), GP

The LA may prefer to use the local NHS or OT saying that
'independent experts' reports are not permitted as part of the

assessment process. At the time of writing, it is not lawful for the LA to disregard reports from independent experts.

After the assessment process is completed, which will include written reports from the professionals who have been consulted, you will have a clear picture of your child's special needs. Plus a detailed outline of the support required to meet those needs.

After the assessment, the LA may issue an EHCP—a contractually binding document—which outlines their commitment to fulfil their duty to meet your child's needs.

The assessment process can stall at many points, most of them will require you to chase up everybody concerned. This is where your notebook helps. You have kept a record of who you spoke to, their job title, the date, and what they said they said they would do.

Thousands of children need support to access education. It's a harsh reality but unless you focus on your child and their needs, they may get lost under a pile of paperwork.

My recommendations for any legal questions you may have is to check the Independent Parental Special Educational Advice (IPSEA) website. They explain your rights and the LA's responsibility in clear terms and also have sample letters if you need to chase up the Local Authority, appeal, complain or go to a tribunal. Or you may contact the local special educational needs support service for your area if you Google SENDIASS.

Assessment reports
Below are a mix of Lucas's behaviours that teachers reported:

- Hypersensitivity to light and loud noises.

- Difficulties with the give and take of conversation required to make friends.
- Easily distracted.
- Love of routine.
- Not using eye contact and gestures.
- He has to be prompted to look at you.
- He often has his own agenda.
- He loves to play with small figures/models/cards of imaginary world.
- He wants to play with his peers but only his games on his terms.
- He does not have good social skills; he finds it difficult to interact.
- He takes time to bond with new adults.
- If he loses a toy, he can become completely obsessed looking for it, unable to concentrate on anything else.
- He has explosions of energy. Before school he runs and runs.
- He cannot cope with changes in routine, teachers, timetables etc.
- He is articulate but unable to explain why he behaves a certain way. Much of what he says relates to his own needs.
- He seems unable to relate to the needs or feelings of others.
- Struggles to understand what is read beyond the literal.

Your right to appeal
If your request for an EHC needs assessment is denied, or anything else happens during the assessment to diagnosis

process, there are many points at which you can appeal the decisions:

1. When the LA has turned down a request for a full assessment.
2. Having carried out an assessment the LA decides not to grant an EHCP.
3. If you disagree with the contents of the EHCP.
4. If you disagree with the named school on the EHCP.
5. If the LA amends the EHCP, including name of school, description of child's special educational needs or the provision.
6. If the LA decides to cease to maintain the EHCP.
7. If the LA consider further assessment is not required.

Mantras

'Knowledge is power.'

'Whatever is wrong can be put right with knowledge, application and love.'

'It's never too late to change any situation. I will react to these difficulties with openness and grace.'

'My child belongs to the universe. He comes with many talents and gifts and his autism is just one of those!'

'I must not be selfish with my child. There are many people who love him and have lessons for him, not just me.'

'I will respond to his anger with love and kindness, especially when everyone else is responding to him with equal anger.'

Lessons Learned

- Take a notebook and write down any questions or concerns you have before you go into the meeting.

- Diagnosis can put a huge strain on even the strongest of personal relationships. If you are in a marriage or long-term relationship, try not to blame each other. Be kind to one another. Communicate. It will get heavy, and if you feel you need to seek outside support, do so with your partner's consent.

- When your child is diagnosed with a disability, accept that part of your child's existence will be shared with the wider community such as the Local Authority, hospitals, health centres, social workers and schools. It can be tough to ask for help but you might need it from various financial or support agencies. There is no shame in this. That's what they are there for. Make a conscious decision to engage and co-operate in the process to achieve the best results.

- Store phone numbers, email addresses and names of key support services. Keep notes of conversations about your case to follow up and hold people to account. Many support organisations run on a charitable basis, so you will need patience, as they won't always have the resource to return your calls or make appointments at short notice. You won't get everything done in one day, so make a list of about 5 things. Try to get these done and then make a new list the next day; especially important if you're working or have other children who need your time and energy.

- Stay calm, patient and polite. Everything will get sorted. "It will be okay in the end, and if it's not okay, it's not the end."

- The financial costs incurred by families on the road to an assessment are often underestimated. You will have to take time off work for hospital, specialist or school appointments etc. In many families I talked to, one parent has ended up giving up their job. If you're a working single parent, like I was, giving up your job isn't an option. Thousands of autism and disability parents have an air of dazed acceptance. They will do anything for their child they love but knowing where to turn for help can be trial and error. As such, I've compiled a list of useful organisations at the end of the book to help you through the maze.

CHAPTER 5

The Diagnosis Zone
What Happens Now?

Getting the right diagnosis

Getting the right diagnosis is rarely easy—it certainly wasn't in our case —and even when we got the diagnosis of ADHD/ Asperger's it was difficult to process. I was relieved, shocked and bemused about the ADHD diagnosis. I associated this condition mainly with hyper-activity, but I realised if it was right, it explained his restless, challenging behaviour and exclusions.

I didn't realise that anxiety, low-self-esteem and poor sleeping patterns were part of the ADHD profile. By this point, Lucas had had 3 assessments with 3 different diagnoses. Now we had a diagnostic report that covered the lot.

The diagnosis was helpful because we could start to tailor support to meet specific needs, instead of mopping up after meltdown spills. We'd endured a lot of shame and misunderstandings to reach this point.

Having a diagnosis and an EHCP meant the school had to provide, by law, the right environment to ensure Lucas's disability would not impair his chances to access the curriculum.

Since the Disability Discrimination Act (1995), which then became the Equality Act (2010), all public organisations (including schools) are required to make reasonable adjustments to ensure every person with a disability receives equal treatment to their non-disabled peers. The reality is that educating children with disabilities alongside their non-disabled friends presents fundamental challenges. Access is just the tip of the iceberg.

If it seems like a long time getting to this chapter, imagine living through it! Lucas had become a sadder version of his earlier carefree self. His behaviour at school was more extreme than in any other area of his life.

Sometimes vulnerable people in distress are judged by others to be angry or aggressive: an 'aggressive gangs of youths,' 'an angry Black woman,' but what if their anger is an emotional state rather than a permanent state of being?

I'm careful about using negative words to describe children that can become truisms. If a child appears lazy or angry, we need to find answers or provide reassurance, rather than accepting their behaviour at face value.

A statement of spring

I got notification of Lucas's statement of Special Educational Needs in 2013, when he was 9, for his Social Emotional and Mental Health (SEMH) issues:

'Lucas is yet to establish many friendships. He is controlling and rigid in his interactions and misinterprets situations. He is yet to develop consistent collaborative play skills and if a child fails to co-operate with him, he becomes angry. Lucas can calm down quickly following an incident and such behaviour occurs during unstructured times when there are changes to his routine. When he is within a large group, he is reluctant to conform. Instead he acts inappropriately by running off, jumping or crawling around the classroom.'

The paperwork triggered a plan and things started to be put in place to help Lucas. The only issue was that the diagnosis wasn't quite accurate. The above wording beautifully describes the presentation of autistic spectrum condition. A child with extreme sensory sensitivity, unable to cope with the noise and confusion of the average classroom, yet unbelievably, the focus was mistakenly on Lucas's mental instability, with scant effort expended trying to work out why he was having these outbursts.

I had an Individual Education Plan (IEP), which provided targets for emotional and academic attainment within a specified timescale. His objectives were to:

1. Develop his approach to learning, to make progress with the National Curriculum.
2. Develop his social interaction and communications skills to enable him to establish friendships.
3. Make progress regarding his behaviour to enable him to follow school rules and teachers' instructions.
4. Enhance his self-esteem to feel more emotionally secure and express his emotions verbally to reduce frustration.

Lucas's ASD and ADHD diagnosis came 3 long years after being initially denied an assessment. The autism label meant Lucas could stay in mainstream school and pursue a life filled with possibility. Without it, we would have disappeared down the exclusions rabbit hole, which for many young boys—diagnosed or not—is a short cut to anti-social behaviour, pupil referral units or even prison (8).

Still it was positive to have some structure in place with a plan attached. Involving Lucas in setting targets for himself, as well as them being set for him, was a positive step.

I spoke with our consultant psychiatrist, Dr Pam, about the parent consultation notes from Lucas's Annual Review. I told her a teacher had commented how lucky Lucas was to have one-on-one support in literacy. She thought this view was unhelpful and pointed out that a child with a physical disability wouldn't be described as lucky to get the support if they needed to get from one classroom to another!

Handing me a copy of an article in *New Scientist* magazine about the impact of standardised education on our children, she surmised that our 'sausage factory' education system—focused on academic results—provides little room for creatives or deviations from the norm, especially those found in autistic/ADHD children.

I realised then the uncomfortable truth about children with neurological disorders. Many of them experience discrimination because their disability is hidden. She was right. I thought back to the attitude of some of the teachers.

Dr Pam warned that his disruptive behaviour would probably return without support. As she predicted, as soon as Lucas caught up with literacy, his one-on-one support ended, and the old issues resumed.

It was evident that the classroom environment itself was a major cause of his anxious and disruptive behaviour.

I was so moved by Dr Pam's insight. I could have cried with

relief. During the whole process, she was the only person who actually seemed to understand our situation.

After a year of one-on-one sessions with Dr Pam, she gently affirmed she was sure about her diagnosis of ADHD and ASD with Asperger's presentation, moving away from the focus on social, emotional and mental health.

Lucas was almost 9 by this point and I felt like I was about 900! But he was lucky. Some people aren't diagnosed until well into adulthood.

She explained how some of his behaviours could be attributed to the ADHD and others were autism traits. She said it was common for these conditions to co-exist, or to use the medical term co-morbid. She handed me a pile of information sheets about support groups.

I was still struggling with Lucas's ADHD label, as the ADHD kids I'd met couldn't sit for hours creating mini-Dr Who character playing cards, or make up word searches, or colour in a detailed picture. I scanned the handouts and my eye landed on the words 'side effects of medication.'

When you add ADHD into the autism mix, you increase the potential for complex, multi-faceted behaviour, which explains why autism can be difficult to diagnose. In spite of the obvious difficulty in identifying his autism, he still ticked every box in the diagnostic book:

- Social communication difficulties.
- Obsessions about a topic(s) which he knew a lot about in detail.
- A verbal tic (a motor tic is also a sign, but in Lucas's case, it was a speech prosody, which refers to the tone).

Reading it back, it seems incredible that his high-functioning autism was missed, misinterpreted or ignored for so long by his educators. Their focus was on punishing him into compliance and making him personally responsible for his neurodiversity.

Some experts claim Asperger's Syndrome and high-functioning autism are interchangeable, while others believe the core difference between the two is the prevalence of delayed language development in those with 'classic autism.'

In some studies, children with Asperger's Syndrome show slightly higher full-scale IQ than those with high-functioning autism; but to the lay person, these differences are negligible. Whether a child's condition is described as high-functioning autistic or Asperger's Syndrome or mild autism, is pretty irrelevant. They all need to adapt or mask their true behaviours to survive and thrive in a neuro-typical school environment.

There such a mishmash of over-lapping symptoms in ASD and ADHD that contradict and conflict each other. If it's difficult for parents and educators to decipher the motives for a child's behaviours, imagine how it must feel for your child to function with such a complicated brain pulling them in so many directions?

Dr Pam was willing to listen and stressed that the most important thing for Lucas was that his needs were properly met at school regardless of the label.

Conversation veered towards Secondary School places. I mentioned I was interested in Reading School, a state-maintained boarding school. Her mood changed. She was concerned that a boarding school wouldn't be right for Lucas, adding that the Local Authority would be unlikely to pay for it. I reassured her I wasn't looking for a freebie. I was keen to consider all options. I truthfully thought a boarding school would be the perfect environment for him. He would be cloistered away from the slings and stones of the state school system we had fought our way through via 4 schools. When you're raising a child who doesn't fit in, your instinct is to wrap them up in cotton wool. In my head, a traditional boarding school surrounded by trees, a chapel and cosy dormitory, like Hogwarts, would offer the sanctuary we craved. Maybe Hogwarts isn't the best example!

I think Dr Pam's negative reaction to the boarding school ideas was based on her personal perspective, rather than clinical insight, but I respected her opinion. Before our meeting ended, Dr Pam said I should check to see whether Lucas was on the borough disability register as it might provide some protection from discrimination.

She also suggested that whatever Secondary School he went to, he would need a clear reward system to assist behaviour management. Ideally, Lucas would need smaller class sizes or higher teacher/pupil ratio to minimise instances of sensory overload in terms of noise and social communication difficulties.

Dr Pam said we should self-refer for occupational therapy (OT) and that she would be sending Lucas's draft assessment to his GP to record her findings. She would draft a few shortened paragraphs to share with the school, borough health and educational professionals.

It felt good to be involved in shaping how Lucas's condition could be understood by his wider network.

The right or wrong diagnosis?
Psychiatrists can and do disagree about diagnoses—neuroscience

is a complex field of study. Even when a diagnosis is made, there is the trial and error process of finding the right drug-regime, especially if the diagnosis is ADHD and medication is recommended. It can take years to get the regime right for some children.

Brain study is fascinatingly mysterious. Due to hormone changes, stress, age, medicines and other factors, our brain functionality changes as we move through life. Evidence of brain plasticity leans towards our brains as living organisms that change and react to positive and negative experiences.

Our brains are particularly responsive to varying levels of stress, which flood our brain with a powerful mix of chemicals.

During this early, post-diagnosis period, Lucas confessed that he would love a brother or sister to play with and was sad not to have one, but especially a brother. The 11-year age gap between him and his older sister, made him feel like an only child.

His class teachers described him as wired during outdoor play and PE. When I observed him (we've all done it. Hung around peeking through the railings to see if their child is playing alone or with friends) he looked like he was in heaven. I saw a child making the most of much-needed peer interaction with lots of little brothers and sisters. I was desperate to understand what the school was doing to build his self-confidence and his ability to socialise better through play.

Although I'd spoken to the school about his strengths (music, art, drawing), I only got negative feedback about his behaviour.

There seemed to be a disconnect; how could he have talents and intelligence in some areas yet not know how to behave?

Did we skip off into the sunset with our diagnosis road map tucked in our pockets? Of course not!

Even with clear documented evidence from a host of experts, some teachers will struggle to understand the impact of your child's autistic behaviours, and fail to understand why they require special treatment.

In the run up to Christmas, an email landed in my inbox from Lucas's psychiatrist. A full diagnostic report. ADHD seemed to be all over his paperwork. It felt too narrow a lens. After 5 years in education, the reasons for Lucas's behaviour had a cause and a name. It read:

'Lucas presents as a child with an autistic spectrum disorder, specifically with elements of Asperger's syndrome and ADHD. There does not generally appear to be evidence of hyperactivity in Lucas, the issues are more with attention. It is worth noting that for some individuals who are on the autistic spectrum, as in Lucas's case, there is a 'high-functioning' aspect. They can cognitively excel in some areas (math, music, art for example) while lacking the finer skills required to navigate everyday life.

His neuro-developmental disorder, which for ease I will describe as the ASD (Autistic Spectrum Disorder) can present itself in the following ways:

- Low self-esteem, down on himself (Asperger's).
- Social awkwardness. Knowing the wrong thing was said or something isn't quite right but not knowing how to remedy this (Asperger's).
- Difficulty in multiple social interaction e.g. the playground (Asperger's).

- Difficulty understanding the nuances or inferences in verbal or written instructions (Asperger's).
- Requirement for total clarity (Asperger's).
- Highly excitable—not knowing when to stop (ADHD).
- Tendency to give up if things don't work out or he can't understand something straight away (ADHD).
- Short temper and frustration (ADHD)
- Inappropriate comments (ADHD/Asperger's).
- A very literal take on the world (Asperger's).
- Extreme sensitivity to external stimulus, noise, light, etc (ADHD/Autistic Spectrum Disorder).
- Need for routine and an understanding of what will happen next (Asperger's).
- Prone to irritation/upset if routine changes (Asperger's).
- Greater sense of 'righteousness and justice' (Asperger's).

Generally, with a clear and structured programme, in a calm and controlled environment, and if time is taken to explain exactly what is required of him, Lucas will be able to deliver what is expected of him.

In a busy, noisy classroom, Lucas will become disorientated and will distract himself and others in the process. He will probably fail to learn. There will be times when Lucas feels so overstimulated, angry, anxious, that he will need time out to rebalance.'

Perhaps it was because of the sensationalist and negative media coverage around ADHD that I felt so resistant to the ADHD part of Lucas's diagnosis. Even with a diagnosis, schools cannot wave a magic wand. There will be bad days, temper tantrums and tears (some of them yours). Classroom strategies will take time to work and need to be applied skilfully, consistently and compassionately.

A diagnosis opens doors to support groups and expert professional advice both of which will go some way to make school and home life more manageable.

Getting my son's diagnosis was a ray of light in the darkness, as well as the first step on a long road.

The link between the diagnosis and the EHCP (or SEN support package) lies in the skills of the teaching and support teams. It is their job (in partnership with you) to ensure your child's diagnosis doesn't mean they are at an educational disadvantage.

Key professionals delivering the support in your child's ECHP are Learning Support Assistants and Teaching Assistants.

Learning Support Assistant (LSA)

The LSA is part of the teaching or classroom team and will work with children who require additional support with their learning. These can be kids with specific learning difficulties, but also children who do not speak the indigenous language or take longer to learn and process information for a number of reasons.

LSAs usually work one-to-one so they can build close relationships with the children they support. Their relationship can be close although I have heard of situations where a child hits out at their LSA.

Benefits

The LSA will provide Enhanced Pastoral Child Development

Support, focusing on the personal, behavioural and social aspects of your child's time at school. A primary function of the LSA is to enable pupils with autism/ADHD to remain in a mainstream school.

Challenges

An LSA can over-support your child to the point of dependency, this can be referred to as 'learned helplessness' where they feel incapable of initiating anything without the prompt or support of their LSA.

You goal is for your child to be as independent as they can be in school, taking into account any disabling factors. Under-supported children can function well at school when the LSA is there and less so if that individual moves job or is absent for any reason.

LSAs in a job-share situation can create a challenge if they have different styles or approaches. LSAs can be an over-used resource in schools, not always in a one-to-one set up. Sometimes they are supporting 5 or more children in a class.

Teaching Assistant (TA)

Additional support also comes in the form of a TA. A teaching assistant is not a qualified teacher, although higher level teaching assistants (HLTA) can teach classes. The TA's key focus is to provide academic and organisational support for the class teacher, such as setting up classroom equipment and displays.

Benefits

TAs spend valuable teaching time with pupils that the class

teacher can't physically get to, so in large classes of 29 pupils or more they are a highly valuable teaching resource.

Teaching assistants are particularly helpful at providing explanations to pupils who need additional support, especially if there is no EHCP in place. In some schools, TAs work across many classes, helping to maintain academic standards, for example by working with middle-tier pupils.

A study by Special Educational Needs in Secondary Education (SENSE) found that children with ECHPs—those generally taught by TAs—spent less time with class teachers (34% compared to 43%) than their peers without S.E.N.D., which raises a question for parents about the aspirations for our children. The reality is children with S.E.N.D. may have poorer attainment levelsbecause of:

- Higher absence from school (illness/appointments/anxiety).
- Less time in lessons.
- More time in lesson with a TA rather than a qualified teacher.

A TA is not necessarily trained in S.E.N.D. as their focus is on academic rather than pastoral or emotional support. Their support is less likely to be one to one. In Primary School, they need to have skills to be able to teach Years 5 and 6.

Rob Webster of UCL's Centre for Inclusive Education London led an initiative called Maximising the Impact of Teaching Assistants' (MITA). The programme raised some familiar issues for TAs in an average, busy, 3-form entry Primary School (3 classes of approximately 30 kids):

- Limited opportunities for teachers and TAs to meet, with TAs often unsure of lesson objectives and outcomes.
- Interactions between TAs and some pupils with S.E.N.D. creating a dependence; where some vulnerable pupils developed a learned helplessness.

The study drew some positive conclusions, especially from the headteacher involved in the study, who after attending the MITA programme: '. . .felt the quality of TA support and S.E.N.D. provision was improving and noted some early indications that this was washing through into pupil progress.'

Most S.E.N.D. parents embrace TA support in the classroom with open arms. Having someone to help your child is infinitely better than them being absent from school due to an exclusion or lack of teaching support.

Special Educational Needs Co-Ordinator (SENCO)
The SENCO is responsible for delivering effective support to children in a school or other educational setting, so they can access the curriculum to the best of their ability. The SENCO is usually one of the first people teachers will consult if they suspect your child's behaviour may be the result of a specific learning difficulty (SpLD).

Understanding a SENCO's role:

- The SENCO does not diagnose. They liaise with and co-ordinate key child development experts. In 3 of the Primary Schools Lucas attended, the SENCOs fulfilled dual roles, doubling as a class teacher, deputy head and school nurse on top of their SENCO duties.

- They will liaise with teaching assistants and the wider teaching team, namely around progressing specific interventions laid out in the SEN support plan or Individual Education Plan (IEP), reviewing paperwork etc.
- Support the class teacher with Local Authority documentation, monitoring children with additional needs, progressing SEN support and EHCP plans.
- Develop provision maps (a document which outlines what support is required and who delivers it).
- Attending parent and LA meetings. The SENCO follows up any specific interventions required to support your child in or out of the classroom and will source trained therapy professionals.

Important note: the SENCO is not trained to diagnose specific learning difficulties. Their role is to work with parents and act as a broker to secure external professional services if required by an EHC plan or an assessment.

Inclusion Manager
The Inclusion Manager's responsibility is that all pupils—regardless of ability, disability, religion sexual orientation, gender orientation—are integrated as fully as possible into the school community. Some schools have an Inclusion Manager as well as a SENCO. In other schools, the SENCO works with, or for, the Inclusion Manager.

Diagnosis or EHCP: not a magic pill
At the beginning of the New Year, still in the adjustment phase

of the diagnosis, I wrote cheery letters to the head, deputy head and SENCO outlining what we'd done in holidays and updating them on Lucas' sleep patterns and growing obsession with Pokémon. He collected and sorted cards day and night.

I didn't get a response until weeks later when I received a call about something that had happened in school. From my perspective, the diagnosis seemed to make no difference in their treatment or understanding of him. I was still getting frequent calls about something Lucas had done: thrown a book across the room, snapped a pencil, pulled someone's hair, didn't want to do his work etc. I recognised them as signs of his frustration and being unable to manage his moods. Things I had no control over as I wasn't in the classroom and things that I expected the school to manage in school, especially considering that they were by then aware of his specific challenges.

Document everything
The Local Authority behaviour specialist set up a team around Lucas. I was invited to discuss strategies for Lucas's progress and behaviour in class now that we had a diagnosis.

The effectiveness of this team was compromised when key individuals didn't show up to meetings or failed to share information with the rest of the team. People would attend from different agencies with different reasons for attending, so it wasn't clear who was leading or who was responsible for taking notes or following up. If you find yourself in such a meeting, my suggestion is to ask questions, get everyone's names, which organisations they're from, and take your own notes!

Some LAs are reluctant to take advice in the assessment process from external professionals if the child has not been previously known to the local services. They can be reluctant to feed information into the assessment process from sources they haven't collated themselves. This isn't lawful. Any clinical and health care professional should be a member of their regulatory body. For example, a SALT will be a member of the Health and Care Profession Council (HCPC) and any report they write about your child will be based on their clinical or professional opinion, which should, theoretically, be free of bias.

Making the EHC plan workable in schools:

- If you don't have one, talk to the teacher about your child's pupil passport (more on this later in the book). There are templates for pupil passports online and they should be as child-centred as possible. Make sure the specific parts of the plan are explained to them in a language that's clear to them. Use visuals, symbols, clear goals, timings and reminders of what their calm-down system is and how it's supposed to work.
- Is their daily routine written into the plan? Is it specific? For example, child checks in with TA/LSA before assembly or registration. Rather than child needs to be well-behaved in all lessons until break time.
- Make sure your child isn't being set up to fail. If they're hypermobile, dyspraxic, or in the middle of a medication change they may not be able to sit still for long periods of time. In line with the law, the school's expectations should be reasonable and not discriminate against the child.
- You may have to try a number of behaviour strategies with the school and your child whilst they undergo

further assessment. This may take time. Everyone needs to be patient. If a child is being assessed, it's helpful if the school doesn't exclude them, especially if they are waiting for a diagnosis. (See chapter on Exclusions.)

- Behaviour policies vary wildly from school to school. Check the school's behaviour and accessibility policies on the website, talk to parents before your child starts the school and ask open questions to different members of staff.

- Collaborate with others inside and outside of school—don't feel you need to solve everything by yourself.

- Each situation is different and the key people around you are likely to change. Remember the one constant you have is you. Be kind to yourself, start each day with a fresh approach. Try to avoid holding a grudge about what you forgot or went wrong yesterday.

- Take copies of your child's up-to-date medical file with you to key assessment meetings: immunisations, diagnosis dates, medical appointments, operations etc. It could save you time and help you get the best out of the appointment time.

- As a parent, you are entitled to see all documentation relating to your child from face-to-face meetings, emails with the class teacher, headteacher, SENCO. But here's a top tip: paperwork doesn't create the right support if the teams don't consider the knowledge and opinions of parent/carers and of the child themselves.

Steps to go from Overwhelmed to Empowered

1. Don't get hung up on the label. Autism is a loaded diagnosis with rising numbers of children being diagnosed. Every autistic child is different and will experience autism in a way that's unique to them. Take your cue from your child. Watch them, discover them, learn how they communicate (and they will, even if they are non-verbal).

2. Buy yourself a lovely notebook and write down the positive things your child does, including their successes and milestones.

3. As much as you can, make your home a haven of safety, calm, order and kindness. You will need a sanctuary when the outside world feels judgmental or cruel.

4. If your child is at nursery, pre-school or Primary School, meet with the senior leaders to find out how they can support your child's, social, wellbeing and academic needs. They're busy people but try to meet them at least once before your child starts anywhere. Your instinct should tell you what you need to know.

5. Schools and nurseries have a duty to publish information on their website about how they support pupils with Special Educational Needs, read that to get a feel for the level of support your child will receive. Your influence

plays a large part in the quality of support you get for your autistic child. Go armed to the meeting with a list of your most pressing questions. Here are suggestions.

- Will they support your child's toileting?
- Will they support your child's eating habits?
- How do they tackle bullying?
- How will your child's communication and language skills be developed?
- Is the level of specialist support enough or does there need to be a needs assessment? (This may lead to an EHCP.)

6. Your child may be autistic, but this doesn't mean they will under-achieve. Schools have a duty to be accessible and inclusive for all children, so your child can and should still achieve their potential. Your child's diagnosis is individual to them. The causes for your child's 'bad' behaviour are as individual as your child themselves. Get details from teachers about your child's behaviour. Ask them to give an example of 'low-level disruption'. This is useful when devising strategies and support.

7. The most important thing is that your child is happy in school and learns at their own pace. Mainstream schools can present challenges for autistic children, so for some children wellbeing needs to be the priority, and the learning will follow.

8. The 3 best places to start your journey for help and support are:

- Your Local Authority website, which will list information about how children with special educational needs are supported in your borough. Search the 'Local Offer' pages.
- The SENDIASS is your Local Authority information and advice service. You should find a contact or helpline number if you put the name of your Local Authority and the word 'Sendiass' in your search engine.
- Go onto the National Autistic Society website www.autism.org.uk and put 'branches' in the search box; you will find a local group.

9. Try not to feel anxious. Your child will sense your anxiety. Approach the diagnosis as a stepping stone to a life of wonder and exploration with your child. Find your calm by reminding yourself that your child is a magical human being and with your guidance, they can overcome the many challenges their difference may present.

10. Monitor you own well-being. Take a break from SEND parenting to do something just for you. Self-care is key.

11. Some Local Authorities and schools have excellent leadership, resulting in high quality pastoral provision and educational targets for all pupils. You are entitled to check the qualifications of the experts who work with your child.

Lessons Learned

- Getting an autism diagnosis for your child can be a shock, which usually mellows down into relief. Your nagging suspicions were right; now you have a name for the behaviours. Once you've got your head around the diagnosis, you probably have hundreds of questions. What are you supposed to do? How will you cope?

- The answers depend on your circumstances, your child and how their autism impacts your daily life. The key message is to take it one day at a time. If you try to sort out therapies and education and childcare all at the same time you will overwhelm yourself and your child. Your child's development may be slower than their peers, so try not to put too much pressure on them. Your child may thrive with some therapies and not with others.

- Part of the challenge of an autism/ADHD diagnosis is that it will mean something different to every family. Some family members might be a bit more understanding around you, but there are no guarantees.

- Siblings or partners may feel immense jealousy at the amount of time and effort you spend supporting and nurturing your neurodiverse child.

- Whatever your experience post diagnosis, at first it may feel like nothing's changed, yet everything has changed.

CHAPTER 6

The Education, Health And Care Plan Zone
Understanding The Process And How It Can Help You

What is an Education, Health and Care Plan?
An Education, Health and Care Plan (EHCP) is a document outlining your child's needs as they relate to school (education), health (medical and mental) and social care, which can take them from birth to age 25.

It used to be called a Statement of Special Educational Needs, but the name was changed to EHCP in 2014 when the law changed, and the Children's and Families Act 2014 came into being.

When you have been through the assessment process, with specialists reviewing your child, the key findings of the assessments will form the basis of the EHCP, which forms the basis of Section B of the EHC Plan (more detail on that to follow).

A good EHC Plan is well written, setting out clearly why your child has an EHCP (the diagnosis), what their specific needs are, and how these needs will be met in an educational setting (equipment, adaptations, one-to-one help, etc). Also who will meet these needs (SENCO SALT, OT, etc) and what the outcomes or targets will be if these needs are met.

There isn't currently a national template for EHCPs. Each Local Authority will have details about their own version online. Your Local Authority may have a template on the Local Offer pages of your council website.

The Local Offer is where you should find information about local S.E.N.D. support services for children, young people and their families including your statutory entitlements.

The EHCP is designed to be a child-centred document. Section A is where the child or young person writes their aspirations, views and opinions, alongside those of their parents. It's useful to include the child's strengths and what they feel they're not so good at in this section.

My son had help from me with the vision and aspirations section. He told me what he wanted to say, and I wrote it up, pretty much in his words. The strengths and weakness section he filled in with his keyworker.

If your child needs help, or there are issues which make it difficult for them to fill in their section, seek advice from a relevant professional, such as a visual or hearing impairment professional or Educational Psychologist.

If your child has been assessed by a speech and language therapist, or any other specialist in the past, the Local Authority may ask that some assessments are re-done to ensure your child's Special Educational Need is accurately recorded and up to date.

It's important to find a baseline measurement—where your child is now—which enables everyone involved with your child to draw up targets for their future.

Your EHCP will be handled by an individual case worker or a team. Either way, the Local Authority is responsible for putting the expert's reports into their template document for you and others, such as teachers, to review.

Legally, the Local Authority must seek the advice of an Educational Psychologist for an EHCP needs assessment. Ideally, they would seek opinions from a range of specialists in connection with a child's needs assessment to get a full picture, including those from independent professionals.

If the Local Authority does not wish to review information from independent experts, against the wishes and feelings of parents, and they subsequently refuse an EHCP, this may be an appealable decision. The Tribunal would be duty bound to consider all of the relevant documentary evidence.

An EHCP is not an automatic right. Education authorities within local councils and the teaching teams will apply a range of techniques to use in class to manage down disruptive behaviour. Some of these will be punitive, which is unhelpful if your child has underlying issues.

Even if the school's interventions are agreed by all to be ineffective, and your child is exhibiting signs of stress, schools are still under no obligation to undertake a needs assessment for an EHCP.

Often, a needs assessment is triggered by a crisis incident, or when either the school or the parents feel they've reached their limit.

Parents can request a needs assessment independently. Ideally it's best to do this with the school's knowledge. An EHCP can open doors to a more comfortable and inclusive life at school for a youngster with disabilities, but it will also incur a financial commitment that the school via its various funding streams, which they may be unable or unwilling to meet.

This is where the EHCP potentially holds its power. It sits under the legal framework of the Children's and Families Act 2014 as a contractually binding document. The Local Authority is duty bound to deliver the content of the plan once it is agreed, regardless of cost.

Unfortunately, due to increasing the pressure on local government spending many initial requests for EHCPs are unsuccessful, even when it is a watertight case.

Initially, we got a Statement of Special Educational Needs in 2012; social and emotional difficulties were the main presenting needs. When Lucas was re-assessed in 2016, his documentation automatically migrated to an EHCP, We didn't ask for it but the school clearly thought there was still a need for it.

His medical and psychological assessments were re-done, new reports written and so on. Only after significant interventions was it clear that expert support was necessary for Lucas to be educated in a mainstream setting.

In total, the assessment and diagnostic process took almost 4 years from the beginning of Primary School in Year 1 to Year 5 at Junior School. In Year 1 the assessment was denied.

Living through an evolution of SEN delivery, a major change in the law and an overhaul in how our Local Authority delivered children's services (by merging with a neighbouring Local Authority to become a social enterprise company) was full on.

There were plenty of strategic, policy and administrative changes that came with setting up a new organisation. It was a long, complex, convoluted and stressful process. Getting an EHCP didn't make us feel like doing a victory dance.

Getting an EHCP

If you're at the start of the diagnosis process and an EHCP is mentioned, this could be exactly what your child needs to tap into the vital resources to improve their time at school.

If the assessment points to specific needs and your child does get an EHCP, the plan will name your child's school or place or learning. The naming of a school is a critical part of the contractual arrangement between all parties: the school, the Local Authority, any experts, your child and yourself. It's a team effort, and everyone must play their part for it to work.

It is the named school and its staff who will be responsible for delivering the educational support for your child's specific Special Educational Needs to enable them to access the curriculum.

S.E.N.D. code of practice

In September 2014, when the Children and Families Act was passed, Special Educational Needs and Disability (S.E.N.D.) provisions were introduced. This reform changed the Special Educational Needs categories and marked the introduction of the new Education and Health Care Plan (EHCP).

The objective was to provide an integrated service for children with SEN that all professionals in contact with the child could feed into.

Having experienced many assessments with Lucas—for his statement and EHCP—my personal opinion is that the EHCP does provide scope for listening to the views of the child or young person, and for parents and professionals to work together to craft a SMART plan i.e. for the individual child. SMART stands for Specific, Measurable, Achievable, Realistic and Timely.

When Lucas was reviewed for the statement and other SEN provisions such as the Individual Education Plan (IEP), the focus was on the number of hours of support that he received, rather than the specific need they met.

Lucas and I were included in the content of the EHCP and active participants in its design. Alongside experts, I drilled down into the deliverables until we agreed on a range of interventions suitable for Lucas's specific classroom needs.

An EHCP is one of the most powerful ways parents or carers can advocate for the children. My top tip is to pay particular attention to the outcomes.

The code of practice groups Special Educational Needs into the following categories:

1. Cognition and learning.
2. Physical, medical, motor and sensory.
3. Communication and interaction.
4. Social, emotional and mental health.

It's useful when writing Section B of the EHCP (your child's Special Educational Needs) to structure it around each of these 4 headings, making it as clear as possible, so you can match the need to the support for those needs.

A close friend of mine decided not to pursue the EHCP route for her beautiful daughter, who had severe social communication issues and hardly spoke when she was at

Primary School. My friend was concerned about her daughter being labelled. Thankfully, her child overcame her social anxieties in late teenage years and blossomed into a happy young woman with an honours degree and a career she loves.

For us though, pursuing the EHCP was the right decision, especially considering the challenges facing boys in schools, Black boys in particular.

Boys from Black Caribbean heritage or socially deprived backgrounds are perceived as aggressive, angry, violent thugs. But lots of these children are young boys with big emotions, in a hyper-competitive world, where it's not cool for men, even very young men, to show their emotions or any sign of weakness.

Culturally, there is still stigma in some communities about any sort of disability, particularly mental or psychological, which makes diagnosis and support even harder.

What to do if the Local Authority does not agree to carry out an assessment

- Appeal to the Special Educational Needs and Disability Tribunal.
- Collate your evidence; you might want to commission your own private assessments. A child can be seen by any Educational Psychologist as part of the assessment process, it doesn't need to one commissioned by the Local Authority.
- Refer to the Special Educational Needs and Disability code of practice 2014 (issued by the Department for Education).
- Get legal advice and contact charitable organisations

like IPSEA or SOS SEN (contacts at the end of the book) who can help point you in the right direction, especially if you're on a low income.

EHCP checklist
- Is the plan clear regarding the amount/type of support your child will get in the classroom? Outside of the classroom on trips? Who will deliver the plan?
- What support is in place for your child during breaks and social time such as lunch time? Is this level of supervision consistent?
- Who is in charge of your child's dietary requirements and/or medication? What is the contingency plan if that person is off sick or absent?
- Is your child adequately stimulated academically and are their pastoral needs met?
- Where does your child go if they feel stressed, anxious or need to calm down? Who would be with them?
- Does the place of learning have a whole school approach to autism, mental health and disability?
- What strategies will be put in place to support your child day-to-day? Who will be monitoring them?
- What happens if there is a crisis at school?
- Who is the lead person to speak to if you feel there are areas for improvement?
- What is the school's behaviour management plan, for children and young people with neurological divergence?

The plan won't be finalised without your consent, including your signature.

What to do if you're not happy with your draft plan

- Raise your concerns at the draft stage. Changes made earlier are easier to implement.
- Submit your evidence like letters and reports to the LA in the drafting process. Keep copies.
- Call or request a meeting with the Local Authority to raise your concerns about any part of the draft plan. Make sure you are content and clear about the contents before you sign anything.
- Refer back to reports or evidence collated as part of the assessment, these will guide you on the wording.
- Write in short sentences. For example, for Section F (the treatment) make sure you are clear about what is being offered and who will deliver it. How many times a week will the therapy be for and how long? Will it be delivered by someone currently in the school or an expert drafted in? Will you be able to chat with the person at any point?
- Make a who, what, where, when, why checklist as you read through the draft. This will help to see if you have everything covered.
- If you've had any independent/private reports, you have a right to express your wish that these are reviewed as part of the EHCP.
- If you need someone to explain the draft plan for you, get in touch with one of the specialist SEN charities, you may be able to get it reviewed free of charge or for a small donation.

Have your say

In Section A, it needs to include details about the child or young person's aspirations and goals for the future. You don't need to include any outcomes in this section). Here are some ideas for what you could include:

- What do you and your child want to achieve at school or college? What job do they want?
- Express your goals and desires for your child too. Think about what your child needs to get through in a typical day without you.
- Be honest about what you think your child is capable of but aim high. Because with the right support, you may be amazed by what your child can achieve and how much potential is in them.
- Outline what has/hasn't worked in the past and why. If your child is able to, ask them their thoughts on this.
- State their views clearly. No one else knows your child as well as you.

The final EHCP

If you've been fully engaged with the drafting of the plan, including the assessments and shaping the outline of what your child needs educationally, it's very unlikely that the contents of the final plan will come as a shock.

The most contentious issue is likely to be the named school or provision. If you've made representations to the Local Authority, they may have already indicated whether they will be naming the school of your choice in the EHCP.

This is where your child's file or elegant notebook get whipped out. With so many cases being handled by Local Authority case officers, they can blur into one.

When you discuss the final EHCP, which ideally will be a face-to-face meeting, you can state your case as to why you believe your child needs to attend the specified school. You will have a stronger case if said school agrees with you.

If you've visited the school, built up a relationship with the SENCO and other staff members and have got a provisional offer of a place, your case will be strong.

Problems arise when the school changes their mind once they have seen the draft or existing plan, or been in discussions with Local Authority officials. At this point, you are in a negotiation process with the school and Local Authority and you need to approach discussions around the EHCP calmly, armed with facts.

If there are a number of state-maintained schools that could meet your child's needs, the Local Authority will need good reason for why these are not suitable, particularly if they have spaces.

Independent specialist schools will often have spaces, but they are costly for Local Authorities. State-maintained special schools may have spaces but require your child to be several hours away from home. Not ideal but don't be discouraged.

If the Local Authority names a provision that in your opinion is obviously unable to meet your child's specific needs, and you have evidence from different bodies or experts to support this, you have the option of disputing the provision. Make an appeal to the S.E.N.D. Tribunal within 2 months of receiving the final EHCP.

Challenging an EHCP at a tribunal
If you decide to go to a tribunal, you cannot challenge the

health/social care elements of the EHCP; this needs to be challenged via separate routes. Only the educational aspects can be challenged in this way.

S.E.N.D. provision is expensive and for this reason some Local Authorities will resist an assessment and diagnosis. This is why some families have no option but to go to a tribunal to fight for their child's right to an education.

Every case is different and children with a host of difficult and different disabilities are being denied education because parents and Local Authorities become locked in stalemate.

Many children are in limbo because parents and Local Authorities can't agree on school provision, or believe their Local Authority is acting unlawfully.

My aim is not to be political and delve into specific cases but to try to present helpful guidance. For many reasons it's not possible to get it right every time, which causes many families' immense strain.

My EHCP Tips

- Keep notes of everything. Take your notepad with you into the meetings. Attention to detail is vital because you may need to take a third party to a tribunal.

- No one knows as much about your child and their history as you.

- An EHCP is a legally binding document. The Local Authority has a duty to carry out what is in the plan.

- If you're unsure, ask for clarification. The plan should be easy to understand. If you as a parent or carer can't understand it, it should be simplified. If technical terms or acronyms are used, the explanation should be alongside.

- Make sure that your plan covers these 3 key areas:
  - What are your child's specific needs?
  - What provision/support will be put in place?
  - How can we measure the outcomes or success of the plan?

- If the plan includes health and social care needs, make sure the educational needs are a priority.

- Does the plan state who will be supporting your child's learning and how?

- Parent/carers can request an EHCP for a child in an Early Years setting to 16+. Children aged 16+ can request one for themselves.

- Schools needs to forward your request for an EHCP needs assessment to the Local Authority. Chase them up because schools can't carry out the assessments.

- Stay on top of the Local Authority. Whether they agree to do one or not, they must respond to the request to carry one out within 6 weeks.

- If the assessment goes ahead, find out which experts they will consult, such as Speech and Language (SALT), Occupational Therapy, Specialist Teachers, GP, physiotherapist, etc. Ask them how long each of the assessments will take.

- Your child's EHCP should be reviewed annually and usually in a meeting setting. Check any suggested changes before you sign anything. You don't have to sign anything in the Annual Review meeting.

- Unhappy with the EHCP? Unsure about whether the provisions in Section F are being met? You can request an interim review to discuss any issues. The school can also request an interim review. You do not need to wait for the Annual Review to voice your concerns.

- Evidence is your best friend. Keep copies of all

conversations, records, notes and your comments. You can monitor whether your suggestions are being implemented.

- In Section E, monitor the outcomes yourself. If they're SMART this should be easier. Get names of who is accountable.

- If things continue to be troublesome, seek specialist advice. There are useful contacts at the end of this book.

- If the EHCP process feels intrusive, time-consuming and overly complicated, don't worry. Lots of us feel like that. Try to commit yourself 100% to this process.

- Suggest to teachers and health professionals changes that would make life less stressful at school. Teachers and health professionals can only contribute positively if they understand what reasonable adjustments would be useful for your child.

Mantras

'Being a parent is the hardest job in the world and the best job in the world.'

'I'm blessed with a child.'

'I am up for the job!'

'I'm my child's best advocate. I know them better than any expert.'

'What I share with the experts is in my child's best interests.'

'This process will bring about positive results.'

Lessons Learned

- The quality of support your autistic child receives depends on a complex spider-web like infrastructure of Local Authority, NHS, charitable organisations, teaching and support staff.

- The quality of this can vary wildly from day to day, but don't under-estimate the power you have to influence decisions.

- Some schools have excellent leadership, innovative and inclusive policies, which helps them to provide high quality educational and specialist provision for their pupils. Other schools, especially if they are still the responsibility of the Local Authority, are battling conflicting political priorities.

- If you're caught in the crossfire between strained teacher workforce and senior leadership who are under pressure to keep costs down, you might need to collaborate with other parents/groups to apply greater pressure. Particularly to ensure schools are acting within the law.

CHAPTER 7

The Exclusions Zone
From Exclusion To Inclusion

Exclusions in the early years

Exclusions were the soundtrack to Lucas's primary education. The many years of exclusions before he was diagnosed created a child who was on edge, defensive and sometimes explosive in pressurised situations. He describes the feeling before a meltdown as a volcano, which he couldn't always control.

By the time he got to Secondary School his generalised anxiety led to a range of mental health difficulties including anxiety, sleep disturbance, reduced appetite and depression.

In the year or so before he was diagnosed, he was withdrawn and he rarely laughed or smiled. He was consumed with his failure, which was dimming the light of his lovely personality.

Pupils are excluded for a range of reasons, but children with social, emotional and mental health difficulties (SEMH), moderate learning difficulties, speech language and communication difficulties and autistic spectrum disorder, appear most prominently in the exclusion statistics. What do those figures tell you?

Those groups of children have difficulty in communicating their feelings, especially if they are in emotional distress. Their inability to communicate builds up a pressure cooker of feelings which eventually explode in harmful or aggressive ways.

They are usually excluded for physical assault against another pupil or adult.

For all of us, behaviour is a language but like all languages it can be misunderstood.

What does exclusion mean for you and your child?
Exclusions have a negative impact on your child's mental health. A child with behaviour bad enough for them to be excluded from school already has problems. The school exclusion adds to their list of problems. The proportion of children excluded from school aged between 4 and 7 is very small. Exclusions at this young age are often a sign of something else going on and not simply being badly behaved or poorly parented.

When Lucas was first excluded, he was 5 and undiagnosed. The Ofsted survey (9) 'Supporting children with challenging behaviour through a nurture group approach' found that a school's exclusion rate was due to a combination of a school's philosophy and whether it had the capacity to meet the challenges presented.

In Lucas's case, I would say that his exclusions were due mainly to the school's philosophy that they believed I was the problem. Further investigations only happened at my insistence.

The exclusions really affected him. He didn't like the change of routine and he missed his friends. When he went back to school, he was hypersensitive and prone to outbursts.

I will never forget that excruciating and emotional reintroduction meeting when the headmaster asked him why he thought he was excluded. Lucas squirmed. He was lost for words. The head then put the words into his mouth and of course Lucas nodded and repeated the headteacher's words, "I won't do it again."

When your child is excluded and you're a working parent, you need to arrange extra childminder/nanny/au pair time to supervise your child. I took emergency leave from work to stay at home with Lucas and paid for the extra childcare. Because I was self-employed, I couldn't recover my loss of earnings. I lost confidence in myself as a reliable employee. I knew deep down that excluding a primary-aged child was wrong, especially as the school had not done enough to find out why he was having outbursts in the first place.

Three strikes and you're out

Autistic pupils are 3 times more likely to be excluded for a fixed period or permanently than pupils with no Special Educational Needs. The 2019 Department for Education overview on exclusions is as follows:

- The number of fixed period exclusions across all state-funded Primary, Secondary and special schools increased by 8% from 381,900 in 2016/17 to 410,800 in 2017/18.
- The resulting rate of fixed period exclusions increased from 4.76% in 2016/17 to 5.08% in 2017/18, which is equivalent to around 508 pupils per 10,000.
- This increase has been driven by Secondary Schools,

while there has been a decreased demand for special schools:

- The rate of fixed period exclusions in Primary Schools increased from 1.37% to 1.40% between 2016/17 and 2017/18 (140 pupils per 10,000).
- The majority (80%) of fixed period exclusions occurred in Secondary Schools in which the rate of fixed period exclusions increased from 9.40% to 10.13% (1,013 pupils per 10,000).
- The rate of fixed period exclusions in special schools decreased from 13.03% to 12.34% (1,234 pupils per 10,000).

Primary, Secondary and special academies all have higher rates than Local Authority-maintained schools.

A 2017 report by the Institute of Public Policy Research (10) entitled *Making the Difference, the link between school exclusion and social exclusion* found that the total number of children being taught in alternative provision for excluded children is far higher than the total number of reported exclusions.

When children are excluded from mainstream or special schools they often end up in a Pupil Referral Unit (PRU) or an independent or non-registered school.

Part of the gap identified by the IPPR is thought to be down to children who were informally excluded and so don't appear in the exclusion statistics. But does appear in the census of children in alternative provision.

Another part of the explanation may be due to children staying in alternative provision for more than a year. So in subsequent years they appear in the alternative provision data rather than that year's exclusion statistics.

But Pupil Referral Units were not designed to be permanent settings for children to complete their compulsory education. They were designed to refer them on to another mainstream or a special school.

Kiran Gill, one of the authors of the IPPR report and founder of charity *The Difference*, states, 'Increasing numbers of children are being referred close to their exams, and end up doing their exams in pupil referral units. Only 1% of GCSE candidates in pupil referral units leave with the 5 good GCSEs they need to continue with their education. Children who are excluded due to reasons of Special Educational Need, or social deprivation, continue to be disadvantaged by their exclusion.'

School inspectorate Ofsted has raised concerns that schools are removing children as they approach GCSEs as a way of 'gaming the system' in performance tables.

Schools strenuously deny this and it's difficult to prove as large numbers of young learners are moving around all of the time.

There also appears to be a group of children who are being repeatedly and informally sent home from school due to difficult behaviour without ever being permanently and formally excluded. These children miss out on large chunks of their education without showing up in the exclusion statistics.

A double disadvantage

Research published by the Education Policy Institute examining unexplained pupil exits in the English school system highlighted the pupil groups most likely to experience unexplained exits from schools. Several vulnerable learner pupil groups are particularly likely to leave school for unknown reasons. Such moves are not accounted for by changes in care placements or changes of address.

Here is a summary from the Education Policy Institute 2019 of pupils most likely to experience an unexplained exit:

- Over 1 in 3 (36.2%) had also experienced a permanent exclusion.
- Around 1 in 3 (29.8%) were looked after pupils (those in social care).
- Over 1 in 4 (27.0%) had identified mental health needs (SEMH).
- Around 1 in 6 (15.6%) were poorer pupils (those who have ever been on free school meals).
- Around 1 in 6 (15.7%) had identified Special Educational Needs.
- Around 1 in 7 (13.9%) were from Black ethnic backgrounds.

Significantly these pupil exits are not identified as exclusions. These exits are not recorded or regulated. But they do show that children from specific backgrounds, who are socially disadvantaged or those with low attainment (which could be the result of an undiagnosed neurological condition) feature prominently in the figures.

Other key findings showed that overall, multi-academy trusts (MATs) have higher rates of unexplained exits.

In light of these figures, the Education Policy Institute recommended that the government should help schools to recognise the complicated causes of pupils' behavioural difficulties by improving their training and reinforce their responsibility to support pupils with S.E.N.D.

The following jumped out at me as I researched this book:

1. Children from Black, Hispanic or dual-heritage backgrounds tend to get a clinical diagnosis (of autism, ADHD) later than other groups. They receive less targeted early intervention, and the intervention that is put in place is more often punitive. Overall, Black and Hispanic children are less likely than their White peers to have an autism diagnosis. In addition, White children are about 19% more likely than Black children and 65% more likely than Hispanic children to be diagnosed with autism. (Maureen Durkin, 2017, Centers for Disease Control.) These are robust studies taken from health and education database from over 1.3 million children aged 8.

2. Initial diagnoses for these children tend to fall into the social, emotional, behavioural or mental health categories, before other root causes of persistent disruptive behaviour are established.

3. Black Caribbean, dual heritage (Caribbean origin) neurodiverse pupils are more likely to be more harshly treated and receive exclusions for similar transgressions than their peers from other backgrounds.

There is no biological reason for the differences in autism prevalence, except maybe things like access to diagnostic and screening services, and access to support may differ across communities.

Early intervention is an excellent indicator of good autism provision, but in reality, accessing autism screening and support depends on many factors that can extend beyond the good policy intentions.

Exclusions figures
- 7,905 pupils were permanently excluded from all state funded Primary, Secondary and special schools (Department for Education 2017/8).
- 78% of permanent exclusions were issued to children with special education needs.

It's important to note that exclusions are attached to enrolments at a particular school and not the individual pupil. Pupils who are registered with multiple schools have each of their enrolments considered separately.

This means schools should be held accountable for their exclusion numbers.

- As in previous years, pupils of Gypsy/Roma (16.52%) and Traveller of Irish Heritage (17.42%) ethnic groups have the highest rates of both permanent and fixed period exclusions.
- Black Caribbean children are 3 times more likely to be excluded than the overall figures (10.46%).
- Pupils of dual White and Caribbean heritage come in at 10.13% - along with Black Caribbean children, these 2 groups saw increases in exclusion rates on the previous year.
- A 14-year-old boy of Black Caribbean heritage, in Year

10, is in the peak exclusion's 'danger zone' according to these Department for Education figures.

- Even if your Black, Mixed or Caribbean child doesn't have a diagnosed Special Educational Need/a significant cause of disruptive behaviour, they are still at higher risk of exclusions than the general school population.
- For many Black Caribbean families, like mine, a diagnosis comes after repeated exclusions.

Children with Special Educational Needs (approximately 14.4% of all children in England) fair badly in terms of exclusions. The figures for children with an EHCP (15.95%) and pupils receiving SEN support (15.10%) are not encouraging (Department for Education annual exclusions data, 2016/17):

- Boys are 3 times more likely to be excluded than girls (boys overall and boys with SEN).
- Pupils with Special Educational Needs are up to 6 times more likely to be permanently excluded from school.
- Pupils with an EHCP have the highest fixed period exclusion rate at (15.95%) over 5 times higher than pupils with no SEN (3.36%).
- Research by charity Ambitious About Autism in 2018 reveals that exclusions of autistic pupils has increased by almost 60% in 5 years.
- Pupils with identified SEN accounted for around half of all permanent exclusions.
- Higher rates of exclusions are seen in areas of high deprivation. Overlaid with other social indicators a child with SEN, living in the West Midlands, entitled

to free school meals, is statistically more likely to be excluded than those living in the South East.

- The number of pupils with SEN in England in January 2019 was 1,318,300.
- There are approximately 351,000 children with a learning disability (0-17) in the UK (Mencap 2019).
- The UK government doesn't provide a number for a category of children with learning disabilities. The categories are moderate learning difficulty, severe learning difficulty and profound and multiple learning difficulty.
- Approximately 2.5% of children in the UK are believed to have a learning disability (Mencap 2019).
- Pupils with Special Educational Needs are 8 times more likely to be permanently excluded than their peers without. (Inquiry from Children's Commissioner, 2012.)

Persistent disruptive behaviour is the most common reason for permanent exclusions and fixed-period exclusions across all school types (Department for Education 2017/8). This is the sort of behaviour most often displayed by children with Special Educational Needs or social, emotional difficulties.

Parents and teachers feel that they're in a depressing groundhog day. A damaging cycle of distress for all concerned.

Can we migrate some of the innovative and life-affirming teaching that happens in some alternative provision placements and weave their positive practices into our more rigid mainstream, or specialist settings?

Or adopt low-sensory and neurodiverse trained teachers in every mainstream school, along with psychotherapists?

It's difficult to understand why vulnerable young people are being excluded in such high numbers when their behaviour is a clear reflection of their distress, trauma, deeper societal issues or poor management of a neurological condition.

Excluding them from school, when they may be unsupervised for many hours a day, creates the perfect storm for the negative cycle to implode.

Teachers and school leaders might be using exclusions to manage 'difficult' children out of the classroom, so they can focus on the other 29, but this just transfers the problem elsewhere.

Assimilating children with various social, developmental and neurological needs into the average classroom is tough, arguably tougher than including children with mobility or other more visible health issues.

Parents, and pupils aged over 18, are able to request a review of the reasons for a permanent exclusion. An independent review panel's role is to review the decision of the governing body, not to reinstate a permanently excluded pupil. The panel must consider the interests of the pupil, including the circumstances in which the pupil was excluded as well as consider the interests of other pupils and people working at the school.

Whichever way you cut it, exclusion statistics are a concern for many parents, causing anguish to thousands of families, and creating major social issues.

A year or so ago, I watched Molly Dineen's television documentary, *Being Blacker*, about a former Brixton-based record shop owner, Blacker Dread, and his experiences of raising his son. It's a moving family story with all of the drama and humour you would expect, but the point that hit home for me was when he and his partner decided to educate their son in the Caribbean because of the difficulties he was having at a London school. Check out the documentary online.

Caribbean youngsters are reported as being louder and more challenging in the classroom. They are reprimanded more seriously than their White counterparts.

UK footballer Ian Wright has been open about his childhood and his experiences at school. He wasn't confident as a reader. His handwriting wasn't good and he wasn't able to concentrate in lessons on the subject in hand. He talks movingly about a compassionate teacher, Mr Pigden, who took him under his wing, give him responsibilities, which helped him feel like he had a use at school.

In *The Times* newspaper, Ian Wright urged schools to try not to expel children, especially boys, to prevent them getting involved in crime. His story isn't uncommon, especially for Black boys. Ian's attachment issues and trauma played a big part in his formative behaviour at school.

There are hundreds of kids, just like him, who need to be guided through their emotions to achieve better outcomes. Thankfully, there are many special teachers who understand the power of listening and praise.

A few hundred years ago, education was the preserve of the elite, but now people of all social backgrounds expect to receive a decent quality of education, particularly in developed countries.

Getting a good education isn't about being a 'scholar' anymore, or studying ancient texts. You acquire skills, qualifications, confidence and a good mindset to become employable in our hyper-competitive global economy.

If we leave challenging children feeling unloved and undiagnosed, we are complicit in setting up their future failure. We are also denying the world some extraordinary talent.

It's not just children that suffer in an over-standardised, mechanised education system. We run the risk of crushing the spirit of excellent teachers under the weight of an impossible job, causing the brightest and best to leave the profession. This is happening already. Bring on the fresh ideas and talent!

Response: consequence: solution

Exclusion should be a last resort when other methods of discipline, sanctions and rewards have failed. If you don't know or haven't engaged in how your child is behaving at school, or how the teacher manages your child, the exclusion letter can come as a shock.

When you're notified that your child is to be excluded, the teachers, especially the headteacher, are sending you a clear message: your child's behaviour is unacceptable in school and they are using forced time out to let you know about it.

It's important to break the cycle after the first exclusion. Without determined intervention from you, the school and your child, the situation can escalate to a permanent exclusion.

Let's not get ahead of ourselves. This book is about help and healing, so try to stay calm if you are facing your first exclusion. Make time to support your child, providing love and guidance.

As soon as the school sees your willingness to work with them, you're not part of the problem, you're halfway to turning the situation around.

Boys tend to be excluded for the following reasons:

- Physical violence.
- Use or possession of illegal substances.
- Carrying, using or threatening to use knives or other dangerous weapons.
- Lashing out on children or members of staff.

Physical attacks are regarded as serious and teachers are not expected to retaliate when they are kicked or punched by a child. These are valid reasons for deciding to exclude children. The exclusion is a consequence of what happened. An exclusion allows the teacher time to reassess and hopefully rebuild their relationship with the child. The school needs to meet the educational and wellbeing needs of all pupils and teaching staff. However, just because a school can rationalise the reasons for excluding your child, it doesn't mean you won't feel sick to your stomach when or if it happens to you.

Meltdowns

At the edge of a meltdown, your child has lost control. This feeling unleashes strong emotions, which the body needs to discharge physically.

If you are near a child in this hyper-aroused state, you may get accidentally kicked. If you are restraining a child in their fight emotional state, they will lash out, scream or bite. You are in the midst of an extreme primal reaction, once the chemical reaction has been triggered in the brain, the body has to follow through.

According to Andy Cutting, Specialist Exclusions and Alternative Provision Advice Coordinator for the National Autistic Society, 2017, 'Parents often report to the National

Autistic Society's School Exclusions Service that their child has no recollection of their meltdown and that when their child is told that someone has been hurt as a result of their actions, they are full of remorse or feel disengaged from their actions. It is this lack of any intention to harm others that might indicate that their behaviour is a direct consequence of their autism.'

The most important part of the exclusion process is the solution. What happens when your child is back at school? How do you, your child and the school move forward?

The solution phase is full of power and potential if it's well managed, and it's possible to achieve great things even after an exclusion.

An exclusion has the potential to:

- Change the dynamics in the class.
- Build trust between yourself and the school/teachers.
- Re-build trust between the child and their class and their teacher(s).
- Improve the perception of your child among his peers.
- Change the energy in the class and make new friendships.

However, most of this won't happen if your child's teacher still holds the same negative opinion of your child, if your child still feels bad about going to school, or if the original cause of your child's behaviour has not been dealt with through preventative and constructive measures to reduce the chance of a re-occurrence.

Parents and educators need to understand what is causing the disruptive behaviour, rather than going straight to punishment.

Warnings don't offer an effective deterrent, instead they

simply back your child into a corner. Teachers need control in their classroom so they can educate in a safe space but excluding a child with violent behaviour becomes an issue for everyone, including other pupils.

A child with a strong personality hoovers up considerable teacher energy. Some teachers handle this without diluting the teaching time for the rest of the class. Others require support staff, training or both.

When the exclusion letter lands

Step 1
Do not panic. Things may feel like they are spiralling out of control, but you can steer things back. Remember, this is not you or your child's failure. This is an experience you will all learn from. Don't be alarmed by the professional and slightly threatening tone of the letter. It's a legal document and is written in that way to comply with the law.

The IPSEA website is a great place to check whether your exclusion is legal. The website has template letters to use if you think your child has been excluded illegally. It happens. The Department for Education website outlines the procedure for legal exclusion and what parents can do. Children and young people can be excluded from state-maintained schools, academies or pupil referral units (PRUs). Make sure you understand your rights about the exclusion, taking into account the age of your child and circumstances for the exclusion.

Read and understand the key elements of the external exclusion:

- Your child is not allowed to be seen anywhere near the school premises.
- The exclusion letter will state the reasons for the exclusion.
- Members of the school governors are copied in.
- Representatives from the Local Authority are copied in.
- Reference is made to your legal responsibility as a parent.
- It explains how your child will be 'reintroduced' into school, after their enforced absence.
- Details are provided about whom to contact if you wish to appeal, especially if you think you child has Special Educational Needs that have yet been undiagnosed or resolved.

The school should call you on the day the exclusion is given and follow it up with a letter including information on:

- The reason for the exclusion.
- Dates and details on how long your child is required to be out of school.
- Your duties during the first 5 days of the exclusion. For example, making sure your child isn't out and about in a public place during normal school hours, whether you are with them or not.
- The procedure for re-entry into school, giving dates, times, locations and who will be present at the re-introduction meeting.

Step 2
- Don't spend days agonising about the letter. It's

a painful sting, but the quicker you start dealing with the sting, the sooner you and your child will heal.

- Swing into action. At times like this, doing is more productive than thinking, and it makes you feel a lot better. Thinking can come later when you're in the solution phase.
- Make a list of priorities. Find a childminder or friend to stay with your child. Organise food and plan schoolwork for him for whilst you're at work. Book some annual leave from work.
- Create a mini timetable of work that includes time for catching up with your child.
- Be kind to yourself.
- Check the school's website in their policies section to help you understand their guidelines on behaviour, inclusion and bullying (or anti-bullying) and S.E.N.D. Depending on the reasons for your child's exclusion, you can check this against the school's behaviour and exclusion policies. If you can't locate the policies online, politely request them from the school office. See if they state clearly the school's grounds for exclusion, are any of these reasons spelled out in your exclusion letter?
- Put the date of the exclusion in your diary and work out what you will do with your child, family and work on those days.
- Plan for your child's return to school date. You need to be there with them. Take notes of what is said during the meeting, and who is going to do what.

Some schools invite you to read and sign copies of their key policies as a contractual agreement when accepting a place in that school for your child. Independent schools are not bound by the regulations of the Department for Education like publicly funded schools are, so you will need to pay particular attention to the school rules if your child goes to a fee-paying school.

Independent school headteachers can be all-powerful so building a good relationship with them is important, especially if you suspect or your child might have an undiagnosed Special Educational Need.

The Department for Education states that it is the school's responsibility to take reasonable steps to set up and mark work for pupils during the first 5 school days of an exclusion.

Missing valuable school and learning time will only set up future problems if you don't pinpoint the reason for the exclusion and make sure that your child has been set an adequate amount of work.

Step 3
- Make sure you understand the legal aspects of the exclusion in terms of what you and your child can do.
- Check that the school has acted legally. If this is a fixed term exclusion and not the first, how many have they had in this academic year? Is your child at risk of being expelled permanently?
- Keep in mind that the law does not allow for extending a fixed-period exclusion or converting a fixed-period exclusion into a permanent exclusion.

Fixed-period exclusions

A child who gets into serious trouble at school can be excluded for a fixed period of time.

Schools can exclude a child if:

- They have seriously broken school rules.
- Allowing them to stay in school would seriously harm their education or welfare, or the education or welfare of other pupils.

Arm yourself with facts

- Only the headteacher or acting headteacher can exclude a child.
- Your child can't be given fixed period (non-permanent) exclusions, which total more than 45 school days in any one school (academic) year. This total includes exclusions from previous schools covered by the exclusion legislation.
- If your child is excluded for longer than 1 school day, the school should set work for them and mark it.
- Work that is provided should be accessible and achievable by the pupil when they're not at school.

Your legal position

The Department for Education and the S.E.N.D. code of practice will provide all of the legal dos and don'ts in terms of what the school is allowed to do, as well as what parents of excluded pupils or the pupils themselves can do.

In summary, schools should engage proactively with parents in supporting the behaviour of pupils with additional needs.

Schools should also cooperate proactively with the carers or children's home workers for looked-after children.

When notifying parents about an exclusion, the headteacher should set out what arrangements have been made to enable the pupil to continue their education prior to the start of any alternative provision or the pupil's return to school. This should be in line with legal requirements and guidance in Section 5.

The S.E.N.D. code additionally provides guidance for:

- Local Authorities.
- Headteachers.
- Governing bodies.
- Academy trusts.
- Independent review panel members.
- Independent review panel clerks.
- Special Educational Needs experts.

Seek early specialist legal advice on your child's rights. Some S.E.N.D. legal experts will provide representation on a lower cost basis if you are a low-income household. Be clear about what you need before you discuss or sign anything. Give yourself time before you appoint a lawyer. Get at least 3 firms to discuss their terms with you.

Children are sometimes illegally excluded, so it's worth spending some time on this. Useful contacts can be found listed at the back of this book.

The S.E.N.D. code of practice
This code is the legal framework that sets out what schools

and Local Authorities must do to comply with the law. Parents need to follow the guidance unless there is a clear reason not to. Like all legal documents, it's a heavy read and I suggest you skip to the exclusion section by searching the code of practice 2015 online.

When notifying parents about exclusions, the headteacher should draw attention to relevant, free and impartial information. This should include a link to this statutory guidance on exclusions and a link to sources of impartial advice for parents.

Children watch and learn from each other in a way that is not always in their best interests. Children love to blame each other for classroom shenanigans. If your child has been excluded, you might feel like a social outcast. I was that lone mum in the playground, too afraid to approach other parents for fear of what they would think of me.

Exclusion to inclusion
The flipside of exclusion is inclusion. The rights and wrongs of inclusion are hotly debated. A one-size-fits-all approach doesn't usually work in reality, but there is a whole armoury of things schools can do to improve their inclusive quotient.

If school becomes a place of punishment or shame for your child, perhaps you can turn it around. Encourage them to get involved in fundraising or volunteer activities or taking part in school productions.

It takes guts to be friendly when you feel everyone is against you and your child—believe me I know! There will always be judgmental parents and their children but once people get to know you and your child, barriers will start to come down.

Smile and introduce yourself to people. It will feel awkward at first and not everyone will be warm and friendly, but it's worth a try especially if you can stay calm and dignified.

If all efforts fail and your child is persistently bullied or excluded and you wish for them to remain in that environment, you have a few last resort options. Assuming you have escalated your concern through the usual channels including the headteacher, school governors and local councillors, you can take a case to the UN Convention on the Rights of the Child (UNCRC, ratified by the UK in 1991).

This widely used human rights treaty sets out what children and young people need to be happy and healthy.

'While the UNCRC is not incorporated into UK law, it still has the status of a binding international treaty. By agreeing to the UNCRC, the Government has committed itself to promoting and protecting children's rights by all means available to it,' Children's Commissioner, 2017.

In relation to school exclusions, the articles of the UNCRC which are of most relevance to this area of policy are:

- Article 2: All rights apply to all children regardless of their personal circumstances and regardless of what they have done.
- Article 3: The best interests of the child must be a primary consideration in all actions.
- Article 12: Every child has a right to express their views regarding all matters that affect them and for these views to be taken seriously.

- Article 23: Children with a disability have a right to special care and support.

Early intervention

Before your child's behaviour gets to the persistent disruptive stage, the school can put in place a range of early interventions in place.

Schools can try a range of activities, monitor and review to see if your child's behaviour improves or seek outside advice.

The Department for Education has full guidance for headteachers on its website. Interestingly, the guidance states that headteachers should, as far as possible, avoid excluding pupils with an EHCP. This should also extend to pupils with Special Educational Needs or those awaiting an assessment. Lucas's red cards and internal and fixed-term exclusions continued even after he got his plan.

Re-introduction to school

When you are nearing the end of the exclusion period, you will need to prepare your child for what happens when they go back to school. There is usually a meeting with the headteacher. They will expect your child to be contrite and ready to be reintroduced to their mates.

Hopefully at this stage the school will suggest new, positive plans to avoid a repeat of the behaviour that triggered the exclusion. Take detailed notes. What support is in place? What is your child to do if they feel angry or upset? Who should they speak to?

The SENCO might be in the re-introduction meeting.

Everyone, including your child, needs to be clear about next steps, which should be confirmed in writing.

I urge you to take a friend or family member with you to the meeting. If your child is in the process of an assessment for SEN, you could suggest that exclusions are paused until the assessment is done.

The school might decline, but it's worth asking. It's a delicate situation, which involves you, your child, the teacher, the other children involved and their parents. Careful handling is needed to act fairly for everyone.

The Department for Education outlines the school's responsibility for putting a plan in place to support your child and help them manage their behaviour, but you should have your own objectives.

The teachers will want assurances from you and your son that the behaviour that resulted in exclusion won't be repeated. Does your child have an early warning system? Are they clear about what they need to do? If you're not satisfied with the support level, ask the teacher to explain what support they are getting from Local Authority. When you child is back in school, will they have a Learning Support Assistant in the classroom or playground?

Our first re-introduction meeting was awful. One of the teachers was almost in tears. The headteacher's back was as stiff as a board as he asked Lucas to explain why he thought he was excluded and what he would do to prevent it happening again. He was 5 at the time. It was like listening to a judge speaking to a hardened criminal. Lucas squirmed in his seat and struggled to get a coherent sentence out. I sat on my hands, trying to make myself invisible. It was literally painful.

When fear, panic and anger fade, you still need a plan. Your child can make a fresh start, especially if they get the support they need. You are still the most important person in his life, whether you realise it or not. He's in pain. He probably hasn't got all the words to speak his feelings, but with you in his corner, he won't fail.

Once your child is back at school, everyone needs to commit to making it work, otherwise your child is likely to be out of school again.

If the headteacher or SENCO uses the phrase 'if your child makes one false move' at your re-introduction meeting, you need to worry.

This is a sign that the school is expecting more disruption and they are leaving you with a clear indication that they won't hesitate to exclude again. A badly staged re-introduction, on top of any uncomfortable or undressed issues, makes it difficult for everyone to move forward.

The impact of exclusion
Their early years are about learning to conformity and fit into the school community. An exclusion is a sign that your child must modify their behaviour to belong, which is difficult if they're not fully in control of it.

Because children with SEN are more often excluded, the experience can crush their already fragile confidence further.

Consider the impact of several exclusions on your child with autism or ADHD. Your child is angry or worried about their exclusion, but may not have the skills, support or experience to prevent it happening again. They may not have the language, processing or social skills to explain their fears or concerns.

On top of this, they probably feel huge guilt about how they have upset you. As children or young adults, they may think they've failed you and their first challenge of school, which is fitting in and making friends.

Depending on where you are in your life, you might feel angry with your child and ball them out, or you may think it's no big deal and it will blow over. Or you may be somewhere in between! Whatever your reaction, your child is watching your response. They have spent their lives trying to please you, so this is a difficult test for them. Find time to talk to your child and tell them why you feel cross or frustrated, sharing your feelings is a good way to open the conversation about how your child feels. There might be big stuff they need to tell you—this is a critical time for listening.

Schools are highly competitive places. Many operate in extremely pressurised environments with the threat of league tables and funding cuts hanging over them. For autistic/ADHD kids, school can feel like a war zone. It's tough when you're going through it. I'll try to help you through.

Considering home schooling?
If this is all too much, a viable alternative to consider is home schooling. At various stages, I considered home-educating Lucas, as the exclusions and punishments got too much.

For some families, home schooling is a perfect solution. It's not a decision to be taken lightly, but sometimes you are left with few or no options.

If approached calmly with lots of research, the home school route provides many social and academic benefits.

There is a sizeable home school community out there and

some of it is made up of parents of autistic or ADHD or other neurodiverse children.

A quick look online will point you in the direction of websites and resources to help you tap into a parallel parenting educational community. Check out the wild schooling website wilderchild.com/wildschooling or investigate the Forest School Movement forestschoolassociation.org/history-of-forest-school.

More families are choosing to educate their kids at home because the long wait for the Local Authority to find suitable provision for their child gets too stressful.

If both parents are working, you will need to organise the practicalities of educating your child. Take into account where you work, your hours, whether you work shifts, whether you can apply for flexible working, and how you will manage on a reduced income if one of you reduces their hours.

If you can manage on a lower income and create a rota for home education, it can be a perfect solution for your family. If you're a single parent, you will need to make sure you access the benefits you are entitled to so you can meet the costs of additional childcare. Whatever your personal situation, you will have to take into account workable child-care arrangements, and the safety and wellbeing of your child if you employ a tutor, or they attend classes or activities away from home.

Don't give up at the first hurdle. You will eventually find a welcoming community of families sharing childcare. You just need to be flexible.

Home school checklist
There are a few rules about opting your child out of mainstream education, here's a checklist.

1. Visit www.gov.uk/education to clarify your Local Authority's legal requirements for elective home education.

2. If your child has an EHCP you must inform the Local Authority if you are planning to home educate.

3. If your child attends a special school, you will need permission from the local council before their name can be taken off the register. They don't usually decline your request, but they will want to make sure you can cope with your child's needs and provide them with a suitable education once they are out of school.

4. If your child attends a specialist unit in a mainstream school, you don't need permission to de-register them. But you would usually inform the headteacher who would advise the local council. In Scotland and Northern Ireland, the rules are different, check your council website.

5. If you are a parent/carer and your child doesn't have Special Educational Needs, but you want to withdraw them from school for another reason, you don't need to contact the Local Authority if you wish to home educate. You need to write to the headteacher who must accept your decision if you plan to take your child out of school completely. The school will let the Local Authority know. But if you want your child at school some of the time and to home educate the rest, the headteacher may refuse your request to remove them from the register.

6. When the authorities are aware that you're opting out of state provision, your decision to home school should

be respected and supported. The council can make informal checks to your home, to ensure your child's education is suitable.

7. There are child protection and safeguarding reasons for making sure that the council is aware of your plans. Social services take a keen interest in home schooled children. It's not personal, it's policy.

8. Check out teaching tools for all National Curriculum subjects online. Many are in downloadable PDF format.

9. If your child is of exam age, find out which exam board your Local Authority will be using for their school's GCSE exams.

10. Contact your Local Authority education team to check where the examination centre will be or contact the exam boards directly if you're unsure about the process.

11. Draw up at least 2 or 3 weekly timetables and rotate them. It will stop you and your child getting bored and ensure you cover all of the topics across the curriculum.

12. Get planning and be organised. Buy a clip board if it makes you feel better!

13. Meet other home school parents through online forums.

14. Make sure your child is well socialised. Look for free, local, affordable activities they can get involved with, such as swimming, sports, music groups, etc.

15. Play to your child's strengths. If your child shows a particular interest or talent, home schooling gives you more time for them to do the thing they're good at.

16. If you're unsure about your own teaching skills and you can afford it, look into getting a home tutor. It's worth the money and means the time you spend

teaching your child the subjects you're strong in, is more enjoyable.

17. Do some of your lessons in the local independent coffee shop to vary the environment. Children with ADHD often crave variety.

18. Take some lessons outside in the sun, snow or wind. It's exhilarating!

19. Make time for the arts and self-expression in your home school timetable. Children with autism/ADHD can excel in some areas, you will have time to explore what these are.

20. Check out Potential Plus UK, their promise is to nurture your child's potential: potentialplusuk.org.

21. Give yourself a pat on the back for being an amazing parent.

Children and young people who are repeatedly excluded from school are later diagnosed with Special Educational Needs, and they can suffer damaging psychological effects for months or even years afterwards.

Persistent disruptive children who are not diagnosed with specific learning needs, usually go the route of alternative provision (AP) such as a Pupil Referral Unit, or permanent exclusion.

Whatever conclusions you draw from the exclusion figures, there is something strangely skewed in an education system that considers large numbers of our future generation to be 'unteachable.' Perhaps there still isn't enough information about what autism and ADHD behaviours look like in the classroom? Although I very much doubt it. I feel we are used to discarding children whose behaviours we don't fully understand or have the recourses to figure out, which is terribly sad.

The resolutions lie in a mix of strategies including teacher and parent discussions about what is achievable within the current structures. The pinnacle of educational achievement isn't going to be a higher education degree for some.

Creativity, kindness and vocational skills can all be achieved without the traditional degree model and they are valuable to any forward-thinking employer.

Diversity in all its formats is good for business. Schools and employers are starting to work more closely with mental health/autism/ADHD campaigners to open up career paths and prospects neurodiverse candidates. This is needed, as the employment rates for disabled people are still lower than they should be at 53.2% compared to 81.8% non-disabled (ONS, 2019). Please note that this figure included all disabled people, not only those with a neurodiversity.

We need a clutch of fresh policy ideas and collaborations. The structural barriers to equality echo the barriers that Black people and other minorities face.

The British Education System legislates that children are deemed to be of compulsory school age by January 1st, April or September following their fifth birthday. This is in contrast to European countries, where children aged 7 are just starting out on their school adventure. Some kids at 5 are ripe and ready to start school, others less so.

There are hundreds of excellent early years teachers who do an incredible job. But if your child has a developmental delay, how confident are you that this will be identified early? The current best practice for SEN is early intervention, as corrective and supportive therapies are more powerful when applied to the younger, more 'plastic' brain.

Is our highly standardised curriculum in bulging classrooms of mixed ability young children working out? Most schools have streaming or sets to cater for different levels of academic ability.

How do we entice teachers into a profession they are leaving in their hundreds? Good teachers are leaving the profession in high numbers. Many are burned out and saying the workload is excessive (18% plan to leave teaching within 2 years, and 24% within 5 years according to National Education Union, 2019). Just as they are getting to the point of being most experienced and valuable.

It's difficult to parent effectively when you need to work round the clock, in fear of your job. It's hard to teach effectively when there are so many pupils to teach and support and not enough hands.

Adults who are diagnosed with autism/ADHD later in life feel a similar sense of injustice. Many feel angry about the lack of support from people who were supposed to help them. The solution to the complex issues of undiagnosed conditions or excluding young talent is everyone's responsibility.

Suzy's 10-Point Plan for Positive Change in Schools

1. Low sensory, chill out zones and visual timetables in all schools.

2. The whole-school SEN concept rolled out widely. All children benefit from adjustments to a school's physical environment, especially those with autism, ADHD, sensory, anxiety or mental health conditions and social or emotional problems.

3. Schools should be encouraged to trial dynamic teaching styles and alternative curricula, using latest technology in all lessons, not just IT.

4. Wider options in mainstream schools for children especially those with specialist interests who show marked talents in specific areas including coding, game design, film and video editing in school curriculum, not just for those sitting GCSEs.

5. Encourage schools to permit children to 'opt out' from some subjects before they take options. Drop French, do extra English, etc.

6. More emphasis on the arts as therapy in schools, to support mood and other mental health disorders.

7. Employ fully diverse teaching teams.

8. Encourage more parent involvement in supporting children with SEN.

9. Dynamic intervention of mental health professionals in schools.

10. More freedom for teachers to explore their specialism with passionate learners.

Whatever the changes, change is overdue. A radical shake up of our mainstream education policies is required as we are consigning a sizable minority of our future workforce to the scrap heap.

Mantras

For parents and their excluded children

'Exclusion is an opportunity for time out. A break from damaging habits.'

'You are an important part of the school community. They just don't understand you yet.'

'This is a temporary setback. We will learn from this and move into the next phase.'

'A diagnosis will help everyone to support my child better.'

'This is a temporary setback. We will learn from this and start to tackle some of the issues that could be affecting my child.'

'My child will soon feel happier and calmer at school.'

'My child is a confident person who has a full role to play in this world.'

Lessons Learned

- Without determined intervention from you, the school and your child, the first exclusion can escalate to a permanent exclusion, off-rolling or a referral. Off-rolling is when your child is taken off the school roll. This means they are not included in the school's permanent exclusion data. Neither can they be entered for any exams. This is not usually in the best interest of the child.

- Anger can be a response to unresolved past hurts or a reaction to current negative events that are unsettling your child.

- There is huge power and potential in the solution phase after an exclusion if you actively get involved in the next steps.

- The potential to re-build relationships and turn the difficulties into a sparkling success story is possible. It just takes will on all sides to make it work, driven by you.

- Work with the school as much as you can. When they see you're willing to work in partnership with them and are not part of 'the problem,' you're half of the solution.

- Hold the school to account with regards to the plans they have in place for support.

- If they've got an LSA in place, set up a meeting and find out what they're planning to do to help your child in class. Ask them what you can do to help.

- If you suspect your child has a Special Educational Need after the exclusion, but the school are slow to follow up, ask for a need's assessment. Document your conversation.

- Encourage teachers to speak to you clearly and explain any educational terminology.

- As a last resort, if your child isn't happy and you sense the school feel they're unable to meet your child's need, consider asking the Local Authority to help you find another school.

CHAPTER 8

The Post-Diagnosis Zone Reflection And Learning

Feeling the need to go back to 'clown school'

After the diagnosis and getting an EHCP (which used to be called a statement), I didn't feel any euphoria or great awakening. It was pretty much business as usual. Teachers don't change their perceptions overnight and children are still cautious of the children who act a bit strangely. Your child doesn't feel like they've won the lottery because there's a complicated document with their name on it. They still have anxious days and sunny days.

Acquiring a label at school is no short-term thing, especially if it's a label you didn't ask for. Depending on how old your child is when they are diagnosed, they will go through their own process of self-awareness. "I'm still me, but I'm different. I don't fully understand why I'm different, but I know that I am."

If your child is non-verbal, or has limited words, they are highly sensitive to how people react to them. I began to feel my way around the post-diagnosis stage, connecting the dots between autism and moods.

I was acutely shy as a child and struggled to fit in, I was aware of my own difference. I had kinky curly hair, brown skin, a gap-tooth smile, sharp curvature of the spine, sloping into a bottom that stuck out defiantly, held up by a pair of athletic legs.

Do neurodiverse kids feel the same sense of alienation that I did? Growing up in a mainly White area of Birmingham, I struggled to speak when I was spoken to, especially by strangers. I developed a zany, incessant chatter, in the hope that this would cover up my shyness or at least fool people into thinking I was funny or interesting.

Children and young people feel socially excluded for many reasons, whatever the cause of this sense of 'otherness,' it is acute.

Autistic children will try to hide their discomfort about being different. Girls in particular are known to mask their emotions.

'In the playground, autistic girls are more likely to hover near groups of other girls, whereas autistic boys are more likely to be isolated.' (Dean M, Harwood R, Kasari C. The Art of Camouflage: Gender differences in the Social Behaviours of girls and boys with Autism Spectrum Disorder. Autism. 2017.)

The negative attention they get from teachers or school chums creates anxiety. We need to be vigilant with neurodiverse children. So many situations and environments leave them feeling isolated, and most of the time neurotypicals are blissfully unaware of the pain they are causing.

Lucas once wrote on a piece of work that he needed to go

back to clown school. It's difficult to imagine the sense of un-belonging he endured.

We owe it to our children and their future life to find positive and encouraging words to say to them at every opportunity. As adult teachers, parents and carers, we need to be mindful of how intolerant and impatient we can be. I've put together some ideas to help you support your neurodiverse child's fluctuating moods.

Managing moods and working with the school
Children's behaviour is affected by the environment around them, such as home life, siblings, poverty, unemployment, divorce—the list is endless. Therapists will tell you that part of managing life successfully is learning that you can't change what happens to you, but you can learn to change how to react to it.

'Life is 10% what happens to us and 90% how we react to it,'
Charles Swindoll, Christian Pastor.

How do you respond to life's trials? I lose it every now and again. In those times, I'm stressed out, shouting, and generally letting the world know I'm peeved off.

When our children see us like this, we are teaching them:

- Mum/Dad has strong feelings, just like me!
- Sometimes their feelings are so strong they lose it, just like me!
- It's okay to rant and rave when things don't go your way, although my family don't do it that often.

It's healthy for our children see us lose it from time to time. It shows them that we're human, and our emotions are as strong as theirs.

A Secondary School class teacher once said to me, "Lucas struggles to accept praise and be positive about the things he does well. He always focuses on the negative. His attitude towards the discipline system is one of expecting to get into trouble, expecting to get red cards and consequently, he acts like he no longer cares about getting into trouble. Whenever I speak to him about something he's done well, he never smiles. His view of himself is quite low and he has gotten himself into quite a negative mind set."

Children with ADHD and Asperger's present difficult behaviours in the classroom. Their neurodiversity inhibits the way they learn and interact with others, which makes it difficult for them and others to communicate successfully.

Educators need to see this behaviour in the framework of the neurodiverse brain. It's totally counterproductive to make comparisons between neurodiverse and typical brain behaviours and attitudes.

ADHD and Asperger's children are repeatedly regarded as wilful and defiant. Understanding your child's dominant preferred activity or communication style can help you and the educator to contain some of their more negative moods.

The high-functioning autism child, some of whom have very long memories of bad experiences, feel a lingering disappointment if things don't go as previously expected. To them, if things go wrong, it feels like a clear path has been obstructed by pebbles and no amount of explaining or path clearing can help them regain their previous feeling of security. They have already worked out their direction of travel and if it's obscured by anything, the re-ordering of thought (executive functioning) creates a sense of powerlessness that follows.

- "Nothing I do ever works out."
- "I'm rubbish at everything."
- "There's no point trying as I always fail!"

I understand how de-motivating this must feel for educators, trained to get the best from their students. Children with ADHD tend to burn off their frustrations more quickly than their Asperger's peers. They can be distracted out of their frustration by introducing a new, exciting idea or theme, assuming they are sufficiently calm.

When they've calmed down, they can and do apologise quickly, especially if they've hurt someone. There is generally no malice in these children's behaviour. On the contrary, they usually internalise their remorse and can be highly upset by their outbursts and lack of emotional control.

A de-escalation approach works well with these children. Most classrooms have an early warning system or recognised behaviour strategy in place, helping children to recognise changes in their own behaviour in an attempt to avoid outbursts.

If the cues are missed and an outburst happens, hopefully a teacher will seek to contain or de-escalate it as quickly as possible.

Resilience Therapy or Cognitive Behavioural Therapy (CBT) techniques are particularly powerful at helping autistic/ADHD children to manage the impact of unexpected change, which happens a lot at school.

There are some limits to the success of the CBT, especially if the therapist isn't used to working with the neurodiverse brain.

Embracing low moods and change in everyday life
Managing your day to day life with your autistic/ADHD child requires forward planning. Okay, that's an understatement. Your neurodiverse youngster will need *a lot* more structure and pre-briefing than their peers. Being closely tuned into your child's life will help both of you to navigate the difficult days together. You will probably have an intensely close bond with them, which won't always be harmonious.

The main cause of Lucas's low mood was dealing with disappointment. Usually this was due to people changing plans at short notice or trying to understand the complexities of burgeoning friendships and why friends weren't always reliable. His low mood would inevitably spike after a bad day at school.

An excerpt from his skills mentor report:

'He is very negative about himself. He says, "I don't like to celebrate birthdays, especially mine. I want to be noticed and have friends." He doesn't accept being verbally praised but likes receiving merit marks in his books. He feels that he is the only one that gets into trouble, even though others are misbehaving.'

Going back to neutral
Focus on the now and get back to neutral. If your child's ADHD brain is already imploding with millions of ideas and

scattered thoughts, trying to introduce lots of new ideas at once will create more stress for them.

A barrage of questions from parent or teachers is overloading. Allow plenty of time for your child to think about what they want and how they feel, with plenty of time for them to answer the question. Then listen without judgement.

Calming distraction activities like cooking, walking the dog or drawing a picture, gives your child space and time to replenish their logical or thinking brain, so they can focus better when they need to. Think of exercise and creative pursuits for the child with ADHD as the re-start or cache clearing mechanism.

Working with feelings
Typical fun things children do such as learning an instrument, looking after a pet, or going for a sleepover can be a trial for children with autism, ADHD or sensory issues.

Some everyday situations create extraordinary reactions; an ice cream on the way home will make their hands feel so sticky and uncomfortable that will outweigh the delight of eating the ice cream. Live music on the radio can be unbearably loud.

I remember during a Christmas concert at Primary School, with a stunning selection of brass instruments crashing away on stage, I spotted Lucas sitting at the back hunched over, hands clasped over his ears. No-one else seemed to notice.

I understand now that for many neurodiverse beings, sounds are like feelings, creating heightened physical sensations in the body. This is why the National Autistic Society's Autism Hour campaign was a breakthrough in sharing awareness about the debilitating nature of sensory overload.

Self-care for parents

It's not selfish to think about yourself when you're coming to terms with your child's diagnosis. It's actually very healthy. If you think about how you cope with stress, and take care of yourself, you can start to merge your individual coping style with techniques for managing your child. It won't happen overnight. It can take years to assimilate the impact of your child's neurodiversity into your life and aspirations for yourself and them.

An autism diagnosis represents a lifelong condition for which there is no cure. Some argue that no cure is required, that we should accept neurological differences in personality and behaviour as part of life and strive instead for acceptance and integration. ADHD, which is considered to be a developmental disorder—although it is neurological in nature—can become difficult for individuals and their families to manage, even creating harmful situations. Taking care of everyone in the mix is vital.

As a parent or carer, one of the best things you can do for your loved one is to start to take good care of who you are. An honest appraisal of yourself and your parenting style will help you, your child and the whole family. Your child will be sensitive to changes in your mood, voice and even the atmosphere in your house. They will pick up your energy and reflect it back at you—good or bad.

As a parent of a child who is experiencing trauma, you need a healing breakthrough, which is when you start to focus more on their recovery and the future, rather than the pain of the past. You cannot provide enhanced strength, clarity of thought and calm representation for your child if you are in an emotional quicksand of anger, frustration, tiredness, blame or guilt.

Look after number one. Tell your inner critic to be quiet. You've got enough critics in the real world.

Our special children
You are not alone in this struggle. In the average UK classroom, of approximately 30 children, at least 5 or 6 will have a specific learning difficulty which is not necessarily autism or ADHD.

Some of these children won't yet be diagnosed. Some will have more than one developmental difficulty. The same child may present different types of behaviour on different days in different classes. Some will be highly intellectual, whilst at the same time, emotionally immature. This is not easy for teachers, who enter the school gates with varying levels of skills and knowledge about childhood disabilities, seen or unseen.

Scientific research seems to confirm there are significant differences between how autism presents in girls and women in comparison to boys and men.

From scientific studies to conversations with hundreds of families, autistic girls are excellent at making eye-contact and mimicking social interaction technique. Studies suggest that autistic girls may look more at faces than autistic boys for example (Harrop et al., under review).

Many studies indicate that autistic individuals, male or female, have difficulty understanding irony, sarcasm, metaphor and deceit.

It's not practical for teachers to apply the same management techniques as parents in a class of 30. Distraction, persuasion, humour and reason may work at home, but school is a different bag of chips.

I preferred a gentle type of discipline, with my signature sharp stare to defuse any temper tantrums at home. Thankfully they were few and far between at home. But everything seemed to trigger Lucas at school. It could be a change in routine, PE lessons, a supply teacher, or a long queue in the dining hall. Activities that other children seemed to be able to manage with minimal fuss.

Advocating for your child at school is difficult for the obvious reason—you're not there! You're reliant on teachers' feedback and your child's account.

Teachers are keen to understand whether your child has boundaries at home and whether the child is aware of the consequences if they cross the boundaries.

Teaching is a rules-based profession and it's natural for them to want to know how you parent at home. Try not to get annoyed if you feel your parenting is being judged.

Maybe there are too many rules in schools, but it's the best way to organise a large mixed community of children. Teachers need to feel they are in control and may come down hard on a child they regard as persistent rule-beaker.

Your understanding of autistic kids and rules is a good conversation opener, especially if teachers have different rules. Being honest about how you parent at home is helpful for the school. It's a starting point to understanding your child's expectations of life in school.

Lucas is like many children on the autism spectrum. He shines, he has a big personality. I believe he's energetic in a spiritual way. If you're tuned into indigo and crystal children you'll know where I'm coming from, if you're not, we will leave it there.

In my experience, autistic and ADHD children are gifted with incredible physical and mental energy, which can be immensely helpful to humankind, especially if we harness this energy constructively in their formative years.

How does it feel for the child? "Other children are impossible to understand. School is like a danger zone I need to be ready to fight back or run away at a minute's notice!"

What's happening here is hyperarousal, sensory overload, meltdowns, followed by remorse and guilt. Once these attributes are highlighted, there's potential for a skilled teacher or mentor to channel these sensitivities into a positive expression for the young person.

Consider the benefits of these hypersensitive individuals working in the caring professions: looking after the elderly, working in a neo-natal unit in a hospital, doing medical testing, where the smallest nuances of change are significant! Such attuned individuals are highly sought after, but they won't be available to make a contribution to society or the workforce in any way if they are excluded from school.

The situation at school filled me with worry. From what I gleaned, some of Lucas's physical outbursts were reactions to teasing by his peers, unwanted touching/restraint and public shaming from teachers.

As punishment for his bad behaviour, he would be prevented from going into the playground or going on a school trip. He had a reputation as a troublemaker. The other children were wary of him, even post-diagnosis.

Lucas wanted to cut links with his painful past. He

announced that he wanted to change his name. He'd always been known by his middle name, Charlie, after his great-grandfather, but he began to associate Charlie with his bad side. One day he said he wanted to be called Lucas. We did just that and things got better. He loved his new name. To him it became his good name, so aged 7 he told everyone who would listen that he was now called Lucas! The name-change marked the beginning of him starting to accept himself.

Self-esteem for good mental health

Self-esteem doesn't bounce-back like a rubber ball. It takes time and effort to rebuild self-esteem. Many adults spend years in therapy trying to re-build their sense of self after difficult childhoods. Why should we expect children to ping back?

Children experience intense damage in their formative years up to around aged 7 if their sense of self isn't systematically restored.

Without the support of a loving parent and possibly professional counselling, some young children autistic/ADHD children grow up to be adults with negative self-belief, which can prevent them from forming relationships.

Difficult or adverse childhood experiences are one of the key indicators of childhood trauma. Early school experiences of bullying, feeling socially isolated and feelings of guilt and shame at being 'different' is deeply traumatising for many children.

Parents in my #happyinschool sessions report how their ADHD/autistic child used to be a joyful soul, with a contagious personality until they started school. Then the mental health issues start to creep in. They talked about mood disorders, self-harm and depression.

This comment in Lucas's school report is a good example: 'We have anxieties about his self-esteem levels and the impact this has on his behaviour and responses in school.'

Rebuilding Lucas's self-esteem after his eventual diagnosis took years. It's a Catch 22. Your child needs to feel confident in themselves and know they can achieve success. Yet when they get things wrongs or get punished for a meltdown, they lose confidence in themselves to do anything right, which leaves them feeling angry at themselves and more likely to lash out. This snippet from another school report illustrates this: 'Lucas is a very intelligent boy with a lot to offer, however his self-esteem is sometimes so low it triggers unwanted behaviour. He lacks confidence in himself and he doesn't see or appreciate what he can do.'

Staying calm when you're breaking
I'd like to share an example of a mother behaving in a calm and positive way in a tricky and potentially dangerous situation. On a packed bus one evening after work, I noticed a mother with 2 small boys of around 3 and 4. She looked zoned out. Her double buggy was weighed down with toys, drinks and coats. They'd obviously been out for the day, but her boys still had plenty of energy!

Feeling frazzled after the long commute and dozing off, I saw a small tornado of a boy fly downstairs in a rage shouting that he didn't want to sit down. I watched with fascination as the scene played out. The older child raced up and down the stairs pleading with his mother to follow. She was speaking to him in a low voice and nothing about her body language suggested she was cross. He swooped on his kid brother, who was out of the buggy, and grabbed him in a headlock.

Mum muttered quietly, "Stop doing that or we'll get off the bus and walk home!"

Incredibly, the older of the 2 boys raced back upstairs, red in the face and shouting at his brother, "You are being so rude, really rude!"

Everyone on the bus tried not to stare but we were all silently gawping and judging. The younger child was now climbing up the side of the bus saying how rude his older brother was. One jolt of the bus and he would have gone flying and possibly hurt himself badly.

I was relieved when they got off the bus, with the older one protesting he didn't want to go.

His mum responded in a calm voice, "I'm getting off whether you are or not!"

Glancing out of the corner of my eye, he was still hyped up as the bus pulled away. Her body sagged with exhaustion.

I thought about her reactions to her kids and came to the following conclusions:

- What other people think about your parenting is not your concern. Only you know your children and the discipline they respond to.
- Reacting like the adult can be difficult when kids press your buttons, but it is possible to remain in control when they act up.
- Speaking clearly and firmly is vital to staying in control. You don't have to get involved in their dialogue or explain yourself. Sometimes a simple 'no' is all you need

to regain your authority. All kids need boundaries, it's up to us to provide them.

- Telling a child off in public is embarrassing and can cause a temper tantrum, but as parents we need to reserve inner strength and confidence just for these occasions. If you need to raise your voice or give the child an ultimatum, that's your business. Being a warrior mother or tiger daddy means loving hard and disciplining hard. Although my personal view of hitting your children in public or private is that it is not advisable. In England, hitting a child in anger is not considered reasonable and is against the law.

- If you routinely hit your children as a punishment, consider looking into alternative methods of discipline, or consider counselling to manage your own anger. No one wants the little boy who has been repeatedly hit to grow up into a 6-foot teenager who beats his mother or girlfriend. A US study found evidence of a cycle of violence among individuals with child maltreatment stories. This indicates that victims of childhood violence perpetrate violence towards their peers or partners later in the life cycle. (National Institute of Justice.) (11)

- Being a parent is one of those jobs where everyone has an opinion about how to raise your child, especially when they act up in public. But they're your child. You are the parent. I'm a gentle person by nature, so asserting myself as top mama didn't come naturally when I became a mother to my first child in my twenties. But I picked it up fast!

- Aggressive, bad boy behaviour is a rite of passage into

manhood. Many cultures celebrate acts of bravado such as extreme physical endurance tests from boys as they approach puberty. This is a way of discharging the surge of testosterone flooding their systems, and to show their peers where they sit in the community's pecking order. Raising boys is taxing, particularly if you're a lone parent and they want to be the alpha male in their household. As a society, we need to relax and ensure boys are provided with plenty of positive outlets for their energy. We also need to make sure we listen to their thoughts and fears as they become men. This is important for all parents but especially for neurodiverse parents, whose boys are prone to mental illness, anxiety, depression, bullying and aggressive tendencies.

Building a good home-school parent-teacher relationship
- Be informed - stay in touch with what is happening at the school. Take time to read information that is shared about your child, the individual class and the broader school community. Attend school meetings and information sessions wherever possible.
- Teachers need to regularly evaluate the quality/ effectiveness of the information being provided to parents.
- Be available - you and your family are unique. Recognise that diversity of families is a good thing. Look for opportunities to contribute to the curriculum. Help with supervision of an excursion, offer to assist with a club or other extra-curricular activity. Think about loaning relevant resources from home.

- Teachers should look for opportunities to involve parents authentically in the class program or routine.
- Be responsive - when your child's teacher asks for information or feedback, take the time to tell them about your child, family and home. Participate in parent-teacher conferences, even if you are confident that your child is doing well.
- Teachers should value the knowledge parents have of their individual child. The insight can be invaluable to understanding the learning needs of that student. Be interested. How well do you understand your school's philosophy, schedule and routines? Do you understand why things happen the way they do? This information can help you to support your child within the school environment. Use the appropriate avenues to ask questions about the class, the academic aspirations for the children, or the workings of the school's community.
- Teachers should consider developing a parent resource library of materials (books, periodicals, articles, website links) that can help parents to understand current educational theory and provide them with practical ideas for supporting their children's learning.
- Be realistic - teachers are busy people and have many responsibilities and personal lives outside of face-to-face teaching. When conversations are likely to require more time, make sure you request an appointment at a mutually convenient time rather than rounding up on them unexpectedly!
- Teachers - consider how available/approachable you are for parents with quick questions or requiring more time.

- Be constructive - when you have concerns, do your best to maintain a solution focused approach in difficult conversations. While you're undoubtedly your child's number one, most important advocate, sometimes the way you feel when things go wrong can prevent you from acting calmly and rationally. Resist the urge to vent on social media, gossip in the playground or on WhatsApp. Address the situation calmly and directly with the teacher and focus on ways to be part of the solution.
- Teachers we understand that difficult conversations are uncomfortable for everyone involved but they have to happen. Recognise that parents are acting out of love and concern for their child and are just looking for ways to work together to reach a resolution that is in the best interest of the child.
- Be kind - shake off the stress of the morning routine and school drop-off chaos and take a second to smile and say hello to your child's teacher each day. Be open, show appreciation and take a friendly interest in your child's teacher as a person, not just a teacher. Your child is watching and learning from these simple, positive gestures. They are learning more than you realise.

Mantras

'The health and teaching professionals are here to help us. I will work with them constructively.'

'I will ask questions clearly and calmly to ensure I am being given the best advice and information to make decisions about my child's health and wellbeing.'

'I may not be a medical, teaching or health expert, but I'm an expert on my child so my views are is valid as everyone else's.'

'I'm a good and loving parent.'

'My child knows I love them and will support them.'

'Sometimes giving support is tiring, and I get annoyed but it doesn't mean I'm a bad person or a bad parent.'

Lessons Learned

Lucas was an intelligent boy with specific interests and could retain his concentration on subjects he was interested in. But on many occasions, he was removed from lessons or put in lower academic sets with a learning support assistant to manage his behaviour.

Before Lucas was diagnosed, his needs weren't clearly identified so the support in place was heavily reactive. It was focused on symptom control like meltdowns. Instead they should have had a thorough understanding of how his brain worked and what tools would enable him to regulate his emotions better and assist his concentration. After his diagnosis, he was doing social skills classes, counselling, or just hanging out by himself in corridors, having some quiet time.

It appears that the focus on negative behaviour, especially by boys with neurodiversity, outweighs the creative input on supportive learning techniques.

- Don't be shy in asking for help. There may be things happening that you don't understand or are worried about. Call in the troops! If you're not getting the help you need post-diagnosis, your local Special Educational Needs Independent Advice Service (SENDIASS) may be able to help.

- In the UK, most Local Authorities have a SENDIASS, a Parent Partnership Service or a Parent Carer Forum. If you don't get anywhere with that try Contact (www.

contact.org.uk), a national organisation with links to various groups across the UK. It's an excellent place to find help and support.

- Alternatively, you can contact your local National Autistic Society representative or an independent S.E.N.D. legal advisor; their numbers are easy to find online. If you want to find a parent support group that's not connected to the Local Authority, there are lots of those out there too.

- It can be a lonely and difficult journey with lots of twists and turns, but it doesn't need to be. Dip your toe in and find a support group that feels right for you.

CHAPTER 9

The Medication Nation Zone
Knowing Your Options Before The Big Decisions

You've had to make lots of decisions on behalf of your child, but the decision to start medication or not is a big one. Our children teach us, as much as we teach them, so including them in the decision is important and will help them to feel involved in their medical care rather than feel like a mere recipient.

Considering your options
When discussions about the ADHD part of Lucas's diagnosis turned to medication, I felt a great sadness. Taking medication to interfere with your child's brain function is big news. Were we consenting to create a different child with a different personality? A child I had not given birth to? Is this the best outcome for a neurodiverse child? To medicate them so they fit in and can pass exams?

New articles about ADHD causes, treatments and impacts are published every year, creating more awareness and confusion in equal measure.

According to the Center for Disease Control and Prevention, an estimated 6.4 million American children aged between 4 and 17 have been diagnosed by a healthcare provider with ADHD (cdc.gov/ADHD, key findings, 2011).

By 2011, 3.5 million children were reported by their parents to be taking medication for ADHD compared to 2.5 million in 2003 (National CDC Survey Data).

England seems to be following this American trend. Almost 75,000 children aged between 6 and 17 received a prescription for ADHD drugs in England in 2017/18 (NHS), with figures wavering between 5% to 8% of children with ADHD globally.

Handwringing won't change the cold statistics but focusing on solutions for change will improve life for thousands of families. You just need to choose a side.

Undeniably, the issue of medicating a child is complex and these decisions should be dealt with on an individual or family basis, in agreement with a trusted medical practitioner.

Prescription drugs are highly effective for a host of brain disorders. Finding the right one at the right dosage is the challenging part, but for many families, it's worth the time to get the dosage right for the immense weight it lifts from the family.

ADHD responds highly effectively to medication. In some situations, the administration of medication helps the individual to succeed in terms of focus and application, where they may otherwise have failed.

This isn't just about exam success. It could be any situation that requires the person to be organised, emotionally regulated with good memory. This is big news. We have found a way to over-ride the part of the brain that doesn't perform as well as it does in people without ADHD. It's not a magic bullet. It's likely your physician will need to try different doses as your child ages or your circumstances change.

If you're at the stage of discussing drug therapies, your main contact is a clinical or consultant psychiatrist. The term psychiatry was coined by the German physician Johann Christian Reil in 1808 and literally means the medical treatment of the soul.

The psychiatric professional is devoted to studying, diagnosing and treating mental disorders. Psychiatrists are particularly concerned with disorders that impact on daily life, especially behavioural, cognitive and perceptual abnormalities such as dementia, epilepsy and ADHD.

It's well documented that governments have harnessed the parts of the human brain that light up the needs, wants and desired areas to manipulate the beliefs and motivations of the masses. You should look up Edward Bernays.

Simple and sophisticated brain manipulation is used widely in advertising campaigns, political campaigns, supermarket layout, right down to school websites. Everything is designed to push our psychological buttons and whisper 'Try me,' 'Choose me' or 'Buy me!'

We've become so used to reacting to our emotional and psychological triggers in our news, social media and the wider environment, that we have trouble working out whether our reactions are authentic.

We are all under the influence to some degree and perhaps this is why children with Special Educational Needs, particularly those that affect behaviour, are so misunderstood in education.

Many autistic children can be piercingly honest to the point of being rude. I call this autistic truism! They don't mean to offend but can be sticklers about honesty. Autistic young people I know speak their truth loudly, laugh frequently, find fun and joy in spontaneous things and situations unencumbered by social norms.

This honesty and spontaneity can cause a huge challenge to an education system or a society that values conformity. I personally wish more people had it!

The response from some educators is to suppress these voices, stifle that joy and reign in that free spirit. Lucas has this in spades. He was brutally honest in situations when a bit of social politeness or tact would have gone a long way. It was a sort of social Tourette's, blurting out whatever was in his head and speaking the truth as he saw it.

Drug therapy for ADHD uses pharmaceutical products (mostly stimulants) to alter the brain chemistry to enable learning. It stimulates the under stimulated parts of the brain. The parts that make learning and concentrating difficult.

The drugs are absorbed into the blood stream and pass into the brain through neural pathways which increases the levels of dopamine in the brain and the body.

Dopamine is one of the feel-good hormones produced in the brain, so the effect of the medication is similar to the feeling you get after eating delicious food or having good sex.

Higher levels of dopamine in the system are documented to improve mood and motivation. Neurodiverse brains are as individual as a fingerprint, so trial and error is required to get the dosage right.

Children with ADHD are probably good at gaming as the games provide constant visual, auditory praise and validation reward to the child, which increases their level of dopamine. In turn it makes them want to keep on playing!

Stimulant medications are also effective at improving academic performance. It increases the levels of dopamine in the mind, providing the same level of focus and concentration ADHD children experience when they're gaming. One of the side effects of stimulants, however, is they are known to suppress appetite.

Building an honest dialogue with your child's psychiatrist will help you decide to what degree you trust them to have your child's brain in their hands. Sometimes the decision will be made for you as your child's behaviour could become so extreme, they are a danger to themselves and others.

You may be faced with the difficult decision of medication to enable your child to remain at home with you.

Talking to the professionals

During one of our behaviour low points, I asked our new psychiatrist at CAMHS about using prescribed medication to help Lucas's outbursts. He talked me through the range of drug treatments. It would take a while to find the right dosage, the correct brand and the best time for Lucas who was still at school to be given the medication. There was also possible side effects such as loss of appetite and mood changes.

I also spoke to our local pharmacist about medications to improve Lucas's sleeping pattern. Some nights he was getting by on just 4 hours and would fall asleep in lessons. The pharmacist told me that the door for medication is always open and only me and my child can choose whether I wish to step through.

There's no rush or time pressure apart from what you

and your child feel comfortable with. A good school with supportive pastoral staff won't rush you into putting your child on medication.

There were times when the reports from school were so worrying that I was close to getting an appointment to review the medication option. I couldn't rule it out and neither should you.

We hadn't gone down the medication route at the time of writing this book but it's still an option. When he was 14, Lucas transferred to a school with highly trained autism staff who made adjustments to his school day, and this massively reduced his anxiety and outbursts.

Medication nation

A diagnosis of Asperger's or ADHD is challenging because some of the symptoms overlap or contradict each other. For hyperactive type ADHD kids their main presenting factor is behaviour.

An article entitled *'Sedation Nation: The cost of taking boisterous out of boys'* (Sydney Morning Herald, 2011) reported that 5 times as many Australian boys are medicated with Ritalin as girls. It's an interesting piece, with the main thrust looking at young male's boisterous behaviours and society's requirement for us to medicate their energy and exuberance to acceptable levels. It's peppered with gender stereotypes too, so make up your own mind!

Some of the reasons why there appears to be an over-diagnosis of ADHD in boys could be the same reason why autism is over diagnosed in males. It's more in your face and sometimes potentially dangerous.

The dangers of girls being under-diagnosed are just as significant. It's dangerous in a different way, due to the harm girls might inflict on themselves.

Carolyn Abraham raises a similar question in her editorial in *The Globe and Mail:*

'Figures compiled for the Globe and Mail by IMS Health show prescriptions for Ritalin and other amphetamine-like drugs for ADHD reached 2.9 million in 2009. More than 2 million were written specifically for children under 17 and at least 75% were for young males.'

The headline, 'Are we medicating a disorder or treating boyhood as a disease?' hits between the eyes. Medicating your child doesn't have to be for life.

'Imaging studies showed brain development in children with ADHD lags 2 to 3 years behind the typical brain, particularly in the pre-frontal cortex, an area involved with thinking, attention and planning.' National Institute of Mental Health, NIMH, 2007.

According to Dr Russell Barkley, approximately one-third of young people will outgrow their ADHD. The rest will become ADHD adults, requiring continued understanding to overcome persistent difficulties with planning, organising, remembering and functioning, in comparison to the majority of the population. My instinct is that gendered behaviours in a mainly female-led primary teaching environment create an unconscious behaviour intolerance. What the hell did I just write? In other words, the sheer physicality of boys in school or in a busy class of 30 is difficult for your average female teacher to teach.

As we've moved towards increasingly digital recreation, many boys have few positive outlets for their natural aggression. Repeated slip-ups in class create an atmosphere where teachers feel it's impossible to teach or reach children who are always on the go.

Medication is an effective therapy for impulsive and disruptive behaviour, but once the dose has worn off, has it dealt with the root of the behaviour?

For some groups, in particular those of Black Caribbean origin, decisions regarding medication and parental choice are more limited. There are some who describe the epidemic of behavioural issues among Black boys as being a 'social construct' having little or no basis in science. Often ADHD, conduct disorder and emotional disturbance are included in this debate.

There are plenty of polemic opinions out there, including that the poor behaviour profile of Black boys at school is due to a number of factors such as sparse in-depth behavioural teaching, a predominantly White teacher and psychologist workforce doing referrals, and the huge profit made by pharmaceutical companies through rampant distribution of psychotropic drug prescriptions for young Black males. There are also plenty of options, suggestions and ideas being mooted in relation to tackling this:

- Greater number of referrals by trained and competent Black (of Caribbean or African origin) professionals.

- Intensive behavioural training for all teachers.
- Investigation and reprimand for teaching professionals who overuse referrals and psychiatric referrals for Black youngsters.
- Better study habits from Black kids.
- Better parental involvement from Black (of Caribbean, African or mixed heritage) parents.

Whatever your thoughts on the clinical, scientific and racial elements of such theories, it seems that the pharmaceutical industry has the power to minimise and manage the symptoms of a host of psychotropic disorders, including ADHD, and for many children they do so successfully.

For those of us who need to make important, possibly life-long decisions about introducing drugs into our child's lives, particularly when they are ill, hospitalised or in the prison system, we need transparency about what we're getting into. A risk versus rewards overview.

To the untrained eye, autism behaviours such as anxiety, processing difficulties, sensory or emotional overwhelm can confuse or bewilder educationalists, healthcare professionals and the police.

They see defiance, disruption, paranoia, emotional obstruction, aggression, emotional dysregulation, inability to follow instructions (defiance), temper tantrums (sensory overload) and so on. Especially in young Black people, whose media image is mostly negative.

If professionals, including teachers, could understand what they are witnessing, the outcomes would be more positive all round.

Autistic and ADHD people are particularly vulnerable in stressful situations involving authority figures. In 2019, the Metropolitan Police launched the Autism Alert Card Scheme, which is particularly helpful for young autistic males who find themselves in contact with the law.

The cards highlight key trigger points, which if not dealt with sensitively, could mean that a young person ends up spending a night in prison. Details can be found at the end the book.

Some children are medicated without parental consent, or are medicated to sedate or control them, which is distressing and traumatising.

In a crisis situation, will your children's extreme behaviour be misunderstood or even criminalised? Does a medicated child or young person reduce their risk of getting into serious trouble? These are big questions I don't have the answers to, but you need to think about and discuss them with your young person and other parents with children of a similar age.

If your child is younger than 11 when they are diagnosed, these issues seem a long way off. If their diagnosis comes in Secondary School, with all of the unpredictability of the teenage hormones and illegal drugs, you need an all-weather plan, to help your child even out their moods in a variety of situations.

I hope you get a helpful, plain-speaking doctor like I did. One who wasn't afraid to answer my questions about the pros and cons of medication.

Lucas's diagnosis of ADHD/ASD came officially (documented) just before his 10th birthday but unofficially—in conversation with the psychiatrist—a few months before that. The consultant child psychiatrist gave me some ADHD handouts.

Hyperactivity – best treatments and clinical evidence
I read the opening paragraphs in the ADHD handouts I'd been given:

'Learning that your child has attention deficit hyperactivity disorder can be distressing. But ADHD can be treated and the right treatment and support can help your child behave better. Treatments can't cure ADHD, but they should help your child behave better so that he or she can develop and learn normally. Behaviour therapy is likely to help your child when combined with drug treatment. We don't know yet whether it helps on its own. Treatments for ADHD have mostly been studied in children over 6 years old. Very little is known about treatments for very young children who are under 6 years old.'

The handouts mentioned other treatments, including complementary and alternative treatments, the use of antidepressants—psychotropic drugs which are used to treat more than one disorder. The dates on the handouts was 2005 and Lucas was diagnosed in 2014.

I found a lot in those few lines. We can treat but not cure. We can help children with ADHD behave better and learn normally. Behaviour therapy works better with drugs.

As I left the clinic with the leaflets about ADHD support groups and medication I stuffed them in my bag and didn't read them until 2 years later.

This is what the leaflets said about ADHD:

- Children with ADHD struggle with paying attention/ maintaining focus/memory/organisation.
- They find it difficult to keep their mind on one thing and may get bored after only a few minutes.
- Can act on impulse. They blurt things out and find it difficult to wait their turn and often talk when it is not their turn. They don't listen and can't follow simple instructions.
- A child with ADHD can find it difficult to communicate and make friends.
- They give up during games and sports that require them to listen and follow rules.
- They have lots of energy and need to run about all of the time.
- Children with ADHD often can't stop and think before they act.
- They can be noisy when they are supposed to be quiet. (American Psychiatric Attention-Deficit Hyperactivity Disorder, 2000.)

I recently discovered a name for Lucas's big emotions. It was called Rejection Sensitive Dysphoria, which is a condition where the person will respond to measured or perceived criticism in a dramatic and overblown way. You will see a disproportionate reaction and feel puzzled because the thing that caused the outburst should not—from the perspective of someone who is neurotypical—have generated emotions that big.

I tried to focus on the content of the sheets, but my brain went AWOL. I walked around like a zombie for days after that final diagnostic meeting. The variety of treatment options for your diagnosed child including medication, behaviour modification, speech and language therapy, group therapy, play therapy, and social skills is mind-boggling. Some therapies draw on a number of techniques or merge into new leading edge treatments.

Unlike autism, which has no cure, ADHD is treatable. National Institute for Health and Care Excellence (NICE) recommends that children of school age should be offered behaviour, stress management and educational support before medication. Some drugs are licensed in the UK to treat ADHD in children aged 6 and above.

As with all experts, you are entitled to ask for the qualifications, experience and credentials of the person working with your child's behaviours or diagnosis. Not all experts are equal. Whatever decision you make is not fixed. There is always room for manoeuvre.

Human behavioural psychology is a big field of study. The more you learn about the complexity of the human being and the vastness of the human brain, the more you realise how little we know. Leave the heavy lifting to the experts but get to grips with the basics. Learn what powers your child's moods, how the medication will work, why eating healthily, cutting back sugar and getting enough exercise and sleep will help to regulate your child's brain function.

You will feel greater empowerment and confidence in advocating for your children. And if you're not sure, just dip back into this book!

There is no cure for autism

An autistic child becomes an autistic adult. Your child may look well and healthy, and in many cases unless there is co-morbidity (more than one medical or developmental condition) but they will need strategies to help them manage their hidden disability throughout life. Especially if they wish to get a job and live independently.

Many successful Asperger's and ADHD individuals have developed innovative coping mechanisms to help them thrive in our predominantly neurotypical world.

If, like my son, your child gets an autism diagnosis whilst at school, this is considered extremely good fortune. Many adults have lived with undiagnosed autism and the associated challenges for years until they reach a crisis in adulthood. Autism is like that. A classic hidden disability.

Autism combined with ADHD makes the medication option trickier. How do you medicate half of yourself? Will your child become more autistic because their ADHD is controlled? Will your child be fine and better able to function at school?

For many children, this is exactly what they need to enable them to follow their dreams to become their unique self in later life. And they will flower in a technicolour cloak of neurodiverse fabulousness.

Securing an education is difficult for many but it can change your life, making your difference, literally work for you.

Lessons Learned

- We need to get beyond labels for autistic and ADHD children, and move towards acceptance of difference, especially in Primary Schools, when children are at their most formative and open minded.

- Medication will alter your child's behaviour, making mainstream education accessible. Be clear about the side effects, dosage and what happens when they come off the medication.

- The body has a tremendous capacity for healing itself, but there is no cure for autism. Autistic life can be comfortable, stress free, joyful, creative and fulfilling.

CHAPTER 10

The Teacher Zone
Working With The School For Positive Outcomes

Working with teachers after Lucas's diagnosis was interesting. Some teachers switched to compassionate mode, keen to make adjustments and concessions. Others struggled and found it difficult to change their perception of the badly-behaved boy to the boy who was, in many ways, vulnerable.

I suggested to the headteacher that Lucas might enjoy being in the gifted and talented sets, as he loved English and music, but he disagreed stating, "That would be like rewarding bad behaviour."

Autism and ADHD parents agree that the UK education system would benefit from a makeover with regards to educating children with neurodiversity.

Organisations like Ambitious About Autism, ADHD Foundation and many others, campaign, lobby and educate to improve education and life chances for ADHD young people and adults, who continue to be misunderstood.

Educational professionals naturally have differing views on diversity and inclusion in schools and since the Black Lives

Matter movement exploded onto the world in the midst of a global outbreak of Covid-19, teachers are in a prime position to examine the nature of their role, as part of a wider culture change.

Many schools have adopted a diverse, pupil-led curriculum, which can have a powerful impact on learning. But the success of inclusive practice in teaching depends on the value that the school leadership places on inclusivity. Also, on how effectively schools agree on inclusive education goals, measurement and investment in training. Until this is ironed out in many more schools, hundreds of kids will continue to be unhappy in school, unfairly or unlawfully excluded and suffer poor mental health.

I was keen to share Lucas's autism/ADHD diagnosis with the school but worried about the impact this would have on him. Our psychiatrist Dr Pam was reassuring, "Don't rush into sharing Lucas's diagnoses unless you feel sure this is the right thing for him. Personally, I think it would help. What you are describing at school is a common reaction for someone with ADHD and ASD. His actions result from the impulsivity and the strong sense of right and wrong. You are seeing his difficulty with social communication in terms of knowing appropriate interaction with those in authority."

I gave it a few months, then felt I had no choice but to draft a note to the SENCO to explain Lucas's behaviour at school.

The following day, I was asked to see the SENCO with Lucas after school. He waved a piece of paper in my direction and slapped it on the table in front of me triumphantly. It was in Lucas's scribbled hand-writing and read 'Lucas is a sucker. Lucas sucks. Lucas is worse than Zane.'

The SENCO said to me, with barely hidden annoyance in his voice, "Lucas is choosing not to use his red card. You need to get in touch with CAMHS to find out how to manage his behaviour!"

In that moment, I realised that the school needed guidance and were relying on me to provide it via the psychiatrist. Although he was a SENCO, it was naïve of him to think Lucas's traffic light behaviour card system would work overnight. I wrote to the headteacher to explain that Lucas was making real efforts to avoid glitches (his word) in the classroom. But unfortunately, the SENCO's red and green behaviour management system wasn't yet working.

The following morning, Lucas and I were bustled into the SENCO's office. He wasn't happy. He'd read the update from the psychiatrist and was concerned that Lucas was leaving the classroom deliberately to avoid lessons he didn't like. The behaviour strategy wasn't working and somehow it was mine or Lucas's fault.

They hadn't grasped the fundamentals of what autism and ADHD looked like in the classroom or the concept that behaviour strategies needed to be modelled over a sustained period of time to embed in the neurodiverse brain. It was unlikely this behaviour system would work as a stand-alone either.

One of the mums cornered me in the playground and whispered conspiratorially, "You know what's been happening with Lucas, don't you?" Not waiting for an answer, she continued, "Well I know someone who has got boys with the same thing as Lucas, you know Asperger's and ADHD!"

She said it like I had won a prize. I burned with

embarrassment. She frog-marched me over to meet the mum called Megan, who was smiley and worn-down looking. She told me her story immediately. She was a single parent of 6 children. Her eldest was 15 and hadn't been diagnosed with ADHD until he was in the last year of Primary School, aged 11. By then, her marriage had broken up. Her youngest, a 6 year old, was currently being assessed for an autism diagnosis.

My head was spinning at the impact autism and ADHD was having on their lives.

She texted me that evening, letting me know I can call on her at any time. She reassured me that it was other people who have the problem with Lucas and we weren't doing anything wrong.

After feeling like a pariah in the school community for so long it was good to have an ally.

Educators are slowly catching up with the accepted knowledge that no 2 children with ADHD/autism are the same. Even with a diagnosis, there are specific triggers and anxieties in individuals, which makes it difficult to capture every nuance or trigger in the scope of a young person's EHCP.

It's unreasonable to expect teachers to remember everything in a child's document or file. This is where a 1-page summary—similar to a pupil profile—comes in handy. It can be slipped into a locked drawer or loaded onto a confidential IT system for easy reference.

Regular termly meetings between teachers and parents can provide a richer seam of information than a thick file that's never looked at.

Small adjustments + big impact = a happier child.

Teacher training and SEN

While researching this book, it became clear that levels of SEN training for undergraduate teachers is variable and on many levels inadequate. Many new teachers I spoke to reported that specialised undergraduate training in SEN was patchy.

Scholars recognise the learning deficit in SEN is particularly apparent in PE lessons. I was interested to read this because Lucas always found PE challenging.

In a 2004 survey by Smith and Green (Including pupils with special educational needs in Secondary School physical education: a sociological analysis of teachers' views, British Journal of Sociology of Education, 25, 5, 593–608) 24 trainee teachers were asked to identify key areas of development in SEN. What emerged from the study was the following:

- Teachers need to further their knowledge about a range of Special Educational Needs, assessments and the partnership of disability organisations.
- 84% of trainee teachers in this study expressed their need for continued education on SEN.

Dr Phil Vickerman's research (2007) showed that both trainee and qualified teachers are keen to acquire skills and knowledge on SEN in order to properly promote inclusive education.

A further study carried out by Lawson, Norwich and Nash (2013), indicated that many trainee teachers struggled to effectively teach children with Special Educational Needs in a whole-class environment. The needs of SEN pupils were at times ignored and due to this they routinely became stigmatised and thought of as 'low ability.'

I believe educating pupils with SEN is a collaborative endeavour that requires children and their parents to be involved in shaping the child's learning programme.

The studies above highlight some of the practical issues faced by teachers in the classroom, who without necessary and continuing education and support, are doomed to fail pupils whose educational needs they do not fully understand.

A sizeable part of the behaviour module in teacher training focuses on maintaining a controlled classroom to enable maximum teaching time and curriculum knowledge. The Lamb Inquiry called for a cultural shift in the way in which schools, Local Authorities and other professionals work with parents and children.

According to the Lamb Inquiry, 'This could be summarised as a desire for greater personalisation of SEN and disability services, or perhaps as a desire for a cultural change towards a more consumer focused/customer service driven approach.'

How is it possible for teachers with limited knowledge about the effect of neurodiverse behaviours and a lack of resources to manage these behaviours? To educate the whole class inclusively and effectively without resorting to exclusion?

There is extensive information available to trainee or student teachers via the S.E.N.D. Gateway. Training materials on this platform are grouped to the 4 areas of need, based on those highlighted in the S.E.N.D. code of practice:

1. Social, emotional and mental health.
2. Cognition and learning.
3. Physical.
4. Sensory.

This platform provides helpful resources for SENCOs who need to provide support for children with a variety of needs. They are helpful because a school or other educational setting can plan to meet a child's presenting needs immediately without waiting for a formal diagnosis.

In 2018 the government published a new Initial Teacher Training (ITT) framework, stating that all trainee teachers should learn how to adapt their teaching strategies so that pupils with autism are fully included and helped to succeed.

This is critically important, as the majority of autistic and ADHD children are educated in mainstream schools. It's positive to read in the framework that trainee teachers, 'should be able to recognise signs that may indicate S.E.N.D. and support common educational needs through review of their teaching, making adjustments to overcome any barriers to progress.'

The requirement is also that teachers/schools are 'able to adapt teaching strategies to ensure that pupils with S.E.N.D. (including, but not limited to, autism, dyslexia, ADHD, sensory impairment or speech, and language and communication needs) can access and progress within the curriculum.'

This is excellent, and if this is comprehensively implemented in all schools, it should make a difference to the quality of life, mental health and educational attainment of children and young people with Special Educational Needs.

Although trainee teachers can opt to undertake additional disability and S.E.N.D. training as part of their Continuing Professional Development (CPD), the reality is, particularly for primary teachers, there needs to be emphasis on learning the wider curriculum.

Therefore, on many undergraduate courses for ITT, S.E.N.D. training or diagnosis take a lower priority to competency in the core curriculum.

As a trainee teacher I spoke to put it succinctly, "With regard to S.E.N.D. we don't know what we're looking for."

The blog, specialneedsjungle.com, goes further on this topic, summarising the report from the Newly Qualified Teacher's Annual Survey 2014 that, 'learning how to teach children with Special Educational Needs is one of the lowest-rated aspects of teacher training for Primary School trainees.'

Elements of this report make sobering reading, as you will realise that in some cases your child will be taught by an NQT unprepared for the challenges they will be presented with and as such may react harshly or unfairly due to their lack of training, or their desire to appear in control (and not lose their job). Until teacher training in this area improves, as parents —who put the care of their child in the hands of teachers we often know nothing about—it is our responsibility to remain informed, vigilant and, where necessary, proactive.

Recognising and supporting SEN in the classroom comes with experience using acquired expertise to adapting teaching styles. The 'Assess. Plan. Do. Review. Model' is a useful way for parents and schools to manage the complexities of identifying and supporting children in school with Special Educational Needs, especially as their needs change as they move through the school.

As parents, we can influence what is happening at school, and this influence is heavily determined by the communications tools such as emails, Apps, letters, book-bag, meetings etc.

A teacher with good classroom management skills can

read situations, take difficult decisions and retain control of their class by:

- Sitting children at the front of the class if they are easily distracted or distract others.
- Separating groups or pairs of children who spark off each other.
- Moving children into another class if there is a personality clash.
- Talking to a child before or after the lesson to see if there is something worrying them.
- Visuals around the classroom that represent 'Kindness. Listening. Difference. Community.'
- Visible emotion zone cards. Frequent reminders.
- Playing down (not ignoring, especially if it's serious) the poor behaviour, using descriptive praising, highlighting the positive behaviour.
- Good collaboration and an agreed plan between class teacher and LSA or TA to manage difficult situations.

Sitting a child at the front of the class allows the teacher to keep an eye on them and interject if there is a likelihood of them interrupting the lesson. Sitting at the front means the child can hear the teacher, ask questions discreetly if they are struggling to understand and the teacher can observe small changes in behaviour and engagement.

Classrooms are competitive and complex environments for autistic children due to constant social interaction due to the multitude of child and adult relationships, as well as the potential for sensory overload.

Even your child's seat in the classroom can create anxiety for them, which the teacher may not be aware of. Gently probe where your child is sitting. Are they near a window (distracted), by the door (noise), underneath a flickering light?

Seating plans require a lot of thought. Teachers learn to build classroom seating plans like a game of Jenga. A simple seating change can improve your child's experience of the classroom and their opportunity to learn.

Teachers are not without bias. They are human beings too. They will like some children more than others. It's important to keep a level head about this stuff. It's basic psychology and it happens in families too. The brother who runs away from home becomes defined by it—a self-fulfilling prophecy. Eventually he keeps running away because that's what everyone expects.

Teachers can change perceptions of certain children, but the best we can expect is that everyone is treated fairly.

How you can support the teacher

- Find out who drives and co-ordinates your child's support in school. If you have an ECHP assessment or diagnosis, find out who the information has been shared with.
- Write a 1-page summary about your child including their likes, dislikes, top line medical history, fears and phobias, areas of weakness, favourite things. This can be separate or tie into the pupil passport. Share this with as many people who think it will be useful.
- Follow the Assess. Plan. Do. Review the process to monitor the outcomes.

- If your child takes medication, make sure you know who is responsible for administering this and at what time. Who does this when the main person is away? Is everyone clear about the dosage? Who is the decision-maker in the event of an emergency or adverse reaction?
- Does your child know the basics of their education and care plan? Use visuals to explain.

List these questions in your notebook. Sometimes systems fall down. Ask for a contingency plan. A mother I spoke to told me that her son was forgotten on a school trip. Literally left behind. He's a masker, shy as a bird and hardly speaks. That event has left him feeling worthless and he now describes himself as the 'forgettable one.'

Everyone who works in a school is ridiculously busy. For some, the time pressures are too much, and they leave the profession. Hopefully, the staff who support your child will appreciate your gentle input and nudges.

The reality is staff change and people move on. Make it your business to take responsibility for your child's administration, as you can't rely on them to do it for you.

A 5-minute chat with tips on what works to calm your child down is gold dust for the teacher. Acknowledge how difficult it is for them with a class of lively kids.

I bought Lucas's class teacher a copy of *The Reason I Jump* by David Mitchell for Christmas. I have no idea whether he read it, but I was committed to building a good relationship with his class teacher. Doing this is your best chance for your child in school when you're not there.

Working with the school

Dealing with the teachers can be more difficult than dealing with the medical establishment. Unused to being a service-user, it was strange having conversations with people who wanted to know everything about us, but I went with it.

There are issues of trust in any personal exchange but if you enter into this thing from a position of power, keeping on top of communication and paperwork, you're giving yourself a better chance of success.

The energy and resources required to support your autistic or ADHD child is beyond the scope of one individual. Within the system, there will be people you click with and some who make you feel like dirt on their shoe. Go with it but keep your wits about you, complain if you need to.

Ideas on how you can help the school

- Give the school your own summary of what your child's (sensory) likes and dislikes are. Don't assume the class teacher will know this, especially if they've moved up a school year or have teachers who job-share. Use bullet points and say what makes your child anxious, what they do when they're anxious, what calms them down, how long it takes to calm them down (see the 'happychild' form at the end of the book as a guide).
- Offer your time in the classroom or on a school trip.
- Ask the SENCO or class teachers for regular updates, feedback etc. Don't wait for them to ask to see you.
- Don't assume everything is going well. There might be things building up they are trying to contain.
- Follow up meetings with a quick confirmation email

stating what you discussed and agreed dates and timings. Don't get into long histories or past battles—just summarise the facts.

- Do you feel comfortable with your child being prescribed medication at school?
- Ask the teacher for their input or ideas on what you could help them with. Don't feel stressed if you can't help but if you can help occasionally it builds goodwill.
- Reply promptly to the school's requests for meetings or information.
- Attend parents' evenings and use the school's communication tools.
- Speak to staff calmly and respectfully, even if you feel angry.

Important

Review Section F (Special Educational Provision) of the child's EHCP regularly. Discuss any questions in person with the SENCO or teacher if you feel the plan isn't being delivered and your child is suffering as a result. Wait up to 3 to 4 weeks to see what happens. If there is no progress, put your concern in writing and wait again. If there's still no improvement, escalate through the school complaints process. See the list at the end of the book for autism charities that can help with complaints.

Ideas for teachers and how the school can help

- Be clear about the specifics of the child's SEN support or EHCP. Share this with the wider teaching team. Some subject teachers, especially in Secondary School think that their role is to teach not support. However, schools with enlightened leadership understand the importance of all staff having baseline understanding of autism/ADHD and how to manage their associated behaviours in the classroom.

- Raise questions or concerns early with parents, colleagues, management and specialists, ideally before any plan is agreed.
- If there are issues in supporting the child with SEN support or EHCP, set up an interim review. For example, one that's earlier than the required Annual Review.
- Review the Section E (outcomes) part of the child's EHCP regularly. Review this often with the parent. Discuss what is working, what isn't and reasons for each.
- If the child is ADHD, are they getting enough physical activity each week? Have you checked how many PE lessons they have each week? Do they need support with games?
- Can they join any after school clubs? If the parent is struggling financially, can the school help with any costs?
- What parent/teacher communication tools are used? Do you tell parents when their child had a 'bad day' more often than you share their successes?
- Do parents have an overview of the behaviour management tools you use at school?
- Have you shared your autism/ADHD behaviour tools with your parents, such as the 5-Point Scale or Zones of Regulation?
- Do you encourage autism/ADHD parents in school to support each other?

- How do you communicate positive behaviour success in the classroom to parents?
- What communication tools do you use with all parents? How do you encourage low-engaged parents to use your communications tools? Do you offer training/refreshers?
- Outcomes for children and young people who are in Year 9 onwards should focus more on preparing for independence and adulthood, in accordance with the child's capacity for this.
- Does the school offer regular parenting courses, especially autism/ADHD specific ones? Check out my workshops and online courses: www.happyinschoolproject.com.

What you can do from home

There are advantages of not working when your child is diagnosed as autistic, but understandably, opting out of the workforce is a last resort for many families as it creates a huge strain.

I worked in a busy press office and in other corporate roles when Lucas was going through the school exclusion phase and found the demands of dealing with the media, the school, long hours, the commute left me frazzled and unable to juggle Lucas's school dramas and medical appointments.

- If you've worked for your employer for a year or more you have the right to unpaid time off work to look after your children.
- You can take up to 18 weeks' unpaid leave before your child is 18.

- You can also take unpaid time off work to deal with unexpected problems, for example when childminding arrangements break down.
- Going from 2 incomes to 1 hits hard at first but there can be many advantages for your child, and hopefully it will only be temporary.
- You're there at the end of the day to help unload and re-pack the school bag, PE kit, checking for lost things.
- You can monitor their mood, before and after school.
- You get an immediate download of the day.
- You don't need to manage the complexities of after school care.
- You can support any eating, sleep, medical or appointments.
- You can build a home/school timetable, including relaxation or exercise regimes to increase security and alleviate anxiety.

If your autistic child is a 'masker' at school (often girls, but not exclusively) they will hide their traits successfully and save the meltdown for home. This is tough on you, especially if the school doesn't see this.

If school is the cause of their anxiety, you need to capture this to share with the school. Using video is intrusive but effective. Ask your child to write a letter to their feelings or create a happiness scale and ask them to fill in a number each day, morning and evening.

Maybe try the truth mirror technique: imagine you're talking to your reflection now talk to it about school? How do you feel during the day? Who are your friends? Do you feel sad going into school or does something happen at school that upsets you?

Many autistic girls have vivid, creative imaginations; so explore this side of their personality to build a bridge into their world. Write down what they say and afterwards thank them for doing this. Tell them you will help them in any way you can.

You may need guidance from a professional counsellor or Cognitive Behaviour Therapist, to help your child get their anxiety in control. Ask your GP or health visitor for a referral to CAMHS and contact your local specialist autism service through the single point of access.

I didn't have the energy to get involved with anyone or anything in the immediate time after Lucas' diagnosis, I did things as best I could on my own. It took years to understand that I had a voice and could advocate for Lucas myself, but once I acquired the skills and the knowledge, we were away!

Trust makes it happen
I love meeting teachers who are keen to develop their knowledge and skills training around SEN, but there are others who call a member of the Senior Management Team at the slightest whiff of trouble.

When faced with an apparently unteachable child, a teacher's decision-making needs to be swift to avoid losing control of the whole class. Their success or failure in the classroom issues rests on the following:

- Relationship between the teacher and neurodiverse children.

- Relationship between teacher and rest of class.
- Relationship between rest of class and neurodiverse children.
- Teacher's understanding of autism and ADHD and how keen they are to learn about the individual child's challenges.
- How the child reacts to sensory overload. If this is extreme, ask if the teacher can provide an alternative teaching environment for certain lessons, e.g. PE, chemistry etc.
- Whether the child is more likely to externalise or internalise in specific settings, e.g. PE, playground, canteen, assembly, etc.
- The relationship between the teacher and the SENCO.
- How well the teacher and SENCO feel supported by their colleagues, in particular the headteacher.
- The relationship between teacher, SENCO and the child's parent/carers.
- Willingness and resources for the teachers are to make accommodations.
- Internal communications between support staff teachers and senior leadership team.

In these narrow moments, unless a good, trust-based relationship has developed, or there is quality back-up, the teacher may feel the easiest and safest option is to remove the child from the class or evacuate the whole class. If there are weak links in the above, it's likely that with or without a diagnosis your child will be ostracised because of their disability.

All elements need to co-exist for a harmonious classroom:

control, respect, laughter, trust, kindness, inclusion and forgiveness. If the teacher demonstrates these attributes, the pupils will follow. Chair throwers can be redeemed.

School and home communications tools

There are many technical tools that schools are using to communicate with parents. Next generation tools enable timely, helpful and interactive information exchange between parents and school such as:

- Class Dojo – uses a points system.
- Marvellous Me – direct to parents snippets of learning-led/praise, news, positive teacher partnership, data managed centrally under GDPR.
- ParentSquare.
- Remind.
- ClassTag.
- Heard.
- Seesaw.
- ClassCharts.

Check out which one your school uses then get stuck in. The newer tools include teacher praise and notes of WWW (what went well), which is great to know so you can boost and praise your kids for the things they've got right!

Better than a poke in the eye

There's the famous incident of Phineas Gage who experienced a personality change after an accident injured the pre-frontal cortex areas of his brain. After the accident he was said to be unable to make rational judgement and become emotionally sensitive, behaving in a socially inappropriate way.

At the time scientists suggested that it was the injury to this specific area of his brain that had created these remarkable changes to his personality.

Brain imaging studies carried out in people with autistic spectrum condition suggest that the connections between the cerebral cortex, the amygdala and the limbic system have become scrambled. As a result, people with ASC may suddenly experience an extreme emotional response when experiencing a trivial object or event. This may be a reason why people with ASC like routines. They follow a set pattern off predictable events, in a predictable way which reduces the possibility of an unforeseen event provoking them into an emotional extreme. It may also explain why a change in routine can feel stressful.

In addition to sensory sensitivity, Lucas wouldn't laugh at the same time or at the same things as other people when we went to the theatre for example. He would often laugh more loudly and for longer than other people, which was embarrassing but sweet. Depending on how well a stage play had captured his attention, he would sometimes ask in a loud voice, "When's the interval?" or, "I'm really hungry," and wiggle about in his seat, saying how uncomfortable it was. His sensory reactions would cut into his enjoyment of the performance, which to an outsider would look rude.

Mental health
During the first years of life, 1 in 5 children will experience mental health difficulty at least once. (Children's Mental Health Matters, Place2be, NAHT, 2016.)

As parents, we may be forced to confront these conditions in our children and learn to manage the effect of their mental health issues in our families. The stigma around mental health may be lessening, but mental health issues in children are still a source of misunderstanding and misdiagnosis.

Take comfort from the fact that even though you feel like you are in a lonely place, you are not alone. I keep repeating this because I felt very alone and ashamed. I don't want you to feel that way.

The S.E.N.D. code of practice (2015) no longer includes behaviour as part of the category of social emotional and mental health. This is because a child's behaviour is perceived as a communication about the child's state of mind and may be caused by a variety of factors for example:

- Anxiety.
- Sensory overload.
- Anger, including anger about pervasive life situations or undisclosed difficulties.
- Response to trauma or attachment difficulties.
- Frustration due to speech and communication difficulties.
- Response to the wrong level of challenge in lessons.
- Grief.
- Physical pain or discomfort, such as hunger.
- Underlying mental health problems.
- Undisclosed physical, mental or sexual abuse.

One afternoon, after a particularly tricky day at school, my daughter gave Lucas a piece of paper and asked him to write down 4 different things that make him angry at school and why. This is what he wrote:

1. People saying rude and mean things to me.
2. When people shout at me.
3. People hurting me on purpose.
4. When people come to me when I don't want them to.

There it was in black and white. Specific situations and events that were stressing him out. Asking him things in quiet moments was a great way to get him to reveal his world and helped us understand how we could help.

It's a great technique:

1. Figure out what external stressors might be: light, noise, too much information, too many instructions. All of these can cause overload.
2. Gently download the events of the day, a couple of hours before bedtime. Straight after school can be too soon for some children. Lucas was so exhausted he could hardly speak after school.
3. Use a favourite toy or teddy as a prop is a great way to get them talking if they find direct conversation too difficult. For example, "Your tractor/race car/elephant looks sad this evening, shall we ask him what's wrong?" Or if you want to go further, "How was school today Fireman Sam? Did anything or anyone make you sad?" I found it effective and had lots of difficult conversations with Lucas via 'Bunny.'
4. Focus on the good bits of school and remind him how

cool they are: football, a school trip, painting, singing, helping the teacher, getting stickers or merits, etc. If your child has difficulties with friendships, praise them for other things they can feel good about.

5. Draw up a contract to minimise over-exposure to stimulating technology. Review it regularly. Put it somewhere prominent. Stick to it as if your life depends on it. Create a new routine for the holiday/weekends. Talk through the list with your child, explain the rules and the reasons for them. Reward them with words when it works. Technology is a friend to many children with autism/ADHD and not a bad thing per se. It's all in the balance.

There are countless examples of teachers who get it right when supporting and educating children with additional needs. Please acknowledge them. They are literally improving our child's current lives and enhancing their potential for an independent, happy future.

Autism carries the secrets of power and potential
I suspect that some educationalists, hopefully just a few, still believe that children with ASD or ADHD possess limited capacity to achieve great things in life. I got this limiting vibe from Lucas's second Primary School before he was diagnosed. If I've learned anything through this process, it's not to judge other people's kids, as you never know the full picture.

Homework SOS
Ah homework. Helping kids with their homework can cause

tensions. Just to make it easy, imagine that there are no rules! Create a system that works for you and your child in your home. Whatever works, great! Just stick to the system. Create a visual timetable and pin it everywhere. As they get older the system will change:

1. Supervise closely to ensure they stay on task.
2. Read out loud. It's easy to misunderstand the questions so reading out loud is so helpful. We all miss things by skim reading, so reading out loud is helpful even for older children.
3. Use humour to diffuse tension.
4. Ask your child to repeat instructions. This is great for improving brain function (language, recall, details).
5. Carry out temperature checks to gauge his feelings and emotions.
6. Break tasks into smaller chunks. Younger children work in shorter bursts of 20 to 40 minutes. Once the task is complete, a break of around 10 minutes is essential. Move around. Be silly. Repeat.
7. Give heaps of positive feedback and praise. This helps to refuel the emotional tank which will be depleted by the intense focus.
8. If your child messes about, try and stay calm. Reacting to anger with anger will only escalate the situation and we will waste valuable learning time implementing the de-escalate button. Quietly restate the task. If you need it done, use a statement not a question, "We need to read 3 pages of your book." Rather than, "Shall we read 3 pages of your book?"

9. Smile and praise in detail when a piece is done.
10. Feed the brain and have some treats. Make sure you have some too!

Lessons Learned
Before and during the assessment period

- Most likely, your autistic/ADHD child will present intellectual and emotional challenges to their teacher. The outcome of these will depend on the skill and experience of the teacher, as in that instant you are not there.

- Teaching is a challenging job, with growing numbers of neurodiverse pupils and strangled resources. We need to recognise this and acknowledge that many teachers are dedicated, talented, inspiring and creative. But they are still human, and neurodiversity is a complex spectrum of conditions that require tenacity, patience and consistency to achieve the level of calm and stability required for learning.

- We need to commit to work in partnership with teachers so try to keep appointments.

- Complete any forms they ask you to. Make sure you ask who will see them and what they are for. Keep copies. Note the date you met.

- Help your sensitive child to be more organised to reduce their stress. You need to raise your organisation game too.

- Keep all officials to tasks. Send follow up emails about what was discussed and agreed.

- Share information—within reason not overly personal or private—that will helpfully inform your child's teacher. No one knows your child as well as you, or how you manage them at home, or when you are out and about.

Lessons Learned
While working with Lucas's teachers post-diagnosis

- Persevere with the teachers. Their workload and level of responsibility is difficult to comprehend.

- Good teachers need to be encouraged and praised. In a pressurised environment, we all like to know what we've done well and not just the mistakes we've made.

- If we don't feedback the good things the teachers and LSAs do, they won't know when they're doing a good job. Similarly, if they get it wrong, they need to know, then move on. Holding a grudge is a waste of everyone's energy.

- Building a good relationship with the class teacher, SENCO and the headteacher will pay dividends. You are, after all, a key player in the trio of your child and their school.

- Getting mad with your child will nearly always make things worse. If they are getting into trouble at school, on the road to a diagnosis or newly diagnosed, your anger simply adds to the pressure.

- Deal with each issue at a time. If your child has hit another child, deal with that. If your child has been excluded, deal with that. If your child is struggling with friendships, deal with that. If you try to do too many things at once either nothing happens, or you will confuse your child. You must prioritise.

- If it happens, an exclusion is always a priority. It's usually the first indicator that school is struggling to educate your child in the existing setting.

- Make regular time for your own self-care.

CHAPTER 11

The Therapies Zone - Working Through Myriad Therapies To Find What Fits

Misunderstandings

Autistic people have a way of communicating, thinking and being that doesn't always mesh with neurotypicals. This means social interactions can be difficult on both sides.

Some researchers use the Theory of Mind, Social Skills and Social Thinking programmes to work around these communication breakdowns.

Communication challenges between neurotypicals and neurodiverse are viewed through the prism of Theory of Mind. This is a psychological concept that suggests that as individuals we all have thoughts, beliefs, desires and feelings that belong to us and other people also have attitudes, thoughts, ideas and beliefs that belong to them, Which may be—wait for it —completely different to our own!

Psychologists have possibly mistakenly observed that because autistic people think, feel and experience life in a way that is different to neurotypicals, they are thought to lack empathy.

The theory is captured in a handout I was given explaining social stories: 'Many people with autism do not understand that other people have their own thoughts, feelings, plans and points of view. Therefore, they think that if I'm angry and want to hit you, you must be angry and want to hit me too. This is frightening. Social situations can become unpredictable and confusing, which can lead to social isolation, exclusion and reduced opportunities to participate. Social stories attempt to address this impairment by giving individuals some perspective on the thought, emotion and behaviours of others.'

Many autistic adults and academics regard Theory of Mind as one-sided and deficit based, and purely reflective of the neurotypical perspective of the academics who developed this concept such as Professor Rita Jordan, August 2019.

It's a spectrum out here, but it can seem like the classroom—as a microcosm of society—hasn't caught up!

Trying to attribute a specific behaviour to lack of empathy denies the autistic child or young person the opportunity of their own personalised individual response, if the neurotypical person is expecting a 'normal' response.

Lucas described the experience of attending a family funeral as enjoyable, which shocked his teachers at the time. When probed about this, he was trying to express his feelings of happiness about seeing so many family and friends, even though it was a sad occasion.

Communication is instinctive and learned. Whoever we are, when we're stressed, we revert to an instinctive suite of communication styles.

Many autistic children feel huge empathy, but whether they trust the other social players depends on the circumstances;

what has happened in the lead up to the communication and their personal and individual motives.

If we expect to see empathy displayed in a neurotypical way, we may miss it entirely. Because autism and ADHD present differences in behaviour and social communication, some intervention is required to support child's learning and development.

Speech and Language Therapy (SALT)

SALTs are health professionals who provide treatment, support and care for children and adults who have difficulties with communication, eating, drinking and swallowing.

They work with parents, carers and other professionals, such as teachers, nurses, occupational therapists and doctors.

SALTs helps ADHD or autistic young people in school with the practical aspects of socialisation like making friends, initiating conversations, taking turns, de-coding body language and working on techniques to managing strong moods and emotions.

SALTs sometimes work in groups with children or one-to-one, which depends on the needs of the individual.

Social Stories

Social Stories were developed by Carol Gray in 1991 and provide a base of template visuals, which depict social interactions or scenarios for teachers to use as a tool.

As a parent I was invited to an event about useful social stories and how parents could use them with their children at home. There's no need to be a Picasso! You can create your own social stories at home, using simple stick drawings. In fact, the less visually busy the better. It's the words and the speech bubbles that provide the key learning.

The teacher describes a situation, using either the 'I' or 'she or he' voice in clear, short sentences and positive language. The story instructs the child how to behave or what to say in a given situation.

They are useful for younger children and are often used before or after an event as a discussion point. They are a brilliant tool, widely used in Primary Schools.

Social stories are usually delivered by trained staff—including SALTs—to children with ASD, autism or social and emotional issues. They are comic strip-style visuals, which help children modify their behaviour by showing alternative ways to interact socially. These interactions are usually between 2 characters but can use more. The stories can be depictions of a daily interaction the child may struggle with such as queuing up, squabbles with friends, forgetting kit, bullying, making friends, etc.

The purpose of social stories is not to change your child's behaviour, but to model an effective response in a variety of situations. Your child will develop an improved understanding of social events and expectations. The use of visuals is a good way to communicate with children who have language delay, limited speech or are unable to easily recognise verbal or body language clues.

Social Thinking

Founded by speech and language expert Michelle Garcia Winner, Social Thinking is designed to help students to develop their social skills in areas they are struggling such as making friends and seeing the perspectives of others.

It is a step on from social skills, which look at how you need to behave. Social Thinking delves into reasons why people do things. Rooted in a number of clinical, psychotherapy and speech and language approaches, social thinking is ideal for older children and young people who need more developed tools of social understanding.

A student of Social Thinking would learn to identify what another person might be feeling and then assign a reason why they might be feeling that way based on a number of social cues, such as the environment, previous comments etc.

They learn to use an emotional vocabulary that helps them to understand others better, as well as express their own feelings in a given situation. It's a useful approach for young people approaching key life transitions, such as going to college or living independently.

The Social Thinking Programme is ideal for older students, ideally those with good speech and language ability.

Zones of Regulation
The hardest part for many parents with autistic/ADHD children is supporting their child's emotional control and self-regulation. It's difficult for teachers too.

Many experts cite the emotional maturity of children and young people with Asperger's Syndrome can be up to 3 years behind that of their peers (12). In addition, finding the right words to voice their emotions can be tricky for them, which looks like a lack of interest. They are also prone to emotional highs and lows.

The world of psychiatry is exploring connection between autism and alexithymia. Alexithymia (13) describes a condition when an individual is unable to identify or describe (name) their feelings and can't identify or describe the feelings of others.

Zones of Regulation by Leah M. Kuypers is a curriculum designed to foster self-regulation and emotional control. Like other social and emotional development programmes, it's not exclusively for pupils with autism and can be used widely in school with any child who experiences difficulties managing their emotions. Using visual tools, the programme consists of teaching aids for parents, therapists and educators, which separates our emotions into 4 zones:

- Rest (blue).
- Go (green).
- Slow (yellow).
- Stop (red).

The 4 zones can help pupils to self-identify their feelings. It can help them work out how to recognise and manage their feelings from each of the emotion colour groups.

Zones is a well-used and respected behavioural tool, which trained teaching and support staff can easily bed into an educational support curriculum. It is not to be confused with the more simplistic traffic light system.

The 5-point scale, created by Kari Dunn Buron, is another visual behaviour management system designed to monitor and evaluate behaviour temperatures in pupils.

Like the Zones of Regulation, the 5-point scale maps emotions in a recognisable, colour-coded way for children. Unlike Zones there are 5 tiers in this scale starting from Level

5 Red which means 'I can't stand this. I'm ready to explode' and down to Level 1 Blue which means 'I'm doing great.'

The 5-point scale is equally a good self-regulation tool and has a downloadable form that children can fill in themselves.

The effectiveness of either model, in my opinion, rests on the skill of the practitioner, the level of empathy between the child and their teacher and the need for the 5-point scale to be applied consistently.

Occupational Therapy

Occupational therapists treat injured, ill, or disabled patients using a variety of therapies to ensure that their patients develop and improve towards the goals of maintaining the skills required to manage everyday life.

For children with autism and ADHD, the role of the occupational therapist is to assess the child's sensory processing difficulties or sensory overload (a possible cause of meltdowns).

The occupational therapist might then instigate a sensory diet, a targeted number of physical activities to help the child remain calm or alert according to the demands of their day. For example, they may suggest a sensory wobble cushion, core body exercises or fiddle toys. They may also look at issues around seating, eating, vision and other physical factors which may affect your child's ability to function in the classroom.

Applied Behaviour Analysis

Applied Behaviour Analysis (ABA) is a technique used to manage children's autistic behaviour, based on the work of behavioural psychologist, B.F. Skinner.

ABA uses the principle that specific learning techniques,

rigorously applied, can change a child's behaviour by changing their learned responses.

Some in the S.E.N.D. community believe that behaviour manipulation in children with autism is cruel. Behavioural training, including ABA, works by modifying clinically diagnosed neurodisorders to the point where behaviour and physical mobility are altered. Put simply, the individual is broken down and re-built to behave in another way.

Others are strong supporters of these techniques due to its well documented effectiveness. Supporters include Dr Ivar Lovaas and many others.

Training someone to use an artificial limb or rehabilitate after brain injury uses similar techniques to ABA by re-programming the brain muscle and firing up chemical reactions, which enable the person to re-learn behaviours.

The application of ABA on an artificial limb sits more comfortably with me than re-training an autistic person who isn't actually 'broken.'

Behaviour programmes require considerable time investment to reach desired goals, they are more effective if started as soon as the child is diagnosed—the younger the better.

Some specialist schools require students who follow an ABA programme to be educated residentially away from parental input or influence.

Lucas's school used a basic behaviour management using a points system and praise for good behaviour (Lego or computer time). I would describe this as behaviour modification.

The use of behaviour controls is effective because it works on the basis of stimulating the brain's reward centre, which floods your system with feel-good hormones. If you opt for

ABA specifically as therapy for your child ask lots of questions, read up on the topic, and talk to other parents if their child has been ABA schooled.

Cognitive Behaviour Therapy

Cognitive Behaviour Therapy (CBT) is a psychosocial intervention. It's a talking therapy, which assists people to interrupt their negative thoughts that can adversely impact their behaviours.

It is particularly effective for improving mental health conditions, encouraging patients to be aware of and change their damaging inner talk.

Eventually, through CBT, children become more resilient in managing their anxiety or anger.

The team at London's South London and Maudsley Hospital recommend that CBT for ADHD should be delivered by specialist trained experts.

CBT can be expensive for schools to buy in, which is why some Local Authorities are developing Resilience Programmes based on the CBT model. It's not essential to have a CBT trained therapist to build your child's resilience, but when you or the school are inviting any expert to liaise directly with your child, try to:

- Meet face to face.
- Request a simple explanation about the therapy (how it works, methods, examples).
- What are the expected outcomes?
- How long will it take approximately to achieve those outcomes?

- What can go wrong?
- How do you manage a crisis?
- How often will they have the therapy?
- Is any follow up required?

Art therapy

Art therapy uses art and expression as a therapeutic technique. It is a particularly powerful tool of expression for children who are non-verbal, or who find verbalising their feelings too emotional.

One of the many positive things that Lucas learned during art therapy was how to verbally express the more positive aspects of his life. By age 12 he had become very negative and withdrawn. Art therapy was a great tool to help him break the negative thought cycle. Some skilled art therapists combine their therapy with CBT.

Drama therapy

Knots Arts, a London-based community interest company (CIC) that describes itself as a 'creative space to untangle social knots,' was a lifeline for Lucas.

When he first started at Knots Arts, he was about a year into his diagnosis and shutting down emotionally. Knots Arts helped him to turn this around.

Each week the sessions started with students sharing their news highlights of the week, preferably positive. Some children would rattle off stories, others were very quiet and struggled to speak in front of their peers, including Lucas. When it was his turn, he spoke quickly, quietly and didn't make much eye contact or he'd say the shortest sentence possible, even if he'd had a full week. It was like he couldn't remember anything good!

By the time he'd been going to Knots for 5 years, he'd learned to relax and enjoy hanging out with other young people. He could also articulate his more complex thoughts to the group and was beginning to listen carefully to the other children.

At the end of each term they put on a play. One year, after a particularly magical production of a Midsummer Night's Dream, the session leaders said such positive things about him. Here's an extract from his end of term report:

'Lucas is showing more confidence this term. His level of eye contact has really improved, and he is beginning to initiate conversations on a regular basis. Lucas showed his increased confidence when he volunteered to be interviewed by Radio 2 (he was interviewed about being autistic and the benefits of being in a group like Knots Arts on the Graham Norton Show). He became a radio sensation! He has showed himself to be thoughtful and articulate. He is a likeable and happy young man and the group enjoy being around him. He thrives on activities when the instructions are precise. He requires processing time, but he is becoming more fluid in activities. He has been a pleasure to have in the group and has proven himself to be a talented performer.'

Being dramatic and artistic may seem a stretch too far if your autistic child is withdrawn, moody or doesn't like to interact, but I recommend you at least give it a go. Going there once a week provided Lucas with an antidote to the rigidity of school. He made friends with the other young people who also had various social communications challenges. But they were accepting of each other.

The professionals in the group helped me to see the bigger picture and suggested from their observations that he might have some processing delay, impacting his ability to listen and follow instructions.

They had untangled him, allowing his kindness to shine through. It reminded us that behind the behaviour was a lovely human being. I wished the teachers had the time to find the person hidden behind the difficult behaviour.

Introducing drama therapy had demonstrated that he had other ways to communicate. He was getting equipped with a new set of tools.

The drama therapy was proving to be an excellent tool of personal and emotional discovery. If you find an activity where your child feels accepted, it will boost their mental wellness and lead to acceptance in their autistic individualism, benefitting them personally and for their future.

Also, social enterprises supporting autism and ADHD children with specific activities, provide much-needed respite for parents.

Mood diary
A mood diary is a useful tool when trying to pinpoint reasons for low mood. For some children the reason is clear. It could be a supply teacher, an educational visit, a change in routine, an inability to do what peers can do, or teasing. Sometimes the trigger isn't as easy to identify and needs a bit of detective work. Pictures or visuals may help if your child struggles to remember or verbalise.

Lucas was highly articulate when speaking about his specialist topics, but when he was asked to explain what caused him to throw a pen, he would clam up or shrug. He switched back to monosyllabic boy, barely making eye contact. It was exhausting for him.

In regular school scuffles, he would own up to all sorts of things, even when he wasn't guilty! When I asked why he did this, he said he didn't know how to explain.

For autistic children, needing to recount a bullying incident is mentally taxing. It's like re-living the whole thing. Keeping a mood diary, even with entries in short sentences, bullet points or drawings, helps everyone to see if there are any patterns or behaviour triggers such as foods, names called, places visited. It's worth the effort.

Complementary and alternative approaches

Although there is no cure for autism, there is a lot we can do to make life calmer and more comfortable for our special children and for ourselves. Here are a few suggestions below.

Hypnotherapy

I read about hypnotherapy and thought we would give it a try. I contacted a reputable practitioner via the UK General Hypnotherapy Register. She had a calming energy the minute she walked into our home.

She explained how it worked and then started to work on Lucas, who was 6 at the time. I stayed in the room quietly observing them. It was so relaxing, I felt he was completely safe. She invited him to listen carefully to her words, using visualisation techniques, such as a magic carpet he could sit on and be completely free.

"Take a ride on your carpet when you're feeling stressed and angry," she said in the softest voice.

I sat in the chair next to him on the sofa and tried not to drift off! She led him into a deep state of hypnosis using soothing words, repetition and powerful imagery. With clear verbal instructions, she created mental exercises designed to get him to focus on his emotions. This helped him discover techniques to help him manage his emotions if they became too much.

The session was wonderful. He picked it up intuitively. I wanted to continue with the full 6 to 8 week programme, but I couldn't afford it. I didn't have 8 weeks to wait either. Things needed to get better at school straight away.

Meditation

We tried meditation, which was effective and not as expensive as the hypnotherapy. You can learn how to meditate by yourself. There are loads of good tutorials online. Once you've mastered it, you just need practice it daily, ideally at a set time each day. It can become part of your self-care ritual.

The techniques to encourage relaxation were similar the hypnotherapy, for example deep breathing and visualisation. The meditation techniques I learned after a couple of sessions could be applied at home.

I bought *Enchanted Meditation for Kids* by Christine Kerr, which was brilliant for Lucas as it calmed and de-stressed him before going to sleep.

Yoga

Yoga worked well and I was amazed how quickly Lucas could get into the various positions or asanas. There is something pure about a child doing hatha yoga. It involves physical movement and stillness, which together promote balance and strength. There's huge growth in specialist yoga classes for children.

Many spiritually advanced practitioners understand the benefits of yoga for children who experience anxiety or hyperactivity, and some won't charge for your child to attend a session. Others run dedicated parent and child yoga sessions. There is a lot of generosity in the yoga community. If you look you will find it and even if you need to make a contribution to the class, the benefits are worth it.

Exercise

If your child is fit and mobile using their body to be active will help them release endorphins. Children with diagnosed or undiagnosed behaviour issues benefit from structured and unstructured activity.

Lucas didn't cope well with rugby or football—too much close body contact and shouting—but he excelled in cross-country and tennis. The fact he managed to run was a pleasant surprise after having joint issues in the years after his arthritis diagnosis. He still had joint flair-ups, usually in cold weather. The doctors said gentle and continuous exercise would ease his joints, unless he was in direct pain.

Sports and other activities, such as indoor climbing or gymnastics help to improve gross motor skills, hand-eye co-ordination and balance, through the movement required to participate. Plus they're fun!

If your child gets angry when they lose a game, playing a competitive sport can help with taking turns, developing team skills, learning how to follow instructions and dealing with disappointment.

CBT is a good way to support children who don't like losing. This would help them overcome their negative belief that they are by default 'a loser.'

A programme could be developed to strengthen their acceptance of their individual strengths and weaknesses. A different approach would be trialled for helping the child to understand rules-based games, such as social thinking or using visuals to describe the game in a more concrete way.

The benefits of exercise are well documented, especially half an hour a day of vigorous exertion to get the blood pumping. If we do this, we get a full body work out, including the brain and heart muscles.

Health professionals recommend we need to retain optimum health for as long as possible. Health care teams are happy to recommend suitable activities for your child's fitness, cognitive or mobility level.

Lucas instinctively liked yoga, which may have been because of its calming aspects and the fact that yoga is not a sport, but still requires a degree of physical strength, builds flexibility and releases emotional tension held in the body.

Lessons Learned

- There is no cure for autism. ADHD symptoms can continue into adulthood, which may require continued medication, therapy, exercise, good eating and sleeping regimens.

- Therapies are designed to provide support, relief and practical strategies to enable autistic and ADHD children to thrive and achieve their goals in a society that sometimes struggles to understand the neurodiverse brain.

- Both of these conditions are spectrum disorders, so will impact the daily life of the individual depending on what the demands of their daily life are.

- Autistic and ADHD children and young people struggle at school for a number of reasons. The demands of the average school day are especially triggering in terms of sensory or emotional overload. Teaching professionals are not always able to separate or identify triggers. Neurotypical teachers with limited understanding or experience may inadvertently be contributing to the autistic/ADHD child's overload. The therapist may not gel with the child. The child is an individual and will respond to the therapy in their own individual way. The school environment may negate the benefits of any therapy provided.

- Find out as much as you can (especially for school-based therapies such as speech and language therapy, occupational therapy and behaviour support such as Zones of Regulation) about the who, what and why of the therapies. What is the therapy? How it is delivered (in groups, one-to-one)? Is it invasive? Will your child be touched during therapy (which can happen in occupational therapy)? Will the child be left alone for any period of time? Is the child rewarded after therapy and what is the reward? Can the therapy be done at home? What equipment will be needed, if any? Does the child understand what the therapy is for and how it may help them?

- If the therapy is something you are paying for privately, although some of these are offered in schools, such as meditation, hypnotherapy, mindfulness, then try to sit in on a session as you might enjoy it! Find out if the session will include other children with additional needs. What professional qualifications does the tutor or session leader have and is he or she aware of your child's specific needs? Are they trained in first-aid?

- For nutritional therapy, for example, find out from the nutritionist about their training, especially if you're investigating whole food or vegan diets for the first time. Will they help you overcome any difficulties if your child is struggling or gagging when they try new foods? Will they help with any of the emotional or sensory issues around food, such as avoidance or restrictive eating in your child?

- All of this may seem a load of work for you. . . and it is! Trying anything new for autistic/ADHD children can be a challenge in itself, be clear about why you're doing this and realise that you need to be as committed as your child.

- Fulsome praise and encouragement are the perfect balm for many a disappointment, especially if things are slow to work or your child is resistant.

- Keep notes, and records, celebrate progress and breakthroughs. Keep smiling.

CHAPTER 12

The Hunger As Healing Zone
'There Is No Hunger That Love Cannot Heal.'

Food and drink

Strong scientific evidence shows that the ingestion of artificial sugars and other food additives or chemicals can disrupt the nervous systems of children, adolescents and adults with developmental difficulties.

I'm not a doctor and cannot comment on medical information, but I think it's important to consider some of the associated behaviour difficulties allegedly caused by food and drink additives.

As a society we are on a steep learning curve about the toxic and curative properties of everything we eat or breathe. Our digestive, emotional and nervous systems play a huge part in our health and wellbeing, so it makes sense that educators, clinicians, and parents should take an active interest in the dietary and environmental input of the children and young people in our care.

We live in a world where our food is coloured, preserved and flavoured and mechanised. Our food products and processes are tested and regulated under strict government guidelines from health standards organisations, to make sure the food on our plates is safe.

Over time, however, chemical additives and even the plastics and aluminium that products are packaged in, create a build-up in our systems. We won't necessarily know what causes a particular ailment until our immune systems or gastro-intestinal systems fail.

It isn't just the ingestion of these additives that creates the problem. It's the widespread use of products as they accumulate in our systems, which may result in toxicity levels that some people find difficult to cope with.

When our bodies are in homeostasis (we eat well, sleep well, exercise regularly and our system is in balance), it is easier for our bodies to rid themselves of the nasty build-up of waste. Stress, illness and anxiety all play a part in disrupting our equilibrium, so we need to think carefully about the quality and quantity of our nutritional load.

The increased demand for dairy and crops means wider use of additives across the food chain. Cattle are given antibiotics to keep them infection-free, crops are sprayed to reduce infestations which results in chemical formulas across so many of the foods we take for granted.

But it's not just foods that have chemicals. We have chemicals in our home, such as cleaning products, perfumes and soaps. It's easy to see how our bodies become overloaded. Our bodies are incredible at keeping us healthy naturally, but are we pushing nature too far?

In neuroscience, glutamate is a chemical that enables cells to send signals to other cells. It is one of the most influential transmitters in the nervous system. It occurs naturally in protein containing foods for example cheese, mushrooms, meat, fish, milk and many vegetables. It is also produced by the human body and is vital for metabolism and brain function.

It occurred to me that eating for brain health is as important for neurodiverse children as eating for body health. You can't have one without the other!

There is a body of research looking at the effects of aspartame and other food additives in children with developmental difficulties, specifically on the central nervous system.

Over the last few decades, as diagnoses of neurological developmental conditions have risen, so too has our consumption of wheat and dairy produce. Industrial farming has incorporated chemical additives, mainly preservatives, to meet growing demand. Further studies are being conducted into the effects of gluten and casein on autistic and ADHD children's physiology and digestive systems.

Food and additives that flagged up in my research as being potentially disruptive for people with sensitive autism/ADHD digestive and nervous systems include:

- Fluorides.
- Preservatives.
- Food colourings.
- High fructose corn syrup (HFCS).
- Aspartame.
- Nitrates.
- Aluminium.
- Mercury.
- Monosodium glutamate (MSG).

Further delving implies that certain additives create a negative immune response causing whole body reactions. Other theories suggest that some chemicals are difficult for autistic/ADHD children to metabolise successfully, meaning they are not excreted routinely from the body and become potentially harmful.

The Feingold Diet was created in the US to improve behaviour in children with ADHD by adopting a strict additive free diet. It's food for thought!

Exploring alkaline foods is another great starting point for your autism/ADHD food journey. If you love a project, create a tailor-made colourful visual food wall chart for your child, based on nutritional needs/things to avoid/eat less of/eat more of/sensory preference needs etc.

Remember to focus on the positives. Eating to suit their specific nutritional needs may help them to concentrate and help them to feel calm, sleep better, improve their skin etc.

Make sure you cover all of the food groups, with sufficient vitamins and minerals. Some GP surgeries have free nutritional advice guides. Seek advice from a qualified doctor, psychiatrist, nutritionist before making any radical dietary changes for a child in your care.

In a world where hunger still exists, I'm grateful to eat most things, but more of us are starting to question the food chain. Many people are choosing to eat more organic or pesticide-free food, less processed food or rejecting some foods entirely.

Our immune systems are as individual as we are and when they fail and we get ill, it's difficult to know where to point the finger.

There's increasing research on the benefits of varied gut

microbes to promote good health. The advice can be confusing and conflicting leaving us not knowing where to start.

Let's start with what we put in our mouths. My choice is to eat a balanced rainbow diet and drink plenty of water to flush any nasties away, with regular exercise thrown in.

Taking care of how we feed ourselves and our children is essential. New books are published every week with nutritious low-cost menu ideas. There are websites offering free resources that are widely available.

We know current stimulant medication for ADHD causes loss of appetite in young people, so feeding them nutritious food is a small thing to do, to balance the equation.

We are what we eat
Family mealtimes can be fraught with problems. The thing to be aware of is that unhealthy habits around food—eating late, snacking, regular takeaways, skipping meals, frequent sugary drinks—set up habits for life.

I used to be terrible for skipping meals or eating at irregular times. It took me ages to realise how important it was for Lucas to eat regularly, little and often. His blood sugars needed to be topped up with slow-release foods to manage his moods.

Getting hungry is to be avoided for ADHD kids. The ADHD part of his diagnosis causes him to burn calories fast. Children with ADHD feel hungry frequently, which is hardly surprising the amount of energy they use up moving around, verbalising, flitting from one activity to the other, having millions of thoughts crowding their brains.

With quick metabolisms, children burn energy faster than adults, more so if they are ADHD and teens. The right sort of food at regular intervals is an important part of successfully managing children with challenging behaviour or neurodiversity. They only realise how hungry they are when they're ravenous, or hangry, due to a drop in activity levels.

Lucas's autism creates different sorts of eating issues such as the tastes, smells, eating the same foods for weeks on end and the need for predictable mealtimes.

For ages, Lucas never used to pick up barbeque chicken wings with his fingers. He didn't like the feel of the sticky residue on his hands. So much for finger-licking good! If these sorts of sensory food needs are not taken seriously, negative and harmful food habits can develop.

The experience of food and eating for autistic and ADHD children is further complicated by anxiety, or compulsive, obsessive traits.

There is growing research on autistic girls with autism, which highlights management of food as an obsession. This can lead to eating disorders, especially if anxiety is present.

Many autistic boys with a comorbidity of ADHD and autism often skip meals because they are focussed on something else or just not feeling hungry.

Avoidance Food Restriction Intake Disorder (AFRID) can also link with Autism Spectrum Disorder. All of this requires careful handling and in some cases professional input.

Take lunch time at school. It's a highly sensory experience with the smells, bright lights, noisy voices, clashing pans, changing menus, the sensory overload of being close to the heaving push of other children. Regulating mealtimes and therefore blood sugar is vitally important. But things didn't always go to plan for Lucas.

He would get caught in canteen queue scuffles and get sent to the back of the queue. He would let others go in front of him to avoid being pushed. If his favourite choices had gone by the time he got to the front, he would skip lunch entirely.

'Wait your turn' is a basic skill kids learn at Primary School. A building block of a well-ordered school community. Enter the impulsive ADHD kid or the autistic child with sensory processing issues and BOOM! We have a recipe for an extremely stressful afternoon.

I would love to see a study of autistic and ADHD children's emotional regulation after the lunchtime/playground experience. Particularly those in mainstream schools.

At Lucas's Secondary School, with autism trained staff, they made excellent adjustments such as allowing him to leave class 5 minutes early to get to the canteen minutes before the whole school crush, at the same time every day, without the anxiety of queuing. He could choose his selection in peace, quickly eat and then retreat to the quiet of the low-sensory centre. This meant he was in a good mood in the afternoon with improved attention. Problem-solved, intelligence applied, everyone is happy.

Expecting a neurodiverse child to work around your flexible eating times does not always work for them. They may not be obviously angry or visibly upset but what we cannot see is the brain activity which is affecting their functioning and emotions.

Ideas for energy dips and preparing food on a (time and money) budget

If you're on a tight budget or have limited time, fiddling about in the kitchen is the last thing you want. Here are a few non-expensive ideas to help you manage energy dips when you're out and about without causing sugar-highs.

1. Get a selection of small containers in different sizes, colours, shapes. Fill with 3 or 4 healthy snacks, e.g. pitta bread strips, chopped apple (a little lemon juice might stop it from going brown), walnuts, raisins, mini yoghurt pots/strips, mini savoury crackers, grapes, fruit cake, mini muffin (shop bought is fine, homemade if you like to bake), individual mini cheeses, cocktail sausages, pretzels, snack crackers, flapjacks, apricots, falafel, grapes, samosa, or sandwiches. Take a selection when you go out. Have a few small boxes for each person on your outing, including you. Using a cool bag is a great money-saving hack too because home snacks are not only healthier than shop-bought snacks, but usually work out cheaper. Selection boxes like this will keep your child's metabolism ticking over, avoiding an energy crash that will wreak havoc with their mood.

2. Involve your child in building the contents of their snack box. If they help to pick the contents and have them in their backpack, they're more in control of their eating, giving them a sense of responsibility. Involve them in choosing the containers and packing them. Make it fun!

3. Celebrations or wrapped chocolates are good, as sometimes only a chocolate fix will do, especially if it's not expected. Space out the chocolate treats as motivation. For example, if there are 2 more places you need to visit before you go home, you could give your

child a treat or snack at this or that place. These should only be small snacks so don't worry about spoiling his/her appetite.

As a busy parent, finding time to prepare nutritious foods can be tricky, but try to limit the amounts of highly processed, ultra-refined foods you eat regularly. I shop at street markets when I can. It's cheaper and helps reduce supermarket packaging waste.

I know immediately if Lucas has had birthday cake or sweets at school or whether his big sister has bought him a cheeky doughnut or strawberry laces. He bounces around the house with his voice getting louder—it's a big giveaway!

In contrast, autistic children may have other eating needs:

- Requirement to eat at specific times every day.
- Prefer to eat the same foods every day.
- Preferences for foods that support their sensory needs, not too spicy, crunchy foods, foods that don't make their fingers feel sticky. The list of idiosyncrasies is as variable as they are.
- Some autistic children get so anxious about food and issues surrounding food, they will stop eating entirely.

A sensory lunchtime would assist so many children. Some schools ask children to pick their lunch at the beginning of the day, which helps children with specific needs to eat at the same time every day without the anxiety of queuing.

Studies show that some children with challenging behaviour associated with ADHD have low levels of zinc and copper in their diet which can affect brain function. Pharmacologist Carl Pfeiffer identified that zinc and copper biochemical imbalances were found in patients with brain disorders including autism and depression.

If you can afford it, see a nutritionist. You don't need to sign up to a whole series of sessions, but they can give you a lot of advice, which you can use as the basis for your own research and food experimenting. Check out nutritionists online and see who comes up that's affordable. Go armed with a list of questions. Ask if they have experience of autistic ADHD youngsters.

When I was a full-time working single mum, I hardly ever ate proper breakfasts. I ignored my hunger pangs until I got to work, where I could buy something at the station. Your child doesn't have that luxury. For them it can be a long time between leaving the house and first break. Half an hour is a long time to a 5-year-old if they're hungry. The trick is to learn to anticipate a child's need. Providing a snack just when they are hungry is like magic for them. You've got them before they even think about whining!

Breakfast and breakfast clubs
Breakfast time. Now don't expect to roll up, eat something and leave the house—no way. You need to plan like you're going into battle. It's one of the hardest times of day for autistic/ ADHD children and their families.

It's a key transition for autistic/ADHD children from waking from sleep which may have been disturbed, then eating food and getting into an uncomfortable school uniform. The prize at the end is a 6 hour shift at school, which for many children, is one of the most hostile environments they have cope with every day. You can't expect them to jump to it.

Like many ADHD children, Lucas was disorganised and easy to anger if he couldn't put his jumper on, button up his shirt, find a pair of socks, find a book—which was most mornings. He would get in a strop, then refuse to eat breakfast or say he wasn't hungry.

After a night's sleep, Primary-aged children need breakfast to reboot and re-energise their system. Breakfast is literally breaking their fast of the night before and if they don't have it, they will struggle. Nothing distracts the brain more than hunger, and missing breakfast impacts on a child's ability to learn. More importantly, the effects get worse over time which can have a negative impact not only for that day but on your child's ability to learn and retain information over weeks.

The good news is that in the UK, nearly half of all state Primary Schools now offer a breakfast club (Department for Education).

Most Primary Schools punctuate the morning with a healthy snack of fruit and milk. If our ADHD/autistic children don't eat breakfast, we are asking too much of their brains to expect them to struggle on until mid-morning before eating.

If they really won't eat before setting off for school, take something in the car for them to nibble on. It's all about their emotions. If they feel stressed, they probably won't eat but if you're calm and matter of fact, they might.

If providing breakfast is a struggle for you financially, tell someone in confidence. There is usually help available. It doesn't mean you are a bad parent. Admitting you have difficulties feeding your child sufficient nutritious food at every mealtime actually means you are being a responsible parent. Many of us encounter periods in our lives when we need to make the decision between bills and food.

Since Lucas's diagnosis, I'm more organised about breakfast and mealtimes. Breakfast can be cereal or toast, but you can throw tradition out of the window and have pasta, samosas or a cold chicken sandwich for breakfast. Anything with a good protein source is ideal.

I have learned which vitamins and minerals are best for levelling out moods and soothing anxiety (vitamin D, B-complex and magnesium). I've rediscovered the dishes my mum used to talk about such as kippers, baked beans, porridge oats with honey, scrambled eggs, sardines, bananas, dark chocolate. Many of these foods have health benefits and some have been proven to contain the essential vitamins and minerals our special children can be deficient in.

Give me sunshine
When Lucas was being treated for juvenile arthritis, one of the consultants mentioned to me after a routine blood test that his vitamin D levels were chronically low. Although Lucas and my family are born in the UK, we have Caribbean heritage, so our genes were probably saying, "Me need a lickel sunshine pon me skin!"

Since then, I add a multi-vitamin and a liquid fish oil supplement, rich in omega 3 and 7, vitamins A and D, to his diet. We've radically increased the amount of fresh fruit and vegetables we all eat.

If your child has sinus problems, there's increasing evidence that taking locally produced honey from the bees in your neighbourhood, pollenating your plants can reduce the impact of pollen-induced allergies like hay fever and allergic skin reactions. You can usually find honey from local bees in shops and greengrocers if you ask or Google locally produced honey. You'll be amazed how many apiaries there are in your area.

Chemical cocktails

If you're worried about the impact of chemicals in food—as all food is absorbed through the digestive system into the blood stream—keeping a detailed food diary is a great way to measure the impact of foods on moods.

Autistic and ADHD children are sensitive to the additives in food and drink too. A food diary can help you isolate what food or drink may be causing the problem. If you see a pattern emerging, the advice is to eliminate that food or drink for a while and monitor what happens when you re-introduce it. This sort of testing should be done under the supervision of a doctor or nutritionist.

Take your food diary with you to appointments to make sure you include detailed information about your child's eating and drinking, such as what time of day, whether they have taken their medication, if they were sick, had an upset tummy etc. And if they had chicken, state whether it was in a sauce or if it was breaded as this detail helps to drill into ingredient detail. Make a note of how much they ate and record everything.

If your child has a severe reaction to something they have eaten you may be referred for an NHS allergy test by a specialist. If your child is already on medication, keeping a food diary is even more important, especially if they have lost weight or you are trying to get their medication dosage right. If you're worried, see your doctor.

Take nothing for granted, challenge and question everything. Due to the changes in global dietary consumption, I wonder whether our environment changed faster than our bodies and our genes could keep up with? Whilst the causes of neurological conditions are hotly debated, we have a golden opportunity to embrace food as a healing force for our neurodiverse children.

Feeding a good night's sleep

Lucas, like many autistic youngsters, had difficulty sleeping. I wasn't sure about Lucas taking medication (melatonin) but was considering it when he was getting about 4 hours a night.

Our local pharmacist explained that a sweet biscuit and a milky drink does the trick before bed, because the body goes into crash mode after the initial sugar spike, making them feel sleepy.

Drinking a glass of warm almond milk before bedtime is also beneficial. It contains calcium, which helps the brain produce melatonin and magnesium, which is important for sleep regulation. Sticking to this routine and making a rule of no screens at least 2 hours before bed did the trick. At least until he reached his teens.

Taking prescription medicine to improve focus and concentration can work against drugs prescribed for anxiety. We managed on milk and biscuits and some very late nights.

Lessons Learned

- Learning the basics of nutrition, especially which minerals and vitamins enhance good brain function, concentration, calmness and sleep, is a powerful way to support your child and advocate for their needs.

- Creating a manageable exercise programme will support your work around nutrition, ensuring your child's body is well oxygenated and flexible.

- Regular exercise doesn't need to be team-based. A brisk 30-minute dog walk counts. Any regular exercise will help your child's co-ordination, gross and fine-motor skills and build their confidence. Exercise will discharge your child's energy, helping to reduce stress or anxiety.

- If you do your research, have good advice and are patient, there are many positives of ADHD medications that help our children to function well in a world that can victimise and demonise them.

CHAPTER 13

The (Right) Secondary School Zone Choices, Decisions And Motivations

Time to move on

Lucas's behaviour improved rapidly towards the end of Year 6. After the emotional rollercoaster of the autism diagnosis at his fourth Primary School it was time to move on. He wasn't one of the little ones anymore.

Some teachers demonstrated extraordinary skill and compassion towards him. His mood swings and volatility were under control and finally he was enjoying school. We were grateful for the school's support but were itching to start afresh in his new Secondary School, and carve out a new identity for him, unstained by his volatile school history.

It was a relief to have an official assessment 3 years into his EHCP that spelled out his diagnosis and outlined areas where he needed specialist support. Now all we had to do was find a good Secondary School.

I was worried that his behaviour history would cast a shadow over his future school. Reading through his plan made my toes curl. On paper, Lucas sounded explosive and unpredictable, with a strong focus on his negative behaviour. It was time to launch Operation Secondary School!

The Local Authority was angling to reduce the amount of in class support Lucas was receiving but the Junior School flagged this as a risk, especially as there were changes ahead. The Local Authority agreed to stick to the same support package until his next Annual Review, which would be once he was in Secondary School.

Lucas hadn't made masses of friends in the Junior School but leaving the few friends he had, was still very sad. Saying goodbye to friends is a big deal when you're 11 years old. Emotions were running high at the Year 6 Leavers' Assembly and I wasn't the only mum to shed a tear when they played the video of Wiz Khalifa's *See You Again* over a slideshow of the kids looking baby-faced in Year 2. A few of the teachers were openly crying.

Different types of school

Major life transitions are hard. I was touched to see the teaching team making an effort to make the Year 6 to Secondary transition successful, especially for the children with additional needs. But issues were already brewing.

Some of the autism parents were suggesting the best option for their kids was one of the specialist schools. Others were betting their money that only the independent sector would deliver. The decision-process was heavy, we were floating somewhere in the middle. The options felt narrow. How do you know which schools are best equipped to support children with SEN either in terms of budget, staffing or culturally?

Children with ASD and ADHD have difficulties with

executive functioning, affecting their organising ability, memory, forward planning, information processing. For some parents, any teaching support is gratefully received.

Intellectually-able children appear to have an advantage over neurotypical children if they have support in the classroom but in reality, they are disadvantaged by emotional, sensory or behavioural impulses, which can impair their learning.

Good SEN support can raise standards for the whole school and there are options. For example, the separate and together (autism unit model) - teaching SEN children in a mainstream school in a calming, neurodiverse friendly environment, e.g. a classroom library or another quiet low-sensory space where they can work independently or with the teacher support or learning aids they need. Away from the busy classroom, they are less likely to experience the bullying behaviour of their peers for being different.

If they feel overwhelmed or anxious, they won't disrupt the learning of the whole class, which is better than being taught in corridors or excluded. Children have the option to learn in the mainstream classroom, where they're supported or they have the option to learn in the 'unit.' This can be arranged according to the lesson type and opinions of the class teacher and support team.

We can upgrade this model by ensuring that all teachers in spaces such as this are fully SEN trained which enables them to teach to a range of learning styles, cognitive ability and neurodiversity. The negative to avoid in this model is to make sure pupils who are educated in another physical location, even within a mainstream setting, are actively integrated into the school's social and academic structures.

There's also the option of a flexible or reduced curriculum, whereby students opt out of specific lessons or even drop subjects early to focus on their stronger subject areas. This may help them avoid the catastrophic thinking, anxiety, obsessive, compulsive traits that may otherwise hamper them.

I've spoken to parents whose children with ADHD are educated in special schools. In most cases, it was the parents' choice to opt for specialist education, having experienced difficult experiences in mainstream schools.

It's a complex decision and we don't always get it right the first time. The most important point is whether your child will be happy in school and feel safe? If these basic needs are met, the rest will follow.

What type of school is 'best' for your SEN child?
There's no easy answer to that question. Many try the 'suck it and see' technique, especially if you are in dispute with the council about funding the place for your preferred school.

A school can look great on paper, fantastic when you get there and the staff are brilliant and friendly, then the headteacher changes and the same school goes down the pan. There's not much you can do about this, even if you did your research.

Mainstream school
This could be an academy. The level of SEN support your child will get is outlined in your child's EHCP. It's during the day only. Depending on where you child is on the spectrum and the skill of the teaching and support team, your child can do well in a mainstream school with SEN support.

Independent mainstream school

This can be day or residential. If you want your child to go to an independent mainstream school which is funded by a Local Authority, you need to have an EHCP. If you have one the LA will agree to name and pay for that school on the child or young person's plan. Usually you need to prove that only the school in question can meet your child's needs and that it would not be an unreasonable public expenditure.

Independent special school

This can be day or residential. Under the Children and Families Act 2014, an independent special school is organised to make Special Educational Provision (SEP) for students with Special Educational Needs.

Mainstream school with specialist unit

This is day-only for SEN support or EHCP covered by the Local Authority. It does depend on whether the unit is autism only or is a mixed SEN community, as well as the skills of the staff and how well the unit is integrated into the whole school community. See if you can check it out and speak to the children there.

Home school

Home schooling can be done individually or in partnership with a group of parents. If you've elected to home school, you may have selected a range of home tutors, clubs and activities for your child in place of the school day.

If your child is being home schooled in a centre you will need to check that they are properly regulated, insured and the staff are vetted etc. Home schooled children are not usually on any school or college roll, but you can opt for part of their education to be in school (flexi-schooling) (14).

Home schooling does not require parents to have a timetable or set hours. You're in charge and you decide how much or how little your child does. However, there are guidelines about what education is age appropriate and suitable.

If you are removing your child from a special school arranged by the council, you need permission from the council before removing them from the register. Every Local Authority has its own policy on home schooling (when you've chosen this, not when they've been excluded) so you should check this to see what the procedures are, especially if your child is also under social services or has an EHCP. The IPSEA website is helpful too.

Free schools
Both academies and free schools are funded by central government and free from Local Authority control (hence the name). While free schools are normally brand-new institutions set up by organisations, academies are usually created by converting existing schools run by Local Authorities. Check on the academy or Free school website.

Get a feel for the culture of the school. Many academies are run on a business-like structure and the headteacher has authority on SEN budgets and exclusions, so do your research. The success of any of these educational settings depends on a number of factors:

- How far along the EHCP assessment process you are.

- Whether your child has a diagnosis of SEN and what it is.
- Whether your child has an ECHP or SEN support.
- How much the Local Authority is willing to spend to support your child's education.
- Whether the school of your choice is in or out of borough (councils prefer children with S.E.N.D. to stay in borough).
- Whether the school of your choice is special or residential (2 of the most expensive options).
- Whether your child will need transport to the named school.

Alternative provision

Alternative provision (AP) is education outside of school for children who cannot attend a mainstream school either for health needs, behaviour issues, exclusions, school refusal, or short or long-term illness.

AP includes settings such as Pupil Referral Units (PRUs), although some pupils who attend a PRU will also attend other forms of alternative provision.

If a child has been permanently excluded, the Local Authority will arrange for them to receive education somewhere other than at school, until they are put on roll at another school. Schools and PRUs can use a range of alternative provision to prevent students from being continuously excluded or to encourage students to re-engage in their education.

Journalist Megan Agnew summed up the current situation well, 'The Alternative Provision System may be inconsistent but one thing is clear, the number of children in this system is rising. There's an average of 42 children excluded from school every day in the UK, an increase of 59% from 2013-14 to 2017-18. You are more likely to be permanently excluded if you are a boy, if you are Black or if you qualify for free school meals.'

Pupil Referral Units

PRUs are schools that cater for children who aren't able to attend a mainstream school. Pupils are referred to a PRU if they need greater care and support than their school can provide. These children might be:

- Permanently excluded from their mainstream school for behavioural reasons or at risk of permanent exclusion.
- Experiencing emotional or behavioural difficulties, including problems with anger, mental health issues, and school phobia/refusal.
- Experiencing severe bullying behaviour.
- Diagnosed with SEN or in the process of getting a diagnosis and unable to cope with mainstream environment without the right support.
- Suffering from a short or long-term illness that makes mainstream school unsuitable.
- A new starter who missed out on a school place.
- Pregnant or young mothers.

Some pupils will have all their lessons at a PRU, while others split their time between the mainstream school where they're registered and a PRU.

PRUs are not special schools. Pupils with more severe special educational needs or disabilities should not be sent to a PRU as a long-term solution.

PRUs don't have to teach the full National Curriculum, but they should aim to provide a broad and balanced education that covers as much of the mainstream curriculum as possible. They should prioritise teaching English, maths, science, computing, and personal, social and health education (PSHE).

Grammar schools

If you're considering a grammar school for your child with behaviour challenges due to autism or ADHD, you need to be aware of the following:

- Grammar schools were traditionally created to cream off the brightest academic talent. Your child will need to pass an entrance test before they are offered a place. If your child meets the benchmark grade and is offered a place, it is at this stage that the school will negotiate with your Local Authority for a support package. Check with the school directly and speak to the SENCO to get a feel for their approach to pastoral support.

- Centres like Kip McGrath (a group of independent learning centres) are set up with the sole aim of helping kids to pass the 11+ and 13+ verbal and non-verbal reasoning selective school tests. Grammar schools are still popular with parents because they offer high quality traditional education at no cost. They are not independent. They are paid for by the state.

- Grammar schools have been a political hot topic for years. Some feel that the school premises are old and crying out for investment. This can make a grammar school a politically sensitive choice. Before you invest your money in π+ cramming, have a look at the schools, meet the teachers, and speak to the SENCO or person in charge of additional needs. Like any educational establishment, they have strengths and their own way of doing things. Some are excellent at accommodating children with autism and other additional needs. If your child has a history of autism/ADHD-related challenging behaviour, ask them directly about their behaviour policy. Some schools are used to making adaptations, even if their dominant teaching styles are traditional and rigid. If you've passed the entrance test, find out before you accept a place.

Lucas sat the entrance test for a popular grammar school in London. I mistakenly thought that children with ECHPs were automatically admitted to selective grammar schools. Wrong!

The entry requirement rests on the test, whether or not they have an EHCP. Cream rises, the saying goes, and so do the marks required to enter these esteemed places of learning.

I sat him for the test anyway and to his credit, he did well, but was still about 20 points off an offer of a place. He went on the waiting list. It was stressful not knowing where he would go. In the end I decided to turn our focus elsewhere.

Managing your child's uncertainly around this key transition is vital and that means managing your own.

State boarding schools
According to the State Boarding Schools Association (SBSA),

'Schools provide high quality boarding at the lowest possible cost. You pay only the cost of boarding as the education at SBSA schools is free. This means that rather than paying £25,000+ a year for an independent boarding school, you would probably be paying less than £10,000 a year at a state boarding school.'

So, state boarding school does not mean it's completely free. They are an unusual hybrid. They can have specific entry criteria and they're neither private nor free.

The school day is usually from 8am to 3pm and is paid for by the state. The boarding element—after school hours—is paid by the family.

If a child with an EHCP attends a state boarding school, additional learning support will usually be provided within the school part of the arrangement. I suggest you go through your child's EHCP to make sure you're clear about the support level during the school day and after school, during the boarding time, and be quite clear about what you will need to find the money for.

If your child needs support to take part in after-school activities, you may need to pay for these separately. State boarding schools are innovative and constantly reviewing their financing models so it's worth checking with each school and website individually.

Assessment and Treatment Unit
You may have read the distressing stories in the news about autistic, Pathological Demand Avoidance (PDA) or young people with complex mental health issues, who were locked in treatment centres, sometimes against their or their parents' will.

These are places where children and young people are

retained and 'treated'. In many cases the treatment makes the child more distressed.

This is at the darker end of being a parent with an autistic/ADHD or complex needs young person. The extreme behaviours are difficult to manage, but there are usually strategies that, if applied consistently with the consent of the child where possible and their carers, which can improve quality of life.

Thankfully, there are many organisations lobbying the government and Local Authorities to change the alleged failures of care in these institutions. Most worrying is that many of these young people were admitted for short-term/respite or investigation and have ended up being away from their families for years, often with limited contact. We need to all do our part to ensure children with high needs are cared for by trained staff in settings that provide humane, compassionate care in compliance with the law.

Our experience of the Secondary School process

Within days our named school had written to me requesting to interview Lucas regarding his place. I was furious. Our Local Authority had named a school that wasn't suitable for him but had shown little regard for the detailed notes in his EHCP about the sort of placement that would meet his needs.

The SENCO either didn't understand Lucas's intellectual learning profile or didn't understand that children with autism don't automatically have a learning disability.

Many children with ASD are not impaired in the classroom because of their intellectual ability. It is the classroom environment itself that presents the challenge. Thousands of children are out of school not because they cannot learn but because the schools cannot effectively manage their behaviours. What a waste of talent!

The requirement for an alternative learning setting is not an indicator of intellectual ability.

Root causes of classroom behaviour must be investigated, especially as neurodiverse students are easily missed. Punishing their behaviour or removing them from the class without understanding the cause is discriminatory.

In 2018, in a school exclusion case, a court made clear for the first time that all schools must make sure they have made appropriate adjustments for autistic children, or those with other disabilities, before they resort to exclusion.

Lucas sailed his overnight boarding test at Reading School, one of the state boarding schools we entered him for. Considering he had difficulties making friends at school, the boarding school experience was surprisingly successful. We picked him up after an overnight stay and he was beaming alongside a group of equally smiling boys.

We also investigated the stunning Christ's Hospital School, which has historic connections with Lucas's Junior School. Visiting Christ's Hospital was like being on a film set. The Open Morning was divine, complete with homemade biscuits to slosh in your tea! The boys were beautifully behaved and genuinely proud of their historic uniform. Listening to the marching band playing as you entered the dining hall daily at noon was a highlight which felt as traditional as if time itself had stopped.

People have mixed feelings about boarding schools. I went to one as a young child, and my experiences were wholly, mystically positive. I missed home, but my mum was a single parent building a teaching career, so the routine and security of my friends at boarding school provided me with comfort and stability.

I wrote to the Local Authority to ask how Lucas's level of support would work at a state funded boarding school. I also asked the question in a session with Dr Pam, the psychiatrist who was assessing Lucas. She told me she didn't think it would be the right environment for Lucas based on what she knew about his ASD and ADHD diagnosis.

By the end of term, Lucas sat 4 Secondary tests in total: the Grammar School, St. Andrews, Reading School and Christ's Hospital. Surely, we would snag a place at place at one of them? We still had a place at the academy, which wasn't a good fit for Lucas.

Things were starting to calm down 3 years after Lucas's diagnosis so I felt strong approaching Secondary School with that clear diagnosis. All we had to do now was face down the gap between the known and the unknown.

Lucas got respectable results in 4 of the selective tests he sat, but sadly he was not selected to go through to the second stages for any of them. He did pass the St. Andrews test with 58%. His non-verbal reasoning score at III was higher than the 100 average, but his score in the English paper was 30%—a fail. It wasn't really a failure considering how far he'd come and how much catching up he'd done, but nevertheless, his place at St. Andrew's was in jeopardy. I didn't know it at the time, but it wasn't only his English test result threatening his place there.

The Junior School had sent a confidential headteacher's report to Christ's Hospital and St. Andrews, neither of which

I had seen, that detailed to their admissions officers there had been significant meetings with parents and that there were lesser behavioural concerns. An Individual Education Plan (IEP) was in place.

An IEP is different to an ECHP as it is funded directly from the school budget. It is routine for Secondary and Primary School headteachers to share information about pupils, but this felt like a betrayal, placing a marker against Lucas's application. Similar paperwork must have crossed between the Junior School and St. Andrew's too. I didn't know about any of this.

In line with General Data Protection Legislation 2018 (GDPR), parents of a child who attends a maintained school have an independent right of access to their child's educational records (Information Commissioner's Office). There is no equivalent legal right to access your child's information if they attend an academy, free school or an independent school.

You can make a subject access request (SAR) which is simply a written request made by or on behalf of an individual for the information which he or she is entitled to ask for under Section 7 of the Data Protection Act 1998 (DPA). The request does not have to be in any particular form. (Information Commissioner's Office).

The most important determiner of the success of your school is based not only on how well they meet your child's needs but also on aspects more difficult to measure, such as the culture of the school, the leadership style or personality of the head, the relationship between your child, and key staff.

I lost myself in Harry Potter-esque fantasies about Lucas going to Christ's Hospital or Reading School but the Local Authority had other ideas.

When we were waiting for Lucas's test results, the Local Authority smashed any dreams I had by naming the unit at the local academy on his plan without my consent. My daughter and I had already done a walk-around of the unit, observed a lesson and agreed it wasn't right for Lucas. Even the head of the unit agreed. I expressed my concerns to the SENCO about the unit's suitability.

It seemed like the negative aspects of Lucas's autism/ADHD personality were too dominant in all of the Secondary School processes and certainly on his EHCP paperwork. Schools get nervous about children with 2 Bs pinned to them: budget and behaviour.

Reading School, Christ's Hospital and the grammar school were out of reach based on results. I'd set my heart on St. Andrews, a local independent school, because of their ethos of raising boys to be men and their good record on pastoral care.

Lucas didn't interview well for St. Andrews. He was quiet. The English result was difficult to talk around and he wasn't sporty. When the rejection letter plopped through the letterbox the next day, I really cried. I had let him down. The only school option left seemed to be the unit in the academy. In my heart I knew that if he wasn't sufficiently stimulated his behaviour would deteriorate. I swung into action. I wrote a letter to the headteacher of St. Andrews.

Excerpt of my letter to the headteacher, St. Andrews:

31st January
'I do not believe that our local LA provision is right for an intelligent child like Lucas. His talents would flourish in an environment like St. Andrews. When I met your admissions

officer last year and explained Lucas's needs, he provided a reassuring account of how the school supports children like Lucas. The stable presence of a single class-teacher throughout the boys' time at St. Andrews is fundamental to this process. My case officer confirms that your school does support boys with Asperger's. I'm not sure how much liaison there has been between Lucas's current school and your SENCO?

Lucas can operate successfully in a mainstream school with a focus on academics as well as a full range of extra-curricular activities. He responds well to a secure and predictable environment and likes to challenge himself. I am particularly keen on single sex education with a male headmaster, and a single class teacher throughout his education. I am at a loss to see where else he could find this without going too far afield. If you were in a position to reconsider your decision, I hope you would not consider this too impertinent a request?'

I also opened up an email dialogue to the (new) SENCO of the Junior School. I sent her a list of specific questions and concerns:

'I haven't seen Lucas's amended statement. Have the LA sent you a copy? Did it go to St. Andrews? Did St. Andrews request a report from the school? I really wanted Lucas to go to St. Andrews because it's non-selective school and they have a good record of supporting children with Asperger's and ASD. My caseworker has left the council and the current 'support' worker has been beyond incompetent. I no longer wish Lucas to be 'labelled' as a child who needs a statement. And I do not wish his statement to refer to historical issues, as now with diagnosis and better management, the situation has improved immeasurably. Will you be contacting the LA about this? I do not wish Lucas to be inside at playtime, so automatically there is a reduction in the number of hours' support he needs. I'm keen to address this urgently.

Lucas's behaviour has improved for a while now, as his behaviour issues were only at school. He's an easy target as he's a sensitive boy. I'm pleased to hear the behaviour plan is being revised.

N.B. A child with Asperger's-ADHD will not behave neurotypically. He will not 'remember to ask for help if he thinks he needs it.' His brain doesn't work that way! He will simmer and think about how rubbish he is, get frustrated with himself and distract himself (or others) from the fact that he can't understand something. I mistakenly thought LSAs were able to teach children and step in proactively to help with learning difficulties in this way, rather than mainly fulfil a behaviour management role?

I'm currently sending emails to a range of prep and independent schools, some local and some further afield. We are way past their entry deadlines and will probably need to wait until offers have gone out before we find out if there are any places. Beyond stressful. I await meeting dates and will work flexibly with you, so we can meet when you are in. Really appreciate your continued support.'

She replied:
'We have discussed supporting Lucas's independence and the development of his self-esteem and confidence. He is being reminded to ask for help if he thinks he needs it. Practice

within the classroom has changed with regard to the amount of time Lucas spends working independently, but we will definitely look at this again.'

I was in a whirlwind of anxiety about Lucas' Secondary School, and tried to analyse the reason for Lucas's St. Andrew's rejection.

Letter to Junior School SENCO, February 2015:
'Could you update me on the issue I raised at the beginning of term regarding Lucas's LSA? He is unhappy with the current situation; it feels like he is being 'policed' rather than educated. After many years of playing inside to avoid playground incidents, he now spends most of his time inside even on sunny days.

One of his past goals was to increase his unsupervised social playtime and develop personal responsibility, both of which are required for successful transition to Secondary School. His 'outbursts' are reduced and I feel he is maturing and improving his self-regulation. Can we reflect his growing maturity with the LSAs including how he spends lunch and break times? I'd like his LSA hours to be reduced ASAP.

It seems like he's haunted by his past at this school; he told me Stephan's mum told him not to play with Lucas as he's not an 'appropriate' friend. That wasn't an easy conversation to have.'

A few days later I received a reply:
'Dear Suzy, thank you for your emails today and over the weekend. I can understand how disappointing the St Andrew's result is for Lucas and for you. I can also see how concerned

you are about the issues you have raised. Please be assured that we will consider and address all of these. As you know, based on his amended statement, Lucas has recently revised targets, specifically to address social, emotional and academic targets. Perhaps we can meet at parents evening to discuss these issues further?'

What if you don't get the school you want?

Writing letters can help, but in most cases you might get a reply with a standard letter or an invitation to go on a waiting list. It depends why you didn't get the place. If it's a selective school and your child passes the test, it could be that they're oversubscribed. Here are some suggestions:

- Contact the school and ask for your child's name to go on the waiting list. Ask what number they are on the list. Most admissions officers will tell you. Ask how many children were offered places off the waiting list last year.
- Consider other schools that have vacancies. If your child goes somewhere else for a year, it is better than them being out of school. You may find you like the new place and want to stay.
- Consider appealing for a place. I appealed for a Secondary School place for my daughter at the only over-subscribed girls' secondary state school in the borough and she was offered a place. Prepare well for the admissions panel. Do your research. You have nothing to lose. If you appeal for a nursery place, it may be more difficult to secure a place as each class is only legally supposed to have 30 children per teacher.

- School admissions are a bit like university clearing. Even if you get a 'no' at first, things change, people move to a new house before the start of term, so occasionally places do pop up.

I held open Lucas's Secondary place at the academy unit, I didn't have a choice as we still didn't have place a Secondary School place. I knew I could decline the offer later on, but I couldn't throw away all of our options.

Nothing beats visiting a school, looking into the eyes of the kids and the teachers. Do the children look bright-eyed? Are they smiling? Focused? Is the receptionist happy? What do the expressions on staff faces tell you?

Some schools live their values, while others put on a shiny façade but when you run into difficulties they stand back and scratch their heads, asking you if there are problems at home!

None of us know what we're getting into in a new school. It's a bit like taking a job offer. It can look great on paper and in the interview, but they don't let on that the person sitting opposite you, who's been at the company for 17 years is a tyrant!

A private assessment
A couple of days passed as I waited to hear from St. Andrews. I considered getting an independent assessment for Lucas. I needed to understand how his autism and ADHD were affecting his learning.

I researched and found a Child Educational Psychologist on LinkedIn. After checking he was fully qualified, I booked an appointment online and followed up with an email—all within 48 hours. I got an appointment costing £400, which lasted for nearly 4 hours and comprised a series of written and verbal tests. This is a sample of his report:

Abilities:
Lucas is of good average ability (above that of 73% of individuals of this age).

Pattern of relative strengths and weaknesses:
Lucas has cognitive strengths in:
- Verbal comprehension and reasoning (above 75%).
- Perceptual reasoning (above 84%).
- Lucas has cognitive weakness in:
- Short-term auditory-verbal memory (above 27%).

Attainments:
Lucas's single word reading (86th centile), spelling (92nd centile), reading comprehension (87th centile) and numeracy skills (79th centile) are commensurate with his age and ability. His reading speed is better than 45% of his same age peers.

Report conclusions:
Lucas's educational needs should be met within the context of the mainstream national curriculum. Lucas would benefit from an academically demanding curriculum and his needs at Secondary level should be explored early, to ensure that he receives the best provision.
It was encouraging to get this detailed read out and gave me the confidence to continue to seek the most appropriate Secondary School based on his needs.

The following day, I got the call I had been waiting for from St. Andrews. The headteacher had carefully read my letter and decided to change his mind and offer Lucas a place! The offer was made on the condition that Lucas read more books during the summer holiday to improve his comprehension skills. I did a jig on the spot in the supermarket aisle whilst trying not to worry about how the hell I was going to pay for this. Focusing on the positive, I was excited that attention was shifting from his neurodiversity to his potential ability. Hurrah for that! The bright lights of opportunity beckoned.

Managing the transition from Primary to Secondary
Whether your child is moving to a Secondary School where his friends will be going, or to a completely new setting, the transition will be stressful. I found a brilliant tool which covers the key transfers right the way from Early Years placement to Primary School, through to Secondary School. It was a Transition Toolkit produced by the Autism Education Trust. One of the key messages in this booklet was that change—for children who don't like change—creates a high level of anxiety.

Here's my summary for a transition:

- Aged 11 peer groups are important, but your child will make new friends.
- If you've chosen a fee-paying school, even if it meets all of your child's academic and pastoral needs, have you considered how you would manage if you lost your income?
- If you've opted for a religious school and you're not religious, how do you feel about your child having to

attend religious services? Say prayers? Fundraise for a cause you may not fully believe in?

- A school's OFSTED is not fixed and can change rapidly for the worse, if key members of the management team, especially a headteacher leaves. Mumsnet or other parent reviews/community forums can provide helpful information before you make your commitment. Always make your own visits and assessments.

- If a school doesn't work out for you in the first year or so, it's not the end of the world. Finding a space in Year 8 is usually much easier than finding a space in Year 7.

- If you don't get the school of your choice, particularly in Secondary School, you can appeal. You can't appeal on the basis that another school (your first choice) is better, because everyone wants their child to go to the best school. However, if there is evidence to support the case that your child would be better suited due to pastoral, health or emotional wellbeing reasons, then it's worth preparing an appeal. Evidence needs to be strong, recent and usually written by a professional (health, social worker, SENCO or educational psychologist) to carry much weight.

- If a school is a Beacon School, excelling in sport, science or the arts for example, and your child shows talent in these areas, check it out, even if their academics aren't as strong as others. Some children show clear focus and desire for a profession, sport or industry even at a young age. Play to their strengths!

- If your child is in the middle of an assessment for an EHCP, see if you can get the paperwork completed in time to include with your school application forms. The deadlines for Primary or Secondary School entry will be on your Local Authority website.

- Start looking for your child's next school early. If they've had a tricky time settling at their current school, you want to avoid a repeat. Keep a record of the schools you've contacted, how they answer the phone, whether you were invited to look around, and how willing they were to discuss your child and address your concerns.

- R-e-l-a-x. Your child will end up in life where they are meant to be. If things go seriously wrong and you get the vibe that a potential school isn't willing or able to support your child in a positive and consistent way, start looking around. It's not advisable to remove your child from a school when you haven't secured a space in another one—more detail about this later but sometimes you have no choice. If things aren't at crisis point, keep your child in school until you've got them on roll in another one.

Coping with a difficult transition

Lucas started St. Andrews in September with a too-big blazer and an alarmingly mature attitude. My late mother's inheritance would cover the fees for 3 years. Things started off well. That should have been the end of this book, but I wouldn't want to cheat you of a dramatic ending!

When Lucas stepped onto the Secondary School playground, he hadn't fully resolved the problems of unpredictable moods and meltdowns due to unsatisfactory interactions with other pupils.

Looking back, there were many unresolved issues with Lucas. In practical terms the transition was easy; he woke up at 6.30am every day to get the school bus and settled down to do his homework in the evenings without being asked.

But the lack of friendships caused things to derail for Lucas. His desire to fit in, but not knowing how to do it in a neurotypical way, caused problems in the classroom and the playground. His peers were rambunctious, always jostling for top dog position.

It began with an iPhone 5, a much longed-for Christmas present. But it wasn't the latest model and the teasing was vile. After a violent temper tantrum on a tennis court, Lucas smashed his precious new phone to pieces, stamping on it and really losing the plot.

On a school trip, a group of boys, including Lucas, were ganging up on another little boy and teasing him. The taunting reached a tipping point when Lucas, after being egged on by his classmates, punched the boy in the face resulting in a nosebleed.

We'd encountered this scenario many times when Lucas was punished for kicking or hitting another child but after further digging, someone had usually put him up to it. Laughing peers would stand by and watch a weak child inflict pain on a weaker one. Anthropologists would put it down to 'pack' behaviour.

It was baffling that the teachers rarely seemed to capture the whole picture or least punish the whole group. It sounded like something out of Lord of the Flies.

Later, when my partner (who had recently become my fiancé) and I challenged Lucas about what happened and why, he tearfully said that other boys were also laying into the child, but they scarpered when the teacher came, literally leaving him at the scene with blood on his hands. I asked him why he'd done it, he said they were egging him on and told him to do it. When pushed, he simply said he wanted them to like him.

Lucas was less in control of his emotions than he was at Primary School. He was so eager to make friends that he was hurting other children to earn his stripes. His testosterone levels may have risen but Lucas looked lost and struggling to find outlets for his hormonal and ADHD energy.

After an uncomfortable meeting with the head of the lower school, it was clear that the school saw a crisis on the horizon and had to intervene to stop the blooded-nose boy's parents from calling the police. We never verified the claim that the other family was threatening to call the police, and the school didn't say whether the rest of the group who attacked the boy would be punished.

In response to this incident and on the advice of the head of lower school, Lucas was excluded from school for a week. On the way home I was thinking that this was worse than Primary School. Prickles of fear ran over me.

An interim annual review meeting was called to discuss how things were going. We filled in the parent section saying how unsettled Lucas was at school, even with an LSA to help him navigate the school day. He wasn't making any real friendships and was becoming withdrawn. Interestingly Lucas's comments on the form were determinedly optimistic: 'My year was pretty bad. There hasn't been a term when I didn't get a red card. My favourite subjects are English and Latin. I've made a couple of new friends and I'll build them outside school. I enjoy tennis, and go to maths clinic. I have got a lot of merits. I also get good grades.'

In spite of the difficult situation we found ourselves in, Lucas demonstrated a level of self-awareness at his review meeting, but it was clear he was still struggling.

He showed remorse about his failure to manage his moods better and knew that he wasn't always able to meet his teachers' expectations. Even with a diagnosis, and my original belief that St. Andrews was the right Secondary School for him, the transition was tough.

The pastoral care didn't seem to extend beyond the SENCO's office. They understood how to manage Lucas in the classroom. If a lesson was tricky they would go for a walk on the field, get some air and review their strategy together. But without the LSA in the classroom, all attempts to self-regulate were not successful.

Once Lucas got into the classroom, he was in the lion's den. Support plans were being swiftly re-drafted, reviewed, and metaphorically torn up each day in an effort to manage his behaviour. He was popular in class but for all of the wrong reasons. He was morphing back into the class clown, the one who would call out, make a funny comment or a rude joke on the command of his 'friends.'

In spite of full disclosure about his autism, many of the class teachers were punishing his autistic traits with red cards and dealing with his genuine neurological condition as if it were a discipline issue. This is a common complaint from ADHD/autism parents.

Lucas was repeatedly and consistently punished for his behaviour if it didn't stay within the class teacher's behavioural norms. There were weekend detentions. Yes, you read that right.

The amount of time the SENCOs were able to provide

support in lessons seemed to be deliberately opaque. I knew they were supporting other boys and I suspected his LSA time was being split between a number of other children, which happens a lot in schools.

Getting support packages, especially those with LSA time are hotly fought. School funding is fiendishly difficult to unpick, and schools are rarely transparent about how your proportion of that allowance is allocated. The hard work of the last few years seemed to be draining away. Taking himself outside of the classroom for time out was not working. Lucas's personality was changing. He was becoming tense, irritable, and sometimes tearful.

One evening, my fiancé and I asked him to tell us what was going on at school. Eventually he confessed that there was a group of boys who were winding him up in class. He knew that what they were telling him to do was wrong and he'd get into trouble, but the temptation to provide them with enormous fun in return for 'friendship' was irresistible.

I called the SENCOs and they hinted that one of the teachers had noticed something was going on, but she was reluctant to tell me what. The head of lower school had organised a class meeting, without Lucas, where he informed the whole class about Lucas's autism and why it was important not to wind him up.

I don't know how the meeting went or exactly what was said. It was nearly the end of the first academic year in Year 7 at St. Andrew's and red card frenzy continued.

Lucas was keeping on top of his schoolwork, but the classroom dynamics were collapsing around him like dominos. The SENCO and the TAs were helpful, but it seemed like the information about how to support and get the best out of Lucas in lessons, didn't extend beyond the SENCO's office. Most of the teaching team only seemed to have punishment in their behaviour management tool in the toolkit.

Another move
One Friday afternoon, on a particularly busy day at work, I got a call inviting me to come into school to discuss an urgent issue with the head of Lower School and his superior. I assumed they were planning another weekend detention. I wearily called home. We were fed up of being summoned to school meetings and treated like we were criminals—or worse—bad parents.

We decided on the spot we wanted to temporarily remove Lucas from St. Andrews to give us time to review our options. I called my Local Authority to speak to my case worker only to discover he had left the council a few weeks before our situation blew up. I was told there was no-one available to take on his case work. I didn't know who to turn to. The team in children's services were overloaded and rarely returned my calls.

I get that it's more work for teachers to tackle the causes of complex neurodiverse behaviour, or bullying behaviour, but skirting around these issues by excluding children and pinning the responsibility on the children themselves, or their parents, creates deeper damage that emerges at some point in the future.

By not dealing comprehensively with neurodiversity in schools, we are making it easier for young adults with difference to be bullied at work, in daily life, and less likely to be able to thrive as adults.

As Tony Attwood describes so sharply in his book, The

Complete Guide to Asperger's Syndrome, 'Because such children are often socially naïve, trusting and eager to be part of a group, they are able to be 'set up' by other children. Another act of bullying is too torment the child with Asperger's Syndrome (ensuring the teacher does not detect the provocation) and enjoy the benefits of the child's reaction.'

Things went downhill fast. The school commissioned an Independent Educational Psychologist to observe Lucas in lessons. A week or so after Lucas's suspension, we attended a meeting to discuss the EP's report with the SENCO, the TA and the EP.

Lucas's class teacher and the head of Lower School didn't attend the meeting. Their absence spoke volumes. The head of Lower School opted to speak to the EP separately, out of my earshot. He'd told her he was adamant that Lucas shouldn't get away with things and shouldn't be treated differently to the other kids. The walls were closing in.

Maybe Lucas was some sort of autism/ADHD educational anomaly. He had been examined and interviewed by so many professionals over the years. When I met the EP I immediately warmed to her. She summarised her report and relayed her observations. She said the school was struggling to cope. As compassionate as she was in her approach, I was aware that she was delivering difficult news.

Here's an extract from her full report:

'The physics classes take place in the lab where Lucas is usually seated in the front row and near his best friend at school. This was Lucas's first day back to school after a week away from school. In the first part of the lesson, Lucas was focused on his work and sat quietly, without getting particularly distracted. When he did get distracted by talking to one of his peers, he responded promptly to his teacher's reminder to stay on task. Towards the end of the lesson, Lucas became more fidgety and started throwing his pen up and down and although he did respond to his teacher's prompts, he got distracted shortly after and resumed his fidgeting. I observed Lucas during 2 lessons, during which Lucas showed restlessness, characterised by fidgeting, interrupting at times and chatting with peers. Whilst it is clear that these behaviours are disruptive for Lucas's teachers and peers in the context of a school with an ethos that promotes a highly disciplined environment, they were by no means extreme, defiant or aggressive. One of the reasons [for the school's lack of support for Lucas] is the lack of consistency between teaching, support and discipline strategies across individual lessons.'

Hearing that the school was struggling was a wakeup call. We had selected this school for their pastoral care, but it wasn't living up to its own hype.

The EP made excellent recommendations for the whole school to implement, but sadly, the school's leadership were reluctant to undertake the re-training required to make the school accessible for children like Lucas. She even suggested that the school invest in a programme of autism awareness and teacher training led by a specialist autism teacher. The more established teachers weren't buying it, especially as it would take about a year to roll out.

I was excited by the programme and could see it would benefit many other pupils but eventually she admitted that the senior leadership team were fundamentally resistant to introducing autism awareness training into the fabric of their school. They got stuck on the issue of having to treat him differently because of his autism. Lucas was facing yet another school move.

Exploring other options

I felt so uncomfortable stepping back through St. Andrews' school gates for a show-down meeting to discuss the next steps. It felt like an ending.

The atmosphere was strained as my by-then husband and I sat politely with the headteacher, several senior managers and the SENCO to discuss the events of the last year. To his total credit, the Head was extremely supportive and didn't immediately suggest that Lucas had to leave. He said it was our decision to make and we needed to think carefully, but he also couldn't guarantee that his teaching team could deliver what Lucas needed. Lucas would have to be the sacrificial lamb. My thoughts, not his words.

It was decision time. All of the professionals in the room stepped outside, allowing my husband and I a couple of minutes to make the inevitable decision to permanently withdraw Lucas from St. Andrews, even though we had no alternative school for him to go to. It was a huge risk, but we knew that as soon as we stopped battling with that school, our energies could go into finding him new school, dragging the Local Authority along with us.

We parted ways amicably, with a gracious apology from the headteacher for not being able to make it work for Lucas at his school. I thought about his original decision not to offer Lucas a place. Now we were leaving I could see it was the right decision.

We didn't find another school to go to or make contact with anyone from the LA. We were shattered from the events surrounding his move and both agreed that staying at that school was harming his mental health. When Lucas went back into school for the last time, to say goodbye to his friends and collect his belongings, he was greeted like a hero. I could almost hear them roar. I'm sure some parents felt the same about Lucas being in their child's class. I don't think they meant to make his life miserable, but he was an easy target.

Whilst he was saying goodbye, my husband and I chatted with SENCO and collected Lucas' bulging file.

Living in the space between schools
It was September, the first half term in Year 8. We had got married in the August and enjoyed a fabulously relaxing 'mini-moon' in Ibiza.

Just a few weeks into our marriage, we found ourselves in a maelstrom of meetings, assessments, doctor's appointments and white-knuckle ride stress with a teenager at home.

We had overcome tricky school situations in the past, but this was a new one. By the end of the process of finding a new Secondary School, Lucas had missed a whole academic year of school. If we had known at the beginning that he would be out of school for so long, we might have been a bit less chilled out, but the removal of the stress was a good thing.

We approached the problem as we had every other family challenge: by talking, sharing, researching online and working it through calmly and methodically.

As the Local Authority was going through its own transition and we still had no case officer, we decided to turn up the heat. We insisted on an emergency meeting with a senior member of the team and were appointed a new case officer at that meeting.

In view of the severity of our situation, the council suggested all of his assessments should be re-done to make sure the next school would really be able to meet his needs. And as law had changed, it was a good opportunity to update his paperwork from a statement to an EHCP.

He left St. Andrews in October and by Christmas he was starting to show signs of stress. He missed being at school and we were only in the early stages of re-assessment.

I threw myself into home school mode and created a timetable of subjects based around the National Curriculum, Key Stage 3. It worked at first, but it's hard to maintain that level when it's just the 2 of you around the kitchen table. We were both disorientated by not having the routine of school to hang our lives around. February was icy cold, but we made it to the Saatchi Gallery, somewhere we'd never been, and the change of scene did us both good.

I had resigned from my corporate job as I needed to focus all of my energy on finding a suitable new school. I partly blamed myself for getting the Secondary School decision wrong. Looking back, it's clear that even with full disclosure and a diagnosis, there are no guarantees that the school your child finds themselves in will be the right one. You need to continue to be flexible and prepare for some setbacks, but you also need to be realistic and make difficult decisions when things aren't working. I tried to stop blaming myself as I didn't want Lucas doing the same.

Our new case officer, Marcus, was engaged and up for the challenge of finding a new school for Lucas. Changing to an EHCP in line with the changes in legislation was a learning curve for all of us, but Marcus was clear that the council didn't want to open up discussions about a new school, until his assessments and EHCP were complete.

They wanted to be sure that the provision would support his needs and provide a clear and an updated profile of what his needs were.

The assessments were happening, but waiting lists for clinicians are long, and after the assessment, we needed to wait for the report to be written up and sent to the lead case officer at the Local Authority.

I had folders containing all the reports, letters and other documents from schools and clinics over the years. I could just about keep track of all his new and old paperwork. Doing any assessment is as much about looking backwards as it is moving forwards.

The weeks rolled into months, and as the spring flowers flourished, so did our boredom and frustration. I was struggling to keep home school going until a friend mentioned that the Local Authority has a duty to provide education if your child is out of school for various reasons.

As I hadn't elected or opted to home school Lucas, I was keen to take up any educational support that was offered.

After 5 months out of school we managed to secure Lucas a few hours one-to-one tuition in core subjects. He had a 2 hour maths session in the morning twice a week, an English session and a general knowledge session. The sessions took place in a youth centre, opposite a Sainsbury's local.

We were both craving an end to this educational no-man's land. We'd been thrown a rope. The tutors there were amazed that he turned up for every session. Many of the young people who find themselves out of school, for whatever reason, stop engaging with education entirely.

The migration from the statement to the EHCP took nearly 8 months. In comparison to some families, this was record time, but it was a long stretch. All we wanted to do was move forward with our lives.

Mantras

'We are all experts in life. Our own journey is unique and precious.'

'My honesty and openness in this situation will create healing.'

'I will take all of the advice given and ultimately trust my instincts with what is best for my child.'

'The diagnostic label is not who your child is. It is designed to describe their condition, not their personality.'

Lessons Learned

- If your child is out of school long-term due to issues around their Special Educational Need e.g. anxiety, depression, school refusal, bullying behaviour, your council has a duty to provide alternative educational provision for them. The Department for Education website has a document about the rules of Elective Home Education.

- Follow up with your council official. What they provide won't match a school day in terms of hours, but they should be able offer something. Keep on asking until you get something.

- The Gov.uk website provides information about alternative provision. There are documents setting out in law what Local Authorities and schools must do to comply with the law.

- Because needs assessments and EHCPs are difficult to obtain, many families find themselves at home with children who are out of school, because the school says they are unable to meet the child's needs.

- If you need to give up work or change your working hours to care for your child, research any financial support that may be available.

- The time delay of waiting for a school place can be stressful on families. Try to talk about the situation in a calm and open way. If you are worried about the situation, it's likely you will pass that anxiety onto your child.

- There are lots of places outside of the home that you can work with your child to avoid both of you getting cabin fever.

- Contact your local autism/ADHD charities and groups. You will find other parents whose kids are out of school. Support each other.

- Do whatever you need to do to spread the load and make the whole experience more manageable. It may be hard to believe but the situation will resolve itself in time.

CHAPTER 14

The New Beginnings Zone
A Fresh Start For Everyone

Finding what feels right

As we approach the end of this book, we entered the rocky terrain of applying for Secondary Schools. What follows next, time can only tell. Applying for a new school means we have to tell the story of our life all over again. We've got used to it.

Raising and educating a neurodiverse child is a team effort. As your young person gets older, they can become a key player in your team. As you start to listen to them, you will learn more about the person they are becoming. As the African proverb says, 'It takes a whole village to raise a child.' This is certainly true. We're playing a game of lucky dip and we're hoping to find the jackpot school but we won't know it's the right one until we've picked it... or they've picked us.

We visited lots of Secondary Schools ranging from mainstream special schools to a couple of local independent schools. My advice to anyone in this position is to visit as many as possible. We visited each one feeling hopeful and nervous, with Dr Pam's positive words ringing in our ears, "A lot of these children end up as inventors, scientists, entrepreneurs, because they see things differently. They see the world differently."

We drew up lists of pros and cons and did lots of research, although nothing beats visiting the school and looking into the eyes of the teachers, the headteacher and most importantly, observing the children. This process helped us to narrow down what we didn't want.

Lucas's assessments came through in dribs and drabs, by this time we had ear-marked a school we thought would be perfect for Lucas. It was a specialist autism unit within a mainstream school, established by one of the UK's leading autism charities.

The unit was run by staff trained in autism and aimed at children with a reasonable level of behaviour regulation who could also manage a percentage of their day within the mainstream school.

I loved the flexible approach. They offered a mix of therapeutic support in addition to exposure to the academic and social demands of a mainstream school. They seemed particularly interested in pupils who had potential to engage in the wider school community. It's an exciting educational model if approached with flexibility.

The unit was only a year old and when we went to visit, and didn't even have a Year 8 cohort, but we all agreed it would be a perfect environment for Lucas.

I met the head of the centre, a softly spoken woman who suggested he would fit in well. There was a small hurdle to jump. The school wasn't in our Local Authority, but in a neighbouring borough.

As this would be school number 6, we waited patiently as the authority's Children's Services teams exchanged paperwork and thrashed out budgets. We made a strong case but there was nothing we could do but wait.

A new school and a new start

I was perched on a bar stool in the kitchen one warm May day when my case officer called with good news to say that the Local Authority had agreed to support Lucas at our chosen school! Whilst not being exactly a royal wedding moment, it was big to me, and Lucas was happy too, in his own low-key way.

Weeks went by before the paperwork was completed and the EHCP named this new school. We were advised he would be in school straight after the half-term break, but it didn't happen.

We used the half-term to go shopping for yet another school uniform. Eventually, he started in the last few weeks of Year 8 before they broke up for the summer holiday. Although he had missed almost a whole academic school year, Lucas was extremely positive about starting school again. He was up bright and early, 6:30am, on the first day of term. It was great to see him getting ready. He relished having a routine again.

I was worried about how things would go socially, but I needn't have worried. The head of the unit created a plan for a meticulously slow and steady transition, paying particular attention to Lucas's flash points in the playground and the canteen.

Other children in the centre also struggled with playtime and had the option to retreat to the low sensory atmosphere in the unit, which was a large, cool area to de-compress with pale blue walls and clear, uncluttered spaces.

The unit had its own eating area and changing area for sports, separate from the main school changing rooms, and there were separate lockers so children could avoid the stress of having to dress and undress quickly in front of their peers. It was a masterclass of good autism design and you could see how harmoniously the experts must have worked with the building contractors to create the space.

In the centre, kids were encouraged to spend approximately 80% of their time in the main school in lessons with the rest of their year group. The remaining 20% was spent in the centre, either having lessons, or focusing on specific therapies like social skills, OT, counselling, Lego Therapy or doing homework.

It's a sensitive solution that helps to create an inclusive school environment. It doesn't work for every child, but that's the same for any child at any school.

At first, Lucas opted to eat his lunch in the centre staying in at lunchtime to play with carefully selected friends. Not full integration, but he was happy and flourishing academically. His willingness to integrate more fully at lunch and break started to increase over time. There was one boy with ADHD who he liked a lot. They talked incessantly about their special subjects and enjoyed each other's company.

A big part of the success for Lucas at school was the time dedicated to developing his social and emotional regulation skills. A good proportion of his 20% was spent doing social stories and speech and language therapy. The meltdowns were diminishing in frequency and intensity.

He talked about his old self like he was another person and was overheard saying, "If that had happened a few years ago, I would have been really angry!"

Since he started at the centre, he achieved so much including a headteacher's award for kindness, an academic award for his work in Philosophy, Religion and Ethics (PRE) and a Jack Petchey Award.

The run up to his 14th birthday was a worry. He was still new in the new school and was not in touch with any friends from St. Andrews.

Friendships weren't prolific, but he enjoyed a successful birthday bowling party with a mixed group of 7 boys. Some were from the centre, some from the main school and a boy from his drama group. One of the boys from school was an unfamiliar name so I asked Lucas about him.

"He hasn't got many friends. He's the weird guy and people are mean to him. He reminds me of how I was at Junior School."

When we met him, he was a slight, serious boy with an inner confidence. His mum was lovely and clearly anxious about him not making many friends at school.

After a successful year at the centre, Lucas had chosen his GSCE options. He'd also had some problems with his joints and arthritis during the winter term, but he was determined to go to school even though the pain was considerable. It was an encouraging sign that showed us how happy and accepted he was at the centre. He'd built good relationships with his peers and the centre staff found him kind with a quick-witted sense of humour. He'd found his laughter again and slowly re-built his sense of self.

And drumroll please... there were no exclusions! I attributed this to his growing maturity and greater awareness of his moods and how to manage them from the intensive therapy work done in the centre.

Why the centre worked (where other schools failed)
- He feels happy (bullying is either none existent or negligible).
- He feels understood and accepted.
- He is supported by teachers at the centre who understand him and are trained in autism specifically.
- The centre is autism forward. By that I mean they talk to the children about their autism and ADHD and how it affects their moods from day to day. They are encouraged to accept who they are and their difference.
- The whole school is committed to the aims and objectives of the centre both as a concept and their commitment to whole school autism training.

CHAPTER 15

The Inclusion, Intersection and Conclusion Zone
You Deserve To Be Heard

Inclusive education is not easy

Education can help people with seen or unseen disadvantage to overcome the challenges society puts in their way. If your child is intellectually able, and learning brings them joy or a sense of achievement, the subject they are good at could be the key to unlocking their future career, independence and happiness.

Even if they are not intellectually able, the act of learning a subject that interests them—in the right setting—can stimulate the pleasure centres of the brain, providing relief from the complexities of everyday life.

Diversity in action or I like to call it living diversity is about bending, flexing and creating an environment where all variants of human beings can co-exist, with a healthy mutual respect for each other.

Inclusive education is not easy. Some autism parents insist inclusion doesn't work in practice. There's not a cut and dried version of inclusivity in education, as the benchmark of success depends on who is sitting on the bench.

My belief is that the opinions and feelings of those being included must be intrinsic to the infrastructure and design of any organisation that strives for inclusion. To what degree are the 'included' ones encouraged to advocate for themselves? The very need for inclusion, implies a particular group has previously been excluded!

It is incumbent on us all to raise our game in the inclusion arena and admit defeat where it doesn't work. We need to collaborate with partners to find alternative solutions for all voices to be heard, and all participants to be able to properly contribute to whatever environment they find themselves in. The rewards will be rich for all of us.

Mainstream and specialist schools can do better. If the policies aren't working in practice, the policies need to change.

The success of the centre at Lucas's school showed me what is possible. The impact of getting it right creates waves bigger than the child and their family. Successful inclusion policies can engulf a school, the wider community and beyond. That's not to say the centre was perfect, but we worked through the difficulties constructively.

Cultural change requires investment from education, health and social care policymakers. It also requires fundamental changes in attitudes and beliefs. If we don't get this right, our children with differences, will become afflicted by social ills that will affect them beyond their disability, anxiety, depression, sociopathy, lawlessness, homelessness, alcoholism.

Investing in young lives in the education and social care system and valuing their uniqueness will not only reduce the future strain on the state, but more importantly marks us out as a society truly worthy of the word civilised. Just like Mahatma

Gandhi said, "the true measure of any society can be found in how it treats its most vulnerable members."

Parent groups across the UK are pooling their resources and taking on their local councils through co-ordinated legal action for their role in cutting S.E.N.D. budgets and failing to deliver their legal obligations.

Law firms lead the way in providing specialist advice to parents, especially those whose children are missing from the education system.

S.E.N.D. training and provision costs money, like all social support services, but the S.E.N.D. and social care community seem to have been hit particularly hard. But they are strong in fighting back, letting councils and central government know that the savings they are making amount to a false economy. Money spent for early intervention can prevent larger sums of money being spent in reacting to court action, tribunals, or many hundreds of social or personal crises.

I salute the many professionals and individuals who are working for:

1. More autism/ADHD training for key S.E.N.D. stakeholders.
2. Appropriate and faster NHS support for young people and teen mental health.
3. Earlier 'hidden disability' detection and intervention.
4. Adherence by all bodies in contact with children and young people to the legislation and code of practice.
5. Raise expectations for all children with SEND.

I would add a few of my own:

1. Review of behaviour policies for children with non-identified S.E.N.D. or social, emotional and behavioural issues.
2. Investment in school infrastructure to enable calm areas for all children.
3. At least one trained psychotherapist and a clinical psychologist per Primary, Secondary School and academy group, to assist with urgent assessment cases.

If we agree that education is the key to a child's future happiness and possible independence, and they are denied that education, then their future is effectively being stolen! A study by an organisation called The Key found that headteachers do not feel that the curriculum meets the needs of all pupils, particularly those with S.E.N.D. It is good to have the research to back up what thousands of parents already know.

Many children with S.E.N.D. are blessed by the love and support of their close family. Schools and teachers must be more receptive to making reasonable adjustments, many of which cost very little or nothing.

Some of these children will make amazing contributions to society if their teachers, mentors and carers look beyond their disability and focus on their ability. We need to get beyond the crippling short-sightedness when it comes to children on the spectrum or with other special educational needs.

Beyond the now

Some young adults require help well into adulthood or for the rest of their lives. Others bounce into adulthood and independence with minimal help. In each scenario there are no short-term fixes. The issues you face at school do not end when your child leaves school or goes to college, instead they change, and evolve.

Your role as a parent is to facilitate as much independence as possible, whilst gently guiding and steering. Think long-term. Use creative approaches and set positive intentions for everything from education, housing, relationships to finances. You may have to change your own ideas on what the future holds but embrace the challenge.

Intersectionality

A groovy word, but what on earth does it mean? For me, it's a junction or a crossroads, where 2 or more paths converge. The similarities between discrimination against people with disabilities and those who encounter race and gender discrimination are close, and whilst different in origin, each can learn from the other.

The strategies required to overcome adversity are universal, although the adversity and prejudice appears in different forms.

As a woman with mixed heritage, I'm on the side of anyone who understands, supports and encourages me to fulfil my dreams. Anyone who provides opportunities for me to participate fully in the society I am part of.

On the other hand, if you struggle to understand me, and prevent me—either directly or subconsciously—from accessing opportunities, developing my talents and using my voice, then, sadly you are against me. And that is your right, as much as it is mine, to exist.

I welcome allies and enemies because both are important to

enable us to have a dialogue that might lead to us understand each other better. I feel this way on all of the hot topics that are fiercely dividing so many of us.

Why would we want to be side-lining innovative future leaders, because of their idiosyncrasies and atypical neurology? Of course, there's an interconnectedness between what happens to our young people in the classroom to what happens when they fall out of the education system!

Rather than watered down inclusion policies we should be dreaming up digital, creative, hubs, spaces where children and young people can consensually step away from harmful institutions to get supervised help, advice and alternative education, with parental or carer consent.

We don't want our children and young people who fall out of the education system to become voiceless. We know their issues will invariably become everyone's issue. But how do we diversify the talent pool of clinicians, therapists, teachers, psychologists, if children from particular ethnic groups or those with neurodiversity are being excluded at a rate that is more than 3 times their peers?

It seems we are locked into a system that is organised to produce clones. But I don't really believe that. We do value diversity, now we need to go beyond value and move into self-examination. That's is our responsibility.

Many neurodivergent young people are gender ambiguous. A desire to express themselves on their own terms. In many ways they are revolutionary thinkers; rejecting the wholesale commodification and standardisation of everything from coffee, education to sexual orientation. I hope I haven't excluded anyone in this narrative.

You deserve to be heard

In this book, I have changed some of the names of the people on our journey , but the experience and the content is real. I hope you take away many positives, even after reading the tricky parts. Using your voice and writing letters does make a difference. Firing off emails was easy for me, but it's not just about communicating in writing it's about your inner confidence and your strength of character.

Don't be afraid to ask questions. Everyone makes mistakes whatever their role or qualifications. You face a delicate balance. You don't want to tell anyone their job, but you are the best expert on your child. You've been to the appointments, written notes, asked questions and sought advice.

If you're not a natural wordsmith, my wish is that some of my words help you. Our children are our teachers, as much as we are theirs. Autistic and ADHD children have special gifts to share, especially if they are non-verbal. Help them to shine and uncover their buried treasure.

I started this journey alone and ashamed. I believed it was my fault and everything weighed on my shoulders. But now we stand proudly as a family and yes, we have our difficulties, like every family, but we are individually strong and collectively unstoppable. We're not victims but strong advocates for individual and collective change.

Bring on the social communication difficulties, obsessive behaviours and special interests. We are a special family and we love it that way.

"I believe it's really important that all children are given the opportunity to succeed in school, so that eventually they will be able to help other people."
Lucas, aged 9 - Pupil Parliament speech.

REFERENCES

1. https://www.adhdfoundation.org.uk/wp-content/uploads/2017/05/ADHD-Bullying.pdf

2. https://theconversation.com/children-with-autism-shouldnt-be-forced-to-socialise-44585

3. https://www.who.int/news-room/fact-sheets/detail/autism-spectrum-disorders

4. https://www.cdc.gov/ncbddd/autism/data.html

5. https://www.autism.org.uk/about/what-is/pda.aspx

6. Asperger Autism Network

7. https://www.sossen.org.uk/information_sheets.php

8. https://www.tes.com/news/exclusions-build-school-prison-pipeline

9. https://assets.publishing.service.gov.uk/government/uploads/system/uploads/attachment_data/file/413529/Supporting_children_with_challenging_behaviour_through_a_nurture_group_approach.pdf

10. https://www.ippr.org/files/2017-10/making-the-difference-report-october-2017.pdf

11. Pathways Between Child Maltreatment and Adult Criminal Involvement (2017)

12. aane.org/significance-asperger-profile-developmental-delays/

13. Term introduced to psychiatry by Peter Sifneos in 1972

14. Department of Education, Elective Home Education Guidance for Parents, 2019.

SUGGESTED READING
Some of my favourite Autism/ADHD reads

Navigating the Social World: A curriculum for Individuals with Asperger's Syndrome, High-Functioning Autism and Related Disorders - Jeanette McCaffe

Like a Virgin - Secrets they won't teach you at Business School - Richard Branson

Asperger Syndrome and Difficult Moments - Brenda Smith Myles, Jack Southwick

Newly Qualified Teacher's Annual Survey 2014 https://www.gov.uk/government/uploads/system/uploads/attachment_data/file/430783/Newly-Qualified-Teachers-Annual-Survey_2014.pdf

Managing Meltdowns – Deborah Lipsky and Will Richards

The Reason I Jump – Naoki Hagashida

The Autistic Brain – Temple Grandin

The Complete Guide to Asperger's Syndrome – Tony Attwood

NeuroTribes The Legacy of Autism and the Future of Neurodiversity - Steve Silberman

The Curious Incident of the Dog in the Nighttime – Mark Haddon

ADHD and Me - Chatterpack.net

USEFUL CONTACTS

ADHD Foundation
www.adhdfoundation.org.uk

Autism Education Trust
www.autismeducationtrust.org.uk

Awake B'ham
www.awakebirmingham.co.uk

#happyinschoolproject.com
www.happyinschoolproject.com (that's me, by the way)

Ambitious About Autism
www.ambitiusaboutautism.org.uk

Ace Education
www.ace-ed.org.uk

British Dyslexia Association
Britshdyslexia.org.uk

British Association for Behavioural and Cognitive Psychotherapies
www.babcp.com

Council for Disabled Children (see IASS)
https://councilfordisabledchildren.org.uk/information-advice-and-support-services- network/about/

Mind
www.mind.org/uk

Children's Legal Centre
www.childrenslegalcentre.com

Department for Education
www.gov.uk/government/organisations/department-for-education

Exclusions: www.gov.uk/government/publications/school-exclusion

Dimensions UK
www.dimensions-uk.org

Family and Childcare Trust
www.familyandchildcaretrust.org

General Hypnotherapy Register
www.general-hypnotherapy-register.com

Heath and Care Professions Council
www.hpc-uk.org

IASS Network Information, Advice and Support, Services Network (see CDC).
Merged with Council for Disabled Children:
www.councilfordisabledchildren.org.uk/information-advice-and-support-services- network/about/

IPSEA
www.ipsea.org.uk

Knots Arts:
www.knots.com

Mencap
www.mencap.org.uk

Mind
www.mind.org/uk

National Autistic Society
www.nas.autism.org.uk
schoolexclusions@nas.org.uk

SOS SEN
www.sossen.org.uk

State Boarding Schools Association
www.sbsa.org.uk

Special Needs Jungle
www.specialneedsjungle.com

Reading Agency
www.readingagency.org.uk

Supplementary Education
www. supplementaryeducation.org.uk

Young Minds
www.youngminds.org.uk

ADVICE FOR EXCLUSIONS

Coram Children's Legal Centre

ACE Education

Information Advice and Support Services Network (IASS, formerly local parent partnership)

School Exclusion Service, National Autistic Society (NAS)

School Exclusion Service (England) or Independent Parental Special Education Advice

About the Author

Suzy Rowland is an author, autism and ADHD Specialist and Trainer, Cognitive Behavioural Therapist and a poet. Suzy's son was diagnosed with Asperger's and ADHD aged 9. Determined to share her experience and expertise, Suzy set up the #happyinschool project, to break down the complexity of autism and ADHD behaviours in education, to parents and educators. She's committed to raising the bar for wellbeing for children in schools, in particularly for autistic and ADHD children. She uses mindfulness, CBT, storytelling and listening as her tools. Suzy works with a range of schools, councils, charities, businesses and parent/carer groups to deliver her unique brand of influence and empowerment.

As a former corporate communications and PR professional turned entrepreneur, Suzy enjoys using her communications skills to provide advice and training to all sectors, in support of her strong belief that diverse businesses and communities thrive better than homogenous ones. She is particularly interested in supporting groups who are disadvantaged by their race, neurodiversity or their additional needs, e.g. boys of Black Caribbean heritage, a group who are statistically, most likely to be excluded from mainstream Primary and Secondary Schools.

Her son is fast becoming an autism/ADHD advocate, he's a successful YouTuber and a distinction-level guitarist, with a Jack Petchey Award in his clutches.

Connect with Suzy Rowland online:
Twitter: @SchoolHappyin & @radiantlady
Instagram: @happyinschool
www.happyinschoolproject.com
hello@happyinschoolproject.com